The Allegory of
Female Authority

Also by Maureen Quilligan

The Language of Allegory: Defining the Genre
Milton's Spenser: The Politics of Reading

The Allegory of
Female Authority

CHRISTINE DE PIZAN'S
CITÉ DES DAMES

Maureen Quilligan

Cornell University Press

Ithaca and London

For my sisters,
Kathleen, Laura, and Susan

Contents

Illustrations

Illustrations

Preface

Throughout the winter of 1970–71, while a graduate student in Oxford, I sat reading manuscripts in Duke Humphries Library at the Bodleian. In preparation for writing my dissertation on the genre, I read a great many allegories that winter, and from time to time Rosemond Tuve's old reading slips would waft out of the odd volume—*Pèlerinage de la vie humaine* or *Les echecs amoreux.* Those signs of her authority were greatly reassuring. I knew when I saw one that I must be on the right track.

At the same time, I was a member of a feminist action group in Oxford. It met at my college (Linacre), no doubt because as an American I was naive enough to get away with hosting such radical guests in so staid a setting. At our meetings we delivered papers to each other and heard reports about international conventions on the Continent. We also went door-to-door through council (public housing) estates, trying to organize a play group for the resident children so that their mothers could have some free time. The play group had for our group a fiercely debated theoretical relationship to our efforts to help organize a strike at a local bakery, where many of the women in the estate worked. Would our helping them to organize as women aid them to organize as workers?

As a Southern Californian, I was terrified to canvass the women at the council estate for fear that as soon as they heard my foreign accent, they would slam the door in my face or become otherwise abusive because I was "an outside agitator"—one of those nonindigenous people whom our American right wing press had held responsible for all the student troubles in California which I had so thoroughly enjoyed in the mid-sixties. And indeed our group, even the British membership, included no public housing mothers among its numbers; this disparity was evident when we figured out how much money the play group might represent in each of their weekly budgets by comparing it to the money one young feminist's parents had paid for boarding her horse. The agenda, however, was entirely focused on the working class. My British co-members all became impatient when I urged that perhaps we might also think about the relationship between women's oppression in society at large and in the university: to them, this was a typically American (that is, bourgeois) concern. I seem to remember that Hilary Wainwright— who has since gone on to become a noted socialist author—complimented me for the activism I maintained despite my inability to theorize my politics in any persuasive way. And so, ardent if untheoretical, I dutifully worked that year in support of the next trades union strike, marching through the winter rain down Cornmarket Street, the towers of Oxford gleaming gold.

As I was simultaneously following Rosemond Tuve through the territory she had covered for *Allegorical Imagery: Some Medieval Books and Their Posterity* (1966), I had no idea there might ever be a connection between my reading of allegories and my problematic position within the action group, but it turns out that in writing about Christine de Pizan I have come again upon the untheorized territory of the activist bourgeois woman, this time inside an allegory.

Some years later, in spring 1982, in the midst of hosting a conference on Renaissance women at Yale University, where I had been teaching since 1973, I received a call from LeAnne Schreiber, a former fellow graduate student at Harvard who had gone on to become deputy editor of the *New York Times Book Review.* She wanted to know if I was interested in reviewing a new translation of a 1405 pro-woman allegory by Christine de Pizan, *The Book of the City of Ladies.* She recalled all the time I had spent in libraries reading allegories and thought I might like to take a look at this one. Although, of course, I knew of Christine from Rosemond Tuve's work on her, I had never even heard of this particular text, or, indeed, known that Christine de Pizan was reputed a notable defender of women. I had a deep admiration for Tuve's own feminism: she chose to spend her teaching life at Connecticut College for Women, moving to the University of Pennsylvania only at the close of her career. And so I explained to LeAnne that if Rosemond Tuve hadn't mentioned *The Book of the City of Ladies*, this particular allegory probably was no good. Apparently LeAnne had had a wager with the editor of the *Book Review:* he had bet her that she couldn't get a publishable review of a "feminist" book written in 1405. And so I said I would take a look at it—but wouldn't promise a thing.

Soon after the close of the Yale conference (which eventually resulted in a volume of essays, *Rewriting the Renaissance: The Discourses of Sexual Difference in Early Modern Europe*, 1986), the mail bag arrived with the galleys of Earl Jeffrey Richards's translation of *Le livre de la cité des dames*. When I opened the book and read the first page, I was staggered. Here was a perfectly generic reading scene, of the sort I knew all too well from those cold days in Duke Humphries. Yet on the very first page, Christine's mother interrupted that reading scene to call her author-daughter to supper! In *The Language of Allegory*, I had devoted a long chapter to arguments about how important this first scene or "threshold text" is to any allegory as a means of establishing the central thematic pivot for the rest of the narrative. And here was Christine de Pizan introducing into that text a generically unorthodox, historical mother. The text of the *Cité* was otherwise recognizable as a self-consciously perfect opening to a conventional allegory. But I had never seen that kind of domestic detail produced by a male author. Sensitized as I then was by the Yale conference's focus on perceptions of "sexual difference" in the early modern period, I was strongly struck by the presence here on the page of a very real sexual difference from the texts of all the male allegorists I had ever read.

I quickly found out that the book had never been published in French. Luckily, however, Beinecke Library, Yale's rare book collection, owned the only manuscript of the *Cité des dames* presently in the United States. As I struggled through the problems posed by assessing a translation of a text different from that of the manuscript I was reading, the critical theorist Barbara Johnson, then a colleague from the Yale French Department, walked into the reading room, came over, and, to my astonishment, announced, "I happen to have a copy of the thesis that edits the French text of the *Cité*. I heard you were doing something with it. You can have my copy." I believe I got it from her that very day. I wrote the review and it was published. LeAnne won her bet.

I narrate this sequence of events because I wish to explain that my decision to write a book on the *Cité des dames*, a text that is, as they say, "outside my field," has owed much to the accidental circumstance of a loosely knit collective of interest on the part of several unrelated women. Their help has made it seem as if my working on the *Cité* was a choice I never actively made; I could only acknowledge that I was already working on it. Doubtless because my argument is that the actual subject matter of the *Cité des dames* has to do with the problem of female authority, I have while writing this book spent more than the usual amount of time wondering by what authority I was doing so. Although I have in fact read many allegories over the years, and many of those in French, I did so for a degree in English, not French, and I have gone on to teach English nondramatic literature, not of the medieval period, but of the Renaissance.

I am aware that in the midst of these specific names of individual women in my past, who have all had their own authority, the names of many notable corporations also figure: Oxford, Harvard, Yale, the *New York Times*. Like Christine's own history, my story takes place at cultural sites that have a distinctly authoritative cultural resonance in the English-speaking world. Yale's Beinecke Library is a far cry from Blackbird Leys', a council estate in Oxford. Yet my effort to write about a French text, when all my training has been in English literature, evokes my fears about being an outside agitator, speaking a different language. So too, Christine de Pizan, an Italian at the court of France, had spoken a different language, at least in her familial setting, from the language she wrote. Yet she aimed to speak for all French women, including those who came from other social strata but had needs she felt she understood. It was this very self-consciousness about margins, I believe, that made Christine de Pizan more than usually aware of the defining parameters that go into making an authoritative core; it made her presciently sensitive to what went into developing a canon.

In order to write successfully, one needs not only the authority necessary to write, but also the authority necessary to be heard. One needs to have access to—if not to be located directly within—the center of dominant power. My hope in this book, a commentary devoted to a single text, is to teach readers how to hear Christine's authority, and so to put her back in her place in the canon. She was the first woman we know of, so far, to make a concerted and self-conscious effort to rearrange the list of privileged French texts of her period, and it will be very instructive to trace her attempt to prevail upon the canon.

As for the necessary institutional support basic to any scholarly endeavor, I thank the staffs of the Beinecke Library, New Haven, the Bibliothèque Nationale, Paris, the Bodleian Library, Oxford, the British Library, London, and the Boston Public Library for their help and also for permission to reproduce miniatures from manuscripts in their collections. I am also grateful to patient audiences at a number of symposia across the country especially for their useful questions and suggestions; the "Diversity of Language" seminar at the University of Pennsylvania, particularly Ann Rosalind Jones; and audiences at the Medieval Club of New York, the Medieval Renaissance Conference at Barnard College, the State University of New York at Stonybrook, the University of California at San Diego, the University of California at Irvine, and George Washington University. I thank kind colleagues at the University of Pennsylvania for their help during the writing of this book: most particularly Margreta de Grazia for her patient and wonderfully generous reading of the manuscript; Kevin Brownlee for all his information, acumen, and expertise; David Boyd for useful bibliography; Joan DeJean for always smart advice; and Stephen G. Nichols for support both early and late. I also thank Nancy J. Vickers for her francophonic patience. I am pleased to acknowledge the funding of a University of Pennsylvania summer Faculty Research Grant for my first foray into the manuscripts and a grant from the American Council of Learned Society for time in which to complete the manuscript. I am also grateful to the May Co. for a grant to defray research and publication costs. My husband, Michael Malone, was not only a tower of strength but a great computer wizard who solved all problems technological and psychological, and I thank him for his patience, humor and elegant editing.

MAUREEN QUILLIGAN

Philadelphia, Pennsylvania

*The Allegory of
Female Authority*

Introduction

Just as Dante's political exile from Florence was an important element of his own self-characterization as a writer—and just as
he puts his exiled self in his poem—Christine de Pizan's socially
marginal position is a significant pivot of her self-presentation as an
author. A brief overview of Christine's career may make her peculiar
position clearer. The details of this "life" are offered here not so much
as the subjective source of her experience which therefore helps to
interpret the writing, as a record of how the writings have constructed the author as a singularly proto-modern woman.

The daughter of the astrologer to Charles V, Christine de Pizan was
brought from Italy to the court of France at the age of four in the
late 1360s. Married, apparently quite happily, since age fifteen to a
courtier-bureaucrat like her father, she was widowed at twenty-five
and thereby left responsible for the support of three young children
and of her mother (her father had died some few months before her
husband). Widowhood brought with it not only the need to take
charge of her own destiny, but also the freedom to do so. Turning her
grief at the loss of her husband into lyric lament, she became a well-
known poet, winning powerful patrons. Simultaneously suing for her
rights in court and writing poems, Christine became what later ages
have called France's "first professional woman of letters." In essence,
she became a professional writer long before the profession existed,
because she had no other identity to which she could lay claim,
neither one derived from a social function, such as an office at court,

I

nor one based upon her attachment to powerful male relatives. She was also something of a scribe and may have, in fact, supported herself in this way, but such a money-making skill would have been subsumed into her identity as writer as soon as she began presenting her own poems to wealthy courtiers.[1]

Christine's choice to write works defending women was a self-conscious literary move, as we shall see, especially in the attack on the authority of the *Roman de la rose*. The *Cité des dames* is a continuation of her anti-misogynist arguments against the *Rose* and a further exfoliation of her uniquely female authority. In form, the *Cité* is a version of the generically conventional allegorical debate, specifically modeled on Boethius's *Consolation of Philosophy*, and is unlike her earlier allegorical poems, such as the *Mutacion de Fortune* (*The Mutation of Fortune*) or the *Chemin de long estude* (*The Long Road of Learning*), which are organized as pilgrimages or quests.

After the generically unorthodox interruption by her mother, the author goes on to read the misogynist booklet she has accidentally come across and then to lament the fact that she was born into a female body. In the midst of her despair, she has a waking vision, in which three august female figures of authority come to console her and to convince her how specifically chosen of God women actually are. Each of these three personifications, Reason, Droitture (Rectitude or Rightness), and Justice, narrates to Christine carefully selected and juxtaposed stories about women to disprove various clichés of misogynist opinion. By this process, they are building a city of ladies, where women will for all time be safe from misogynist attack.

In the first section, Reason tells of great female city builders and women who founded cultural institutions. In the second section, Droitture narrates stories about secret traditions of female prophecy and about the more domestic questions of parent-child and husband-wife relations. In the final section, Justice recounts a series of lives of saints—most of them martyrs.

What follows is essentially a page-by-page commentary on the *Livre de la cité des dames*. The reasons for casting this book in such terms were both practical and polemical. All allegories demand com-

---

[1]For Christine's work as a scribe, see Charity Canon Willard, *Christine de Pizan: Her Life and Works, A Biography* (New York: Persea Books, 1984), pp. 45–47.

mentaries, and given the major, indeed generic, importance of narrative sequence in allegory, as well as the centrality of the reader's experience of the interpretive process, it was important to explain how Christine's text developed through time as a reading experience. Her architectural metaphor (the construction of the city of ladies from foundation stone to turrets and towers) is in danger of seeming merely quaint to modern readers not used to the bracing architectonic struts particular to this genre or the incredibly powerful analytic effect of such narrative structures. The close juxtapositions and placement of narratives, articulated by the architectural metaphor, are the text's own signals for activating the reader's analysis. Such a commentary pulls the allegory of city construction *forward*, so it acts as a frame, its underpinning gridwork not merely subtending the text but organizing analytic perception. So too Christine's subject—and her method—in writing the *Cité des dames* is the revision of tradition necessary before that tradition is capable of articulating a female's experience of history; hence Christine's own revisions of her precursor texts are part of her text's point. The presence of the subtexts, juxtaposed and rearranged in a certain order, is just as important as any conjuncture in Christine's text, and it is not only far easier to keep them straight in an episode-by-episode analysis, it is also the process by which their revision becomes a topic of the text. Christine may choose to narrate Boccaccio's second story first because Dante had already placed that story in an unusual first position.

Even though it is prose, the *Cité des dames* has the formal resonance of an allegorical poem. Only with page-by-page attention could the intricate web of interrelationships, both across the surface of Christine's text and among various precursor texts subtending hers, be acknowledged with the amount of detail sufficient for coming to any useful understanding of what is going on in the *Cité des dames*. The significance of Christine's revision of her *auctores* extends all the way to individual lexical choices and comprises her single most important achievement in the *Cité*, an intervention into the canon.

As France's "first professional woman of letters," Christine has inhabited an odd position in French literature, singularly out of context in any number of ways. As Italian-born and therefore foreign, as a "professional" long before the profession was possible, and finally, as a woman, Christine possesses a unique alienness to the usual contextualizing grids by which one locates an authorial practice, an alienness that makes those frameworks all the more problematic as critical tools. It is somewhat of a paradox then to realize that the one framework in which Christine's literary practice makes the greatest sense is the canon. I say "the canon" advisedly, for Christine positioned herself with respect to the medieval list of world-class texts—works written by men such as Plato, Aristotle, Cicero, Virgil, Ovid—with the greatest possible specificity. Because more recent candidates—such as Dante and Jean de Meun—for the roster of famous names had not yet been decided upon in 1405, Christine, it appears, was able to be one of the writers engaged in its formulation. Christine's selection of a list of authorities providing a context in which her own work was possible and made sense did not merely happen by chance to coincide with the canon subsequently selected by later readers; her own intervention was so aggressively spectacular and well staged that we may indeed wonder if it was not one of the forces giving ultimate shape to our sense of the crucial texts in medieval literature. That she herself has dropped out of the canon of French literature or has remained a name only in the genre of lyric is a function of later uses of this remarkably powerful tool. In her own hands, the process of canon formation was used to position her work with the greatest possible visibility. The commentary form helps to make clear all the details of her canonical maneuvering as she creates for herself a place in the list of texts by constructing the list through her own deft revisions.

Writing a commentary has had the further salutary effect of making my book absolutely dependent upon Christine's. Because my primary aim is to help to make the text of the *Cité des dames* readable, I deem it a small price to pay to have my own text remain not entirely readable without the *Cité*. To position a critical work vis-à-vis a text in such a way, however, is to court being called old-fashioned—subservient to author and to text—when criticism, and especially theory, ought to stand on its own. So too, my method of comparing, in fairly minute detail, Christine's rendition of a story with her precursors' versions begs complicated questions about authorial intentions which have only recently been put into powerful play. Why write a book that seems so old-fashioned? Why concern oneself with literary "authority" when the "author" in modern criticism has been pronounced dead and when it is a very real question whether, indeed, any such creature actually existed in the Middle Ages? I have chosen this critical task because it seems to me that we may finally not do literary history justice if we do eliminate the author as a powerful position from which to produce text before any *female* author can usefully inhabit that position. The peculiar achievement of the texts signed by Christine de Pizan is that they represent an authorial persona of a remarkably distinct type, for either sex, of any period; a persona with even a very well-defined and recognizable, repeatable visual image. She was her own scribe. We have her handwriting, even in some instances her written instructions to miniaturists. Pictures of her illuminate her collected works, "collected" by herself for presentation to powerful patrons such as Queen Isabeau of Bavaria and the duke of Berry. In other words, we have all the elements of what a modern author has traditionally been. How can this be so? How can a medieval woman, for whom writing itself was a most unlikely act, become a modern "author"? I suggest that to see how this is possible, we need only consider Catherine Belsey's demonstration that the family may appear as a possible social unit aimed at providing a "private realm of warmth and virtue" long before it becomes a prevalent feature of social organization—as, for instance, she argues happens in Holbein's famous painting of the family of Sir Thomas More.[2] In a similar bit of prolepsis, Christine de Pizan very early anticipated the position of "author," and inhabited it—however briefly—becoming an accidental occupier of a theoretically possible social slot in part *because*, as a female, no other cultural model was available to her.

Of course, we now understand, as Belsey notes in the same essay, that "in post-structuralist analysis . . . subjectivity is not a single unified presence but the point of intersection of a range of discourses, produced and re-produced as the subject occupies a series of places in the signifying system, takes on the multiplicity of meanings language offers" (p. 188). But it is also important to point out that Christine positioned herself within discourse in such a way as to reproduce in her text a female authority that, although it replicated in many elements the prevailing master discourse about femaleness, also contended with it and instated a difference that took on the hard

[2]Catherine Belsey, "Disrupting Sexual Difference," in *Alternative Shakespeares*, ed. John Drakakis (London: Methuen, 1985).

outlines of an established subjectivity. Although she herself assumed otherwise, the "difference" authored by Christine in her careful and minutely significant variations from her authorities is not due to a natural, essential difference. Rather, we see her ably maneuvering in the available discursive spaces. While she managed to look with suspicion on much official discourse about women, she did not mount a critique of the notion of god-granted essences. She did, however, redeploy an essentialist definition of the "natural" woman in order to enable her to revise tradition, presenting portraits of women which were very different from their male-authored originals.

The problem of the mother, who interrupted the first page of the *Cité*, continues to worry Christine's text, and so my commentary on it. From the first moment of the appearance of Christine's mother, it was obvious that her mere mention there on the threshold made the notion of actual motherhood a central problem to be worked out by the allegory. And so in many of the stories, the problematic relationship of the notion of the mother to all other possible sites of female authority is tested and analyzed. Because of the question of mother/son incest, so central to the foundational story of Semiramis, it became important for me to be able to organize the conversation about these recurring questions into some larger framework. Therefore, although this book began as a commentary, it has had to have recourse to a great deal of psychoanalytically derived theory. It is something of an accident that the theorists to whom I appeal are almost entirely women. Julia Kristeva, Luce Irigaray, Hélène Cixous, Nancy Chodorow, Jessica Benjamin, Elaine Scarry, Elaine Pagels, Kaja Silverman—these are the theorists and historians I have used to help me excavate Christine's allegorical city. In large part, they themselves stand as more-or-less self-consciously feminist commentators on male *auctores*. For example, Kristeva, Irigaray, and Cixous, as well as the American object-relations psychoanalyst Chodorow and the film theorist Silverman are essentially commentators on Freud, standing somewhat in the same relationship to Freud which Christine had to her *auctores*—essentially in agreement, but offering corrections, especially where the male *auctor* misstates the case about women.

Such recourse to theory, however, has been driven by what I assume are primarily generic stimuli. From the moment of the mother's appearance as a boundary marker to the threshold text, the idea of mother is necessarily going to be central to the allegory: not merely the notion of relationships of mothers to sons, but that of the relationships of mothers to daughters.

As in much recent work on feminist theory, the central problem addressed by the *Cité* seems to be female-to-female relations, generationally: the relationship between mother and daughter; the relationship between motherhood on the one hand as a site of reproduction of roles, as well as reproduction of the species, and, on the other, as site for determining what parts females will play in our society. A commentary on the *Cité* is not, however, the place to try to decide all or any of the present questions in contemporary feminist debate. And I regret that the vocabulary developed in that debate is not yet as fully formed as it would have to be in order to be easily applied to a text written in 1405. But it is the vocabulary we have, and I have tried to translate, as a feminist theorist and as a scholar of allegories, between those discourses. The *Cité* deserves to enter our canon. We have no hope of having it take its place there if it is not allowed to speak past history to our own murky understanding of contemporary problems. And so it does. In positing the mother as a site of contestation over the proper definition of woman, the *Cité* is doing no more than what our contemporary psychological and psychoanalytic theory has done and continues to struggle to do.

A final word of direction is in order. Christine has recently come under virulent attack by feminist Chaucerian Sheila Delany for her reactionary politics.[3] According to Delany, it is not enough for a woman simply to write in order for her to be of interest, or of use, to a radically political feminist criticism. While Delany, angered by excessive claims for Christine's radicalism, overstates the case against what she sees as Christine's anachronistic antidemocratic position, it is true that Christine conservatively looked to a sovereign authority as the guarantor of social order in a time of literally murderous turmoil and civil chaos. Delany has indeed brought up an important problem: Christine's politics are a major part of her oeuvre, they are distinctly conservative, and they need to be taken seriously.

[3]Sheila Delany, " 'Mothers to Think Back Through': Who Are They? The Ambiguous Example of Christine de Pizan," in *Medieval Texts and Contemporary Readers*, ed. Laurie A. Finke and Martin B. Schichtman (Ithaca: Cornell University Press, 1987), pp. 177–79.

Delany's moral objections are peculiarly appropriate to her subject: Christine herself had objected to Jean de Meun's *Roman de la rose* on similar grounds of the author's morality and the impact he would have on his readers. She instituted Jean de Meun as something like a modern author to be held accountable for the effect his texts had on his readers, and her intervention into the canon formation ongoing during her literary moment was designedly political, just as Delany's is. For Delaney is arguing as much against what she fears to be an increasingly quietist academic feminism as against an overvaluation of Christine's radicalism.

The terms in which Delany couches her critique are, however, deeply unfortunate and occlude discussion rather than illuminate it. To argue, as she does, that Christine's defense of her royal patrons makes her the "Rosemary Woods of her day" is, while undeniably startling, to make a rhetorical gesture that sacrifices accuracy to polemic. It is also anachronistically to hold an author up to a litmus test of political purity few authors of any period could pass because the terms of comparison are incongruent. Rosemary Woods was Nixon's personal secretary, who by virtue of her sex, privatized position, and personal sentiment owed her deepest loyalties to her "boss," whom she served even when he was not president. Christine de Pizan, in contrast, debated in a public, written arena with royal secretaries who were all male and who owed such a public, bureaucratic office as secretary to class position, elite education, and patronage—not to personal choice. What gets lost in such a statement as Delany's is not merely this kind of historical detail but the necessary notion of the "alterity" of the Middle Ages, its difference from our own historical moment. The difference in such a term as *secretary*, which the Middle Ages gendered "male" just as generically as we now gender it "female," is a case in point. Christine wrote much serious advice to her aristocratic patrons in genres in which critique traditionally masqueraded as compliment. In a letter to the then reigning queen-regent, Isabeau of Bavaria, Christine risked—and earned—loss of favor by her admonitions to make peace among warring baronial factions. Rosemary Woods as secretary would never have circulated a public letter to Nixon advising him to stop being a crook, but this, in essence, is what a very unpliable Christine did—so taking upon herself the public voice of an entity called "France," constructed as a virtual nationhood.

Delany has also argued in condemnation of Christine that "if Martin Luther King is your idea of a radical then the leap to Christine de Pizan is not hard to make." It may not be accurate to call Martin Luther King a "radical," yet he has been a figure of enormous cultural force, eminently worthy of consideration and political analysis. Even in feminist scholarship, it should not be necessary for one to be a radical far to the left of Martin Luther King in order to be worthy of historical study. To argue otherwise is to police literary study for an ideological purity that will severely limit the historical figures open to research. In a similar vein, Delany's denunciation of King's notions of passive resistance, self-sacrifice, and eventual martyrdom as politically nugatory is to have a severely limited grasp of the exercise of a force that can cause political change without recourse to violence. In deriding King's slogan "If there is blood in the streets, let it be ours," Delany shows herself incapable of appreciating the power of self-sacrifice. Such an incapacity is not in general disabling; yet because the last section of the *Cité des dames* is a martyrology, for a student of Christine self-sacrifice becomes a crucial political test case. Passive resistance and political martyrdom are not in the final analysis only medieval maneuvers, politically dismissible because authorized by a sentimental Christianity. Neither Gandhi nor for that matter the Ayatollah Khoumeni was Christian (or medieval), but both understood the aggressive and revolutionary political force of both those positions. Nonviolence and bloody self-sacrifice can go to the roots of social change and in this sense qualify as "radical."

Christine de Pizan was not a political revolutionary. But she was one of the first women to assume a position of literate authority and to write from it about women and about large political issues. My assumption here is that this act is itself a problem worthy of serious consideration. If, in answer to the question "how" did Christine manage to construct a speaking position for herself, we find that she chose to speak in defense of a conservative rather than a radical politics, we need to ask about all the possible connections there may be between her construction of female authority and political absolutism. In the final chapter, "The Practice of History," I outline those connections, locating the sequel to the *Cité des dames—Le trésor de la cité des dames*—in the context of Christine's remonstrating letter to the queen and her general program for secular, political female authority in the chaotic court of Charles VII. In the process of correcting some of Delany's overstatements about Christine's backwardness in arguing against popular rule, I attempt to theorize her construction of a subjectivity through absolutist sympathies by comparing her pro-monarchical stance to that of two seventeenth-century English pro-woman authors who also held to a problematic political conservatism. Finally, in a brief discussion of Christine's last poem in celebration of Joan of Arc, a woman whose most authoritative act was the crowning of a king, I try to put into clearer historical perspective the problematic politics engaged by the close relationship of royal to female authority.

Chapter 1

The Name of the Author

If at the end of the Middle Ages, *auctores* became like men, men became more like *auctores*.
—A. J. Minnis, *Medieval Theory of Authorship*

Aux estrangiers povons la feste
Faire de la vaillant Christine—
Affin que sa mort accoutine
Le corps, son nom dure toudis.

For the benefit of foreigners, let us
Celebrate the valiant Christine.
So that, although death has taken
Her body, her name will endure always.
—Martin le Franc, *Champion des dames* (1442)

"Je, Christine." These two words, the author's peculiar signature, open Christine de Pizan's *Ditié de Jehanne d'Arc*—the only poem to be written about the warrior saint in her lifetime. Furthermore, another collocation of personal pronoun and specific name directly addresses the poem's subject: "Tu, Jehanne."[1] The words "Je, Christine" are unique in literary history for two reasons: First, they are spoken publicly and prophetically, by one woman to another.[2]

---

[1] Christine de Pizan, *Ditié de Jehanne D'Arc*, ed. Angus J. Kennedy and Kenneth Varty (Oxford: Society for the Study of Mediaeval Languages and Literature, 1977), ll. 1, 169.

[2] While, for example, Margery Kempe speaks in *Book* of her meeting with fellow female mystic Julian of Norwich and quotes Julian's direct charge to her to "set all your trust in God and fear not the language of the world; for the more despite, shame and reproof that you receive in the world, the more is your merit in the sight of God," Margery was herself unlettered, and her text is by an amanuensis. Hence the author is referred to in the third person: "Much was the dalliance that the anchoress and this

Second, as an author's signature, they indicate a practice that we ordinarily associate with the self-naming Renaissance. Michelangelo's famous carving of the inscription "Michelangelo hoc fecit," across the Pietà stands witness to the later age's resolute refusal of anonymity.

While the appearance of the formula "Je, Christine" is not entirely anomalous in medieval literary practice, its repetition throughout Christine's oeuvre—especially in that the *Livre de la cité des dames*—makes its idiosyncratic frequency a signal mark of Christine's authority, a "signature" in more ways than one. It invites us to examine the lessons, in Christine's own experience, in the historical conditions then obtaining, and in the potentialities of the literary system, which taught her to establish her authorial *self* by such a naming, and specifically by a signature seen as a gendered term.[3] Another way of asking this question is to wonder what it was in the late fourteenth-century literary system that provided the interstices into which Christine could insert her specifically female authority.[4] What was it about those interstices which formed (or allowed Christine to form) that authority in such strikingly proto-modern terms?[5]

---

creature had by communing in the love of Our lord Jesus during the many days they were together." Cited by Catherine Jones, "The English Mystic: Julian of Norwich," in *Medieval Women Writers*, ed. Katharina M. Wilson (Athens: University of Georgia Press, 1984), p. 271. See also Clarissa W. Atkinson, *Mystic and Pilgrim: The "Book" and the World of Margery Kempe* (Ithaca: Cornell University Press, 1983).

[3]Centuries earlier, Marie de France also named herself as the specifically female author of her lais, although in her case such self-naming (in the third person) has not proved useful for identifying with real certainty a specific historical woman as Marie. For a discussion of Marie's self-reference and the various candidates, see *The Lais of Marie de France*, trans. Glyn S. Burgess and Keith Busby (London: Penguin Books, 1986), pp. 8–11. For a discussion of the relationship between signature and gendered authorship in modern critical theory and literature, see Peggy Kamuf, *Signature Pieces: On the Institution of Authorship* (Ithaca: Cornell University Press, 1988).

[4]For a discussion of the Elizabethan "literary system" and a set of categories which covers a spectrum of positions including "amateur," "professional," and "laureate" authors, see Richard Helgerson, *Self-Crowned Laureates: Spenser, Jonson, Milton and the Literary System* (Berkeley: University of California Press, 1982). Helgerson's argument that a system both produces the range of individuals and remains a product of those individuals would require the assumption that "female author" was a category already possible by the time Christine inhabited that position.

[5]The extreme self-consciousness of Christine's construction of her own female authority makes her sound not merely proto-modern, but proto-feminist—another label currently very problematic in its application. In her biography of seventeenth-

As the work of critics like Foucault and Barthes has shown, what it means to be an "author" is today a complicated question.[6] It is important to understand the term's implications in postmodern critical usage; but the term was also a problematic one in medieval theory as well. Before we can truly understand what Christine so peculiarly attempted and seems so uniquely to have achieved, we need to look briefly at contemporary practice in authorial signatures at the time Christine wrote and to scrutinize an exemplary instance of a medieval male author's self-naming. By gauging Christine's difference from her male contemporaries and from her own most privileged model, we will be in a better position to assess the uniqueness of her construction of a "modern" authority for herself.

Self-Naming in the Prologues to Chronicles

Christine's practice of naming herself mimics in part a trend in a particular genre of medieval writing—the chronicle. Although the chronicle is a literary type very different from the allegorical narrative of the *Livre de la cité des dames* or the lyric prophecy of the

---

century writer Mary Astell, *The Celebrated Mary Astell: An Early English Feminist* (Chicago: University of Chicago Press, 1986), pp. 17–18, Ruth Perry argues for the legitimacy of applying the term "feminist" to Astell: at bottom, according to Perry, the term denotes "the recognition of women as a separate class, quite aside from any other social or economic grouping, and a woman-centered identification with that class." She also adds a second criterion: the desire to improve conditions for women, to champion their cause. In this sense of the term, Christine de Pizan *is* a "feminist"; however, I use the term "proto-feminist" to insist upon the real difference that the stretch of time between 1500 and 1990 involves and to put aside, for the moment, the complicated political questions implicit in using the label "feminist" for any historical figure.

[6]Michel Foucault, "What Is an Author?" in *Language, Counter-Memory, Practice*, trans. Donald F. Bouchard and Sherry Simon (Ithaca: Cornell University Press, 1977). Foucault explains, "When a discourse is linked to an author, . . . the role of 'shifters' [personal pronouns, adverbs of time and place, and the conjugation of verbs] is . . . complex and variable." The "I" of such a text "gives rise to a variety of egos and to a series of subjective positions that individuals of any class may come to occupy" (pp. 130–31). Foucault is more interested in the sort of "author function" which establishes "the endless possibility of discourse," such as that fulfilled by Freud and Marx. See also Roland Barthes, "The Death of the Author," in *Image-Music-Text*, ed. Stephen Heath (New York: Hill and Wang, 1977), pp. 142–48.

poem to Joan of Arc, it will be helpful to pause at the outset to situate Christine's self-consciousness about this new possibility for autho-rial self-representation. Her rather unusual use of the chronicler's self-naming not only inaugurates her strange "modernity" as an au-thor but also marks her practice as essentially gendered, specifically when she redeploys the chronicler's signature to make her own fe-maleness a social category supporting her authority.

In the fourteenth century, writers such as Froissart began using a new, fixed formula for establishing their authority by citing their individual names in the prologues to chronicles. Diverging from older usages, which indicated the named author in the third person, the new formula included the "first person pronoun followed by the author's name and surname, title and rank (which situate the writer socially), followed by a verb indicating the act of writing."[7] Thus: "I, Jehans Frouissars, treasurer and canon of Chimay," or "I, Jehan d'Or-reville, of Picardy, named Cabaret." Christine herself used the for-mula in the prologue to her *Livre des fais et bonnes meurs du sage roy Charles V* (The Book of the Deeds and Good Customs of the Wise King Charles V), although she alters it slightly: "moy Christine de Pisan, femme soubz les tenebres dignorance"; "Christine de Pizan, me, a woman beneath the shades of ignorance."[8]

The chronicler's designation indicates a unique person who is located in a specific social context: both identifications, of name and of social place, echo the "juridical" act of signing a will or other legal contract, and as Christiane Marchello-Nizia has argued, may have

[7]Danielle Régnier-Bohler, "Imagining a Self: Exploring Literature," in *A History of Private Life*, vol 2, *Revelations of the Medieval World*, ed. Philippe Ariès and Georges Duby, trans. Arthur Goldhammer (Cambridge: Harvard University Press, 1988), p. 379. See also Christiane Marchello-Nizia, "L'historien et son prologue: Forme littéraire et stratégies discursives," in *La chronique et l'histoire au moyen âge*, ed. Daniel Poirion (Paris: Presses Université Paris-Sorbonne, 1986), pp. 13–25. Charity Cannon Willard has noted in *Christine de Pizan: Her Life and Works* (New York: Persea Books, 1984), p. 47, that the formula "Je, Christine" is legal language with which Christine would have become familiar when suing for her rights in court as a widow in the early 1390s, as well as through her participation in the Parisian book trade. This legal and admin-istrative background trained her to give exact dates; she records both the beginning date, October 5, 1402, and the completion date, March 20, 1403, for the composition of her work *Le livre du chemin de long estude*.

[8]*Le livre des fais et bonnes meurs du sage roy Charles V*, ed. Susan Solente (Paris: Honoré Champion, 1936), p. 5.

been intended to confer upon the act of writing a truth-value generically important to the chronicle. Danielle Régnier-Bohler summarizes: "The individual thus designates him- or herself as unique person in a precise social context and stakes his or her claim to truthfulness" (p. 379). Christine's indication of her status as a (humble, uneducated) female, however, changes the formula subtly by substituting a reference to her gender in the place reserved for mention of a social category such as class (Froissart's position as treasurer) or a city (Enguerran de Monstrelet refers to the actual physical place in which he wrote). By so doing, Christine makes her gender the precise social position she occupies, as specifying as Enguerran's social class ("yssu de noble generacion") or Mathieu de Coussy's native city ("homme Lay, natif de Quesnoy"). The "place" from which such a precisely located social being as Christine de Pizan—"femme"—writes, however, is not a named city, but an allegorical landscape, "beneath the shades of ignorance," a realm of women that is by definition marginal to the very act of writing. Christine names herself as a female author and thus occupies a position that is defined by the special authority conferred upon her by a traversal of the conventional categories—she is *both* an ignorant woman *and* a learned (because self-taught) author. Her presentation of her authority, even in her act as a chronicler, is thus unlike that of her male contemporaries. Equally subtle and different, of course, is her substitution of "moi" for "je." Object rather than subject of her own sentence, Christine emphatically marks the difference of her own gendered use of the formula.[9]

Far more important, in the *Livre de la cité des dames*, Christine diverges from the practice of the chroniclers, who confined their self-naming to the prologue, acknowledging some formal boundary between the authority of the writer and the authority of the event to be chronicled. Instead, she names herself again and again throughout the text of the *Cité:* "Je, Christine, qui ces choses entendoye de dame Rayson . . ." (p. 734); "Je, Christine, encores dis a elle" (p. 761);

---

[9]The grammatical difference may indicate not so much the difficulty a female encounters in taking up the position of the speaking subject as that even here she moves to constitute her "self" as the subject of speech. It thus indicates as well Christine's insistence upon her authority precisely as a woman to speak of recent history, to gather the materials of a "novelle compilacion."

"Adont, je, Christine, ouyant la parolle de la dame honouree, dis en cest maniere" (p. 786).[10] In this work in particular, her own experience as a female subject engaged in conversation with other female authorities ("entendoye," "dis," "ouyant") becomes quite literally the subject of her discourse. This is no mere play on words. She can make herself the active agent of her own sentences, which are on the topic of her own opinions, ideas, and experiences. Uniquely Christine de Pizan not only names herself as author but makes her own gendered subjectivity, indicated by the signature, the fundamental authority subtending her text. "Experience," of course, is as discursively constructed as any set of purely textual traditions; but, as we shall see, Christine's positing of an essentialist assumption about experiential difference allows her to construct an alternative authority within the textual practices she has inherited.

By such outright courting of the gendered position, Christine not only differentiates herself from the practice of her male contemporary chroniclers, but also seems to insist upon an authority that goes contrary to modern constructivist feminist practice.[11] Monique Wittig has, for instance, argued that for a modern woman author to use the first-person pronoun is to stake a claim to the authority of a

[10]There may be numerological significance to Christine's self-naming in the *Cité*. In part I, Justice addresses her once, and she refers to herself three times. In part II, she uses the locution "Je, Christine" nine times. In part III, Justice calls her directly by name three times; only Justice addresses Christine with her name. Part II: "Et je, Christine, dis adont a la dame qui parloit" (p. 838); "Apres ces choses, je, Christine, dis ainsi" (p. 872); "Adonc je, Christine, dis ainsi" (p. 885); "Derechief je, Christine, dis a elle" (p. 925); "En procedant oultre, je, Christine, dis derechief ainsi" (p. 926); "Je, Christine, dis ainsi" (p. 955); "Et je, Christine, respondi" (p. 961); "Et je, Christine, dix adonc" (p. 963); "Et je, Christine, a tant respondis" (p. 970). Part III: Justice addresses her directly with her name (p. 974); Justice tells the story of the naming of St. Christine, Christine's patron saint (p. 1000); Justice addresses her directly with her name (p. 1027): "Que veulx tu que plus je t'en die, belle amie, Christine?"; "Je ne scay que plus t'en diroye, Christine, amie" (p. 1030). Such repetition is important in establishing the formula as a "signature." Jacques Derrida, in "Signature Event Context," emphasizes the repeatable sameness of the signature as the basis of its functionality: "In order to function, that is, in order to be legible, a signature must have a repeatable, iterable, imitable form; it must be able to detach itself from the present and singular intention of its production." *Margins of Philosophy*, trans. Alan Bass (Chicago: University of Chicago Press, 1982), p. 328.

[11]For a discussion of the various affordances essentialism may provide, see Diana Fuss, *Essentially Speaking: Feminism, Nature, and Difference* (New York: Routledge, 1989), in particular chapter 3, an analysis of Monique Wittig's anti-essentialism.

locutor who is an "absolute subject," speaking with a universal and abstract authority. She notes that in French, however, the moment the first-person pronoun receives its first past participle, it is gendered and by being gendered, it is particularized, and so deprived of any universal application. "The result of the imposition of gender, acting as a denial at the very moment when one speaks, is to deprive women of the authority of speech, and to force them to make their entrance in a crab-like way, particularizing themselves and apologizing profusely. The result is to deny them any claim to the abstract, philosophical, political discourses that give shape to the social body."[12]

In diametric contrast to this modern polemic against gendering, Christine's practice of immediately—even ostentatiously—gendering her first-person pronoun by particularizing it with her own Christian name announces a practice that embraces the already stated differences of gender and establishes an authority by means of that very difference. As a woman writer, Christine de Pizan knew herself to be valued for the sheer novelty of the thing. By her insistence on this novelty, she became "France's first professional woman of letters" (Willard, p. 15). Paradoxically, she also became, in some fundamental sense of the term, France's first "modern" author, that is, self-named, autonomous, biographically and historically specific, a "professional," possessed of a social authority that substitutes gender for traditional class status.[13]

These two anomalies embedded in Christine's career—her appar-

---

[12]Monique Witting, "The Mark of Gender," in *The Poetics of Gender*, ed. Nancy K. Miller (New York: Columbia University Press, 1986), p. 67.

[13]Danielle Régnier-Bohler, *Imagining a Self*, p. 358, implies that the first privatized individual subject would necessarily have had to be a woman: "By praying until everyone in the house had gone to bed and then making sure that all doors, windows, and chests were tightly closed, an autarchic inner world was eventually created. The individual, wholly devoted to God, stood in the dead of night face to face with herself." In a summary discussion of an answer to the question, "Did the twelfth-century discover the individual?" Caroline Bynum states a useful difference in *Jesus as Mother: Studies in the Spirituality of the High Middle Ages* (Berkeley: University of California Press, 1982), p. 87: "When we [twentieth-century people] speak of the 'individual,' we mean not only an inner core, a self; we also mean a particular self, a self unique and unlike other selves. When we speak of the 'development of the individual,' we mean something open-ended. In contrast . . . the twelfth century regarded the discovery of *homo interior*, or *seipsum*, as the discovery within oneself of human nature made in the image of God—an *imago Dei* that is the same for all human beings."

ent modernity as an author and her female gender as a writer—are connected. The sheer particularizing repetitions of her name in conjunction with the first-person pronoun make the autobiographical marking of her text a necessarily different operation from that of the chroniclers and even from the writings of such nonchronicling authors as Guillaume de Machaut, who uses a lyric "je" and occasionally mentions his own name.[14] Dante held in the *Convivio* that no one should speak of himself without real reason, although, as Ernst Curtius points out, Dante admits that there could be exceptions and that such distinguished authors as "Augustine and Boethius might name themselves."[15]

The Model of Dante

Dante, of course, named himself in the *Commedia*, a poem Christine knew quite well. Because she appears, in fact, to be positioning herself in relation to this moment in her first self-reference in the *Livre de la cité des dames*, his naming of himself will reward a brief consideration.

The passage is famous. Dante inserts his signature once in the *Commedia*. Before he actually sees her, Beatrice calls out his name in Canto XXX of the *Purgatorio*. The centrality of this moment of self-naming arises from both the uniqueness of the self-reference and the crucial conjunction of literary history and authority within it. Dante

[14]For a discussion of the tradition behind the "lyric je" and the transformations wrought with it by Guillaume de Machaut in the generation before Christine, see Kevin Brownlee, *Poetic Identity in Guillaume de Machaut* (Madison: University of Wisconsin Press, 1984), chap. 1. Machaut's self-naming is far less frequent than Christine's and is often in anagram. Her signature remains, if not unique, then exceptional.

[15]Ernst Curtius, "Mention of the Author's Name in Medieval Literature," in *European Literature and the Latin Middle Ages*, trans. Willard R. Trask (New York: Pantheon, 1953), pp. 515–18. Curtius argues that the reasons for anonymity varied widely through the centuries and across geographical areas, nor was it always required, the twelfth century in particular showing an "unadulterated pride of authorship." A. J. Minnis surveys the secretive self-naming through wordplay and acrostics of late medieval authors in *Medieval Theory of Authorship: Scholastic Literary Attitudes in the Later Middle Ages*, 2d ed. (Philadelphia: University of Pennsylvania Press, 1988), pp. 170–77.

has turned to speak to Virgil, translating Dido's famous confession of passion—"Adgnosco veteris vestigia flammae" (*Aeneid*, IV. 23)—but Virgil is gone.

> "conosco i segni de l'antica fiamma."
> Ma Virgilio n'avea lasciati scemi
> di sé—Virgilio, dolcissimo patre—
> Virgilio, a cui per mia salute die' mi!
> (Purg., XXX.48–51)

"I know the tokens of the ancient flame." But Virgil had left us bereft of himself, Virgil, sweetest father, Virgil to whom I gave myself for my salvation.[16]

Translating "vestigi" as "segni," Dante turns a mark into a sign, signaling thereby the evolution in the ontological status of the flames. While Dido feels the return of a long-dead flame that will end in a libidinous passion for Aeneas and the betrayal of her faithfulness to her dead husband Sichaeus (a betrayal that warrants Dido a place in the first circle of Dante's hell), the "sign" of the return of Dante's love for Beatrice represents a far better love. The translation of "vestigi" as "segni" may in fact label what Dante is doing to his pagan tradition, turning the trace of an empire-threatening physical love into a symbol of divine favor. It is both a translation from one language to another and a transformation of the "flame" of libidinous love into the *caritas* hidden in the triple mention of Virgil's name in a single terza rima, the form paying homage to the triple figuration of the divine. At this moment Beatrice speaks:

> "Dante, perché Virgilio se ne vada,
> non pianger ancor, non piangere ancora;
> ché pianger ti conven per altra spada!"
> (Purg., XXX.55–57)

"Dante, because Virgil leaves you, do not weep yet, do not weep yet, for you must weep for another sword!" (p. 331)

---

[16]Dante Alighieri, *The Divine Comedy: Purgatorio*, trans. Charles S. Singleton (Princeton: Princeton University Press, 1973), p. 329. For further discussion of the problematic figure of Dido in Augustine, Dante, and Christine, see below, pp. 172–73.

The pathos of paternal loss figures the transfer from one authority to the next, from male pagan *pater* to female Christian beloved.[17] Charles Singleton has argued that the triple repetition of Virgil's name within a single terza rima mimics a similar triple call in Virgil's *Georgics*—when Orpheus says goodbye to Eurydice just before she descends to hell. Hence the triple naming echoes the master's text at a point where the topography of Mount Purgatory delimits the upper limit of Virgil's reach, a boundary Dante now crosses, leaving Virgil behind.[18]

The episode thus marks Dante's full inheritance of his literary patrimony in a poetic succession from one *auctor* to another. Dante names himself here by having Beatrice call to him. The first half of line 48 enacts his initial homage to the pagan poet upon their first meeting at the foot of the mountain, celebrating his possession of the epic poem whose verses have made him a poet: "Dante, perché Virgilio." At this moment, Dante makes clear that he is Dante because Virgil has been Virgil.[19] The number *three* figures importantly in the dense layering of texts by which Dante bids farewell to his pagan auctor and pater, specifically in the terms which that pater had used to describe the return of sexual passion, a passion now transformed, if no less deeply felt. Beatrice mentions Virgil's name three times but calls out to her own beloved only once.

The misogyny by which Dante compares his loss of Virgil to Eve's loss of paradise marks the transfer of authority from male to female psychopomps. It would have been a move of interest to Christine de Pizan, and it may indeed have been for his emphasis on Beatrice's authority that Christine recommended Dante as an alternative authority to Jean de Meun. In her famous attack on the misogynist authority of the *Roman de la rose*, she had compared the two poets, referring to them in significantly different terms.[20] She had written to Pierre Col:

[17]For a fuller discussion of multiple gender reversals in this passage and Dante's relationship to Virgil generally, see Rachel Jacoff, "Models of Literary Influence in the *Commedia*," in *Medieval Texts and Contemporary Readers*, ed. Laurie A. Finke and Martin B. Schichtman (Ithaca: Cornell University Press, 1987), pp. 158–76.

[18]Charles S. Singleton, *The Divine Comedy, Purgatorio: Commentary* (Princeton: Princeton University Press, 1973), p. 741.

[19]I am indebted to Nancy Vickers for this point.

[20]For a discussion of Christine's entry into public Parisian intellectual life with this attack on the authority of Jean de Meun, see Pierre-Yves Badel, *Le "Roman de la rose"*

Mais se mieulx vuelz oïr descripre paradis et enfer, et par plus subtilz
termes plus haultement parlé de theologie, plus prouffitablement, plus
poetiquement, et de plus grant efficasse, lis le livre *que on appelle le
Dant; . . .* la oyras autre propos mieux fondé plus subtilment, ne te
desplaise, et ou tu pourras plus prouffiter que en ton *Romant de la
Rose,*—et cent fois mieux composé; ne il n'y a comparison.

But if you wish to hear heaven and hell described more subtly and
theologically, portrayed more advantageously, poetically, and effica-
ciously, read the book *which is called Dante. . .* Without wishing to
displease you, you will find there sounder principles, and you will be
better able to profit from it than from your *Roman de la Rose.* It is one
hundred times better written; there is, be not offended, no comparison.[21]

To underscore the contrast, Christine refers to Jean's text by its title;
Dante's poem she calls by Dante's name, as if text and author were
one, thereby privileging Dante as an auctor and denigrating Jean's
claim to true authority.[22]

The first time Christine names herself in the *Livre de la cité des
dames* she uncannily echoes Dante's emphasis upon the numerologically significant third term. Justice is specifically the *third* figure of authority introduced in the *Cité.* It is she who calls Christine
by her Christian name for the first time in the text, only moments
before she announces her own name.

Aprés parla la tierce dame qui dist ainsi: "Christine amie, je suis Justice,
la tres singuliere fille de Dieu, et mon essance procede de sa personne
purement.

au XIVe siècle: Etude de la réception de l'oeuvre (Geneva: Librairie Droz, 1980),
pp. 411–46.
    [21]*Le débat sur le "Roman de la rose,"* ed. Eric Hicks (Paris: Editions Honoré Cham-
pion, 1977), pp. 141–42; emphasis added. Translations are from Joseph L. Baird and
John R. Kane, trans., *"La Querelle de la 'Rose'": Letters and Documents,* North
Carolina Studies in Romance Languages and Literatures (Chapel Hill: University of
North Carolina Department of Romance Languages and Literatures, 1978), p. 138.
    [22]For a discussion of Christine's establishment of her own authority against Jean's in
the "querelle de la *Rose,*" see Kevin Brownlee, "The Discourse of the Self: Christine de
Pizan and the *Rose,*" *Romantic Review* 59 (1988), 213–21.

Afterward the third lady spoke and said, "My friend Christine, I am Justice, the most singular daughter of God, and my nature proceeds purely from His person."[23]

The specific allusion works by structural analogy rather than by verbal echo. Justice, a woman, names Christine, just as Beatrice, a woman, names Dante. Justice is the third figure after Reason and Droitture (who is both Righteousness and the Law in a secular sense) to address the interlocutor, and the tripleness itself may be a possible allusion to the *Commedia*'s intricate triplicities (as in the terza rima and the three repetitions of Virgil's name). A further structural parallel is that Justice narrates the third section of the *Cité*, which, like the *Paradiso*, is populated by saints. Her character is as different from Droitture as Paradise is from Purgatory: both Justice and the *Paradiso* are heavenly and both give special relevance to the specific identities of their respective poets, although in Dante's case the identification concerns not his name but his patrilineal forebear, while Christine's name is granted to her patron saint.

Of equal importance to the similarities between the two moments of naming, however, are the striking differences between them due simply to gender: when Beatrice reprimands Dante, she addresses an interlocutor who is gendered "other" from her. Dante does not name himself, but allows Beatrice to place his name with Virgil's; by her authority she not only chastises him but grants him the same status as named *auctor*. With modesty, he both excuses and emphasizes his self-naming in the text: "mi volsi al suon del nome mio, / che di necessità qui si registra" (Purg., XXX.62–63); "I turned at the sound of my name, which of necessity is registered here" (p. 331). His particularity as an individual sacrifices no universality to his masculine identity because it is stabilized by her female otherness. In the plot development of the narrative itself, the transference from a pagan to a Christian authority is further underscored by a switch in the gendering of authority. While Virgil plays both father and mother to Dante, he is male. Beatrice retains the authority of the female, and

[23]"The *Livre de la Cité Des Dames* of Christine de Pizan: A Critical Edition," ed. Maureen Curnow, 2 vols. (Ph.D. diss., Vanderbilt University, 1975), p. 635; all further quotations of the French text are from this edition, hereafter cited in the text. The translation is from *The Book of the City of Ladies*, trans. Earl Jeffrey Richards (New York: Persea Books, 1982), p. 13, hereafter cited in the text.

1. Boethius and Lady Philosophy, Ms. Ffr. 1728, f. 221r. Paris, Bibliothèque Nationale

the future lessons Dante receives from his blessed guide conform more nearly to the usual paradigm of the allegorical debate in which, traditionally, a male poet questions and is questioned by a female figure of authority—as, for example, in Boethius's *Consolation of Philosophy* or Alain de Lille's *Complaint of Nature*.[24] Two illuminations will make this usual transaction clearer: In Figure 1 Boethius confronts Lady Philosophy in the capital that opens Jean de Meun's translation of the *Consolation of Philosophy*. Figure 2 is a later fifteenth-century illumination that shows Boethius in prison while Lady Philosophy attempts to give him comfort. The gender of this

---

[24]Christine uses Boethius's *Consolatio* as her basic auctor in the reading scene of *Le livre du chemin de long estude*, ed. Robert Püschel (Paris: H. LeSoudier, n.d.), ll. 205–9.

2. Boethius and Lady Philosophy, Ms. Ffr. 809, f. 29v. Paris, Bibliothèque Nationale

conventional scene is due essentially to the exigencies of grammar: personifications of abstractions such as Philosophy and Nature take the feminine form primarily because allegory always works narratively by literalizing lexical effects. The gender of abstract nouns made from verbs in Latin is always feminine—*auctoritas* itself, for

3. Boccaccio and Lady Fortune, Ms. Royal 20 C V, f. 198r. London, British Library, by permission

instance, is feminine—and so the personifications embodying these concepts take on the gender of the words: Lady Philosophy, Lady Nature, Lady Fortuna.[25] In Figure 3 Boccaccio confronts a multi-

[25]Joan Ferrante, *Woman as Image in Medieval Literature: From the Twelfth Century to Dante* (New York: Columbia University Press, 1975): "Many of the classical personifications were female because the abstract nouns they represent are feminine, though grammatical accident is not the only factor in determining gender" (p. 38). Chapter 2 gives a thorough survey of the range of female images in allegory (pp. 38–64). Male figures of authority are rare and seldom hold a masculine gender that goes against the grammatical grain. A significant example is Gerson's attempt to make the character of Eloquentia masculine in the "querelle de la *Rose.*" Although Eloquentia is male in Gerson's text, the other interlocutors refer to the character as female. Gerson

armed Lady Fortune in the incipit illumination to the *Cas des nobles hommes et femmes.*

In contrast to such representations, in the *Cité des dames* two females confront each other at any given time. Both are, moreover, female characters who self-consciously identify themselves as females, sharing a similar stance in opposition to a misogynist male tradition. In essence, what Christine does is simply to take very seriously the metaphorically feminine gender of allegorical figures of authority—decreed by the grammar of romance languages to be feminine—thereby literalizing them through a verbal play generic to allegory and transforming them from female figures of authority into female spokespersons for a vast range of pro-woman (anti-misogynist) positions. In itself, it is a curiously different staging of auctoritas. Even in comparison with so hospitable an author as Dante then, Christine's difference from her male precursor is striking and is underscored by the loss of misogynistic reference, for even Dante chooses to remind his readers of the tradition that locates the origin of all loss in Eve, our "antica matre" (Purg., XXX.52).[26]

Christine's preference for Dante over Jean de Meun had doubtless many motivations. First, it is important to recognize that—like any other writer who was attempting to enter the canon—she would necessarily undertake a rewriting of that canon, one that might *allow* her entry.[27] Her attack on the *Rose*—indeed her engagement in the "querelle de la *Rose*" (which subsequently developed into the Renaissance "querelle des femmes")—seems to have been quite self-consciously aimed at establishing the specific possibility of female authority.[28] She had closed her first letter with a distinct self-defense:

---

writes, "Eloquance Theologienne . . . par grande auctorité et digne gravité, il, . . . telement commensa sa parole et sa cause" (Hicks, *Débat sur la "Rose,"* p. 66); Pierre Col responds, "Premierement donc dame Eloquance Theologienne dist . . ." (Hicks, *Débat sur le "Rose,"* p. 92).

[26]The verbal echo may underscore a similarity between the erotics of the Virgilian "antica fiamma" and the biblical "antica matre."

[27]See John Guillory, "The Ideology of Canon-Formation: T. S. Eliot and Cleanth Brooks," *Critical Inquiry* 10 (1983), 173–98. For a persuasive and thorough discussion of Christine's construction of her authority in the early lyric poetry that specifically builds on the *Rose*, see Kevin Brownlee, "Discourses of the Self." Brownlee argues that Christine "confronts and displaces Jean de Meun as authoritative vernacular clerk with a historically 'real' self-presentation as learned woman author" (p. 201).

[28]Pierre-Yves Badel, *La "Rose" au XIVe siècle,* p. 436: "La querelle lui permet de

Et ne me soit imputé a follie, arrogance, ou presompcion d'oser, moy femme, repprendre et redarguer aucteur tant subtil et son euvre admenuisier de louenge, quant lui, seul homme, osa entreprendre a diffamer et blasmer sans excepcion tout un sexe. (Hicks, p. 22)

And let it not be imputed to me a folly, or arrogance, or presumption for me to dare, a mere woman, to reprehend and to criticize an author of such subtlety, whose work is acclaimed by praise, when he, a single man, has dared to undertake to defame and blame without exception an entire sex. (My translation)

Her entry into the canon is thus positionally gendered from its inception in this polemic prose.

Christine's praise of Dante's Italian allegory may secondarily have been an attempt to capitalize on the great admiration felt in France at that time for the beginnings of Italian humanism and therefore to defend against any handicap her Italian birth may have been to her. Hence she advises Pierre Col to have someone explain Dante to him because it is written "souverainnement" (superlatively) in the Florentine language.[29] Ultimately, Dante's tripartite form may have been an aid in her selection of the three-part form she uses in the *Cité* and other allegorical-vision poems (for instance, *Lavision-Christine*).[30] The specific use of Justice as the third figure of authority to address the poet (a figure who then narrates the third section of the text) indicates the tripartite form of Christine's own allegory, modeled after the numerologically significant shape of Dante's poem. As Christine was only the second person in the history of French literature to mention Dante (her colleague at court,

---

conforter sa réputation de femme de lettres et de hâter une ascension que couronne, le 23 juin 1402, une première édition de ses oeuvres complètes." In 1616 Ben Jonson became the first English "author" to publish his nonposthumous collected *Works;* Christine's manuscript collection predates his by 204 years.

[29]Hicks, *Débat sur la "Rose,"* p. 142. Willard, *Christine de Pizan,* p. 74, points out that the exchange of letters in the Rose controversy may have owed something to the Italian humanist practice of engaging in literary debates. Jacqueline Cerquiglini, "L'étrangère," *Revue des Langues Romanes* 92 (1988), 239–51, suggestively argues that Christine's own experience as a foreigner engaged her in a cultural sense of exile which she wrote into a number of different "translations," ending with her self-constitution as the writing subject.

[30]*Lavision-Christine,* ed. Sister Mary Louise Towner (Washington, D.C.: Catholic University of America, 1932).

Phillip de Mézières, has the honor of being the first), she may not have expected anyone to recognize these subtle echoes. But her positioning of herself in relation to Dante's unique self-reference in the *Commedia* in her own first self-naming in the *Cité* remains a move entirely logical, given her overall attempt to install herself in a literary tradition that specifically privileges him. That she then goes on to name herself over and over marks her difference from him specifically in her very different allegorical practice.[31]

Writing *The House of Fame* (1372) some few decades before Christine wrote the *Cité*, Chaucer parodically recalls this same moment in Dante. His imitation suggests that the passage of self-naming could become pivotal to subsequent poets, especially to one who was considering—as Chaucer distinctly was in this aptly titled text—his own authority.[32] The eagle comments on Chaucer's fatness—"Saynte Marye! / Thou art noyous for to carye" (ll. 573–74)—and later calls him by name: "Geffrey, thou wost ryght wel this" (ll. 729–32).[33] Chaucer differs significantly from Christine in his comic use of Dante because he not only recalls Dante more directly, conflating his dream of being carried by an eagle in Purgatorio IX with the moment of naming from Purgatorio XXX, but also imitates the unique instance of Dante's self-naming. Geoffrey is "Geffrey" only once in the three-part *House of Fame* (indeed is mentioned nowhere else throughout the rest of his corpus). Christine, conversely, names herself continuously. Wherever she first found it, her constant repetition of the practice of self-naming puts a distinctly different textual weight upon both the narrator's representation of her authority and its intensification of her gender. Her name's usual scribal abbreviation with the Greek letters Chi-Rho (Xpine) makes the very word stand out on the manuscript page, as it carries within it the initial Greek letter in the name Christ, which means "anointed." As we shall see, the authority that the term is made to carry by this verbal

[31]See below, pp. 242–43.

[32]For a discussion of *The House of Fame* as Chaucer's elaborate consideration of the various authorities available to him as a writer, see Jacqueline T. Miller, *Poetic License: Authority and Authorship in Medieval and Renaissance Contexts* (New York: Oxford University Press, 1986), chap. 2. See also Maureen Quilligan, *The Language of Allegory: Defining the Genre* (Ithaca: Cornell University Press, 1979), pp. 247–48.

[33]F. N. Robinson, ed., *The Works of Geoffrey Chaucer*, 2d ed. (Boston: Houghton Mifflin, 1957). *The House of Fame* ends inconclusively with the appearance in the very last line of "A man of gret auctorite," who, however, does not speak (l. 2158).

wittiness, a gesture generic to allegory, becomes the culminating drama of the last section of the text, where Christine avails herself of the highest possible authority by deriving her patron saint's name, and therefore also her own, from the name of Christ.[34]

The caption to the portrait in Figure 4 reveals the usual scribal form of Christine's name, and the portrait shows her giving moral guidance to her son, the one position that could be an instantly recognizable stance of authority for a woman, whose motherhood allowed her all the socially sanctioned power of physiological nurture. As the miniature also makes abundantly clear, however, Christine de Pizan occupied her position of motherly authority with all the accoutrements of an entirely different tradition of authority. Her paradigmatic presentation in her study, surrounded by books, doubles her authority: it is both "natural" *and* cultural, both physical and scripted. The books in Figure 4 confer an authority that also allows her to write a book of moral proverbs for a male audience. The replication of the woman in Figure 4 in the miniature in Figure 5 demonstrates the transference of the authoritative stance of maternal nurture from one to the other, a transference that "naturalizes" the bookish authority.

A rather more surprising representation of female authority is the incipit miniature to the *Livre des fais d'armes et de chevalerie*, a practical manual in which Christine revised outdated chivalric rules.[35]

In Figures 4 and 5, Christine is portrayed almost as if she were barricaded behind the table upon which the open book lies, one hand touching the text, the other gesturing speech, but in the commencement to the book on chivalry (Figure 6), Christine stands before Minerva. While in the first two miniatures the woman becomes a conduit for the book's authority and occupies a stance similar to the

---

[34]See below, pp. 216–17. William Langland uses his own name as part of his allegorical program in *Piers Plowman:* As "Will" he represents the appetitive faculty of the will; he has also lived "in lond, my name is long wille." Shakespeare, of course, does this throughout the sonnets, but he is a Renaissance writer for whom the gesture is less surprising. For further discussion of the name-play in allegory see Quilligan, *Language of Allegory*, p. 164.

[35]Willard, *Christine de Pizan*, pp. 186–87, points out that William Caxton's early translation and printing of the text in 1489 kept in prominent position Christine's female authorship, but the early French printed text published by Vérard in 1488 suppressed the author's gender entirely.

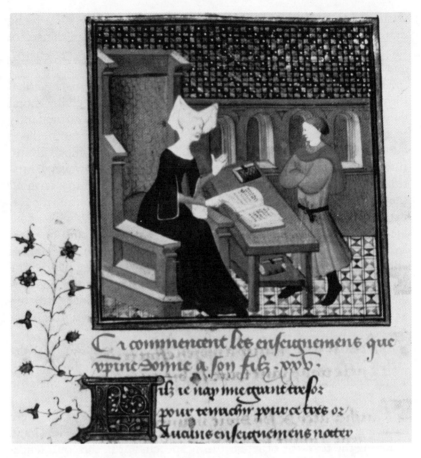

4. Christine de Pizan and her son, Ms. Harley 4431, f. 261v. London, British Library, by permission

picture of Philosophy herself holding the books in Figure 1, in the more transgressive text on warfare, Christine receives the information directly from a goddess Christine figures elsewhere as another Italian woman. She does not touch the books, as if there is no need to do so when the female authority (Minerva) is herself physically present.

One way of indicating the interconnections between various authorities available to Christine as a woman writing in the late fourteenth century is to consider what those depicted books may have meant to a reader attempting to understand the unique position

5. Christine de Pizan, the incipit to the *Proverbes moraux*, Ms. Harley 4431, f. 259v. London, British Library, by permission

occupied by Christine in these miniatures. What place did a woman have in the medieval system of auctores?

The Authority of the Auctores

A. J. Minnis has recently argued that there was a theory of authorship in the later Middle Ages which can be best discovered through a survey of the academic prologues to numerous commentaries on

6. Christine de Pizan and Minerva, the incipit to the *Fais des armes et chevalrie*, Ms. Ffr. 603, f. 21. Paris, Bibliothèque Nationale

scripture and secular Latin literature throughout the period. The theory focused on the function of authorship: an author, or auctor, was "someone who was at once a writer and an authority, someone not merely to be read but also to be respected and believed." Only the work of an auctor was marked by authenticity, a status bestowed when "later writers used extracts from his works as sententious statements or *auctoritates* . . . or employed them as literary models."[36] Most important, in order to be "authentic, a saying or a piece

---

[36]A. J. Minnis, *Medieval Theory of Authorship*, p. 10. Minnis summarizes the grammarians' derivation of the term "author" from four main sources: "*auctor* was supposed to be related to the Latin verbs *agere* 'to act or perform', *augere* 'to grow' and *auieo* 'to tie', and to the Greek noun *autentim* 'authority'. An *auctor* 'performed' the act of writing. He brought something into being, caused it to 'grow'. In the more specialized sense related to *auieo*, poets like Virgil and Lucan were *auctores* in that

of writing had to be the genuine production of a named *auctor*"
(p. 11).

Minnis's excavation of one form of authority is of particular importance to Christine's practice in the *Cité des dames,* as well as to all of
her major auctores for that work. A "special literary activity and a
distinctive literary role" belongs to the writer Minnis calls a *compilator,* whose participation in the writing function is distinctly
different from that of an auctor: "Whereas an *auctor* was regarded as
someone whose works had considerable authority and who bore full
responsibility for what he had written, the *compilator* firmly denied
any personal authority and accepted responsibility only for the manner in which he had arranged the statements of other men [*sic*]"
(p. 192). It is notable that all of the sources Christine mentions in the
Cité are writers who presented themselves as compilators of one sort
or another—Jean de Meun, Boccaccio, and Vincent of Beauvais. Indeed, she herself is a compilator, the *Cité* being an exquisitely arranged compendium of stories about the lives of notable pagan and
Christian women, framed by an allegorical *débat* or *consolatio.*

The care with which a compilator would distinguish his own lack
of authority from that of his auctores may be exemplified in the
method used by Vincent of Beauvais to warn his readers of his own
opinions: according to Minnis, "he carefully labelled those few asser-
tions for which he was prepared to accept personal responsibility
with the term *actor*" (p. 193), an actor having far less authority than
an auctor.

Such distinctions are important for the characterization they allow of Christine's practice as a female writer from text to text, and
also because they had a peculiarly pivotal part to play in the nuanced
shadings of authority granted to specific author-positions within a
changing literary system. For example, Minnis points out that in the
later Middle Ages, "the traditional protestation of the compiler is
well on its way to becoming a 'disavowal of responsibility' trope"
(p. 198). Jean de Meun was notoriously able to exploit the moral
ambiguity of the compilator's humble position and to use the typical
"apologia" to defend himself from charges of obscenity, and most
significantly, of misogyny:

---

they had 'tied' together their verses with feet and metres. To the ideas of achievement
and growth was easily assimilated the idea of authenticity or 'authoritativeness'."

> D'autre part, dames enourables,
> S'il vous semble que je di fables,
> Pour menteeur ne m'en tenez,
> Mais aus aucteurs vous en prenez
> Qui en leur livres on escrites
> Les paroles que j'en ai dites,
> E ceus avec que j'en dirai;
> Ne ja de riens n'en mentirai
> Se li preudome n'en mentirent
> Quil les anciens livres firent.

> And furthermore, most honorable dames,
> If you think I say things that are not true,
> Say not I lie, but search authorities
> Who've written in their books what I have said
> And shall. In no respect speak I untruth
> Unless wise men who wrote the ancient books
> Were lying, too.[37]

In a recent attempt to interpret the significance of medieval misogyny as a pervasive discourse that cuts across many generic boundaries, R. Howard Bloch has most usefully pinpointed its character as "a citational mode whose rhetorical thrust is to displace its own source away from anything that might be construed as personal or concessional and toward the sacred authorities whose own existence, as often as not, is the absent . . . Theophrastes."[38] Late medieval misogyny, especially as exemplified by the classic form it assumes in the *Roman de la rose*, makes the best response to any challenge a recourse to the auctores: just as Jean explained, he was not criticizing women, but only following what wise men had already written in ancient books.

---

[37]Guillaume de Lorris and Jean de Meun, *Le roman de la rose*, ed. Felix Lecoy, 3 vols. (Paris: Editions Honoré Champion, 1965), 0:15215–24; *The Romance of the Rose*, trans. Harry W. Robbins, ed. Charles W. Dunn (New York: Dutton, 1962), p. 320.

[38]Howard Bloch, "Medieval Misogyny," *Representations* 20 (1987), 6. Bloch problematically posits a far more general relationship between misogyny and the scandal of the fictive than would a scholar adopting a more social historical approach. In his formulation that "the danger of woman . . . is that of literature itself" (p. 20), he loses the specificity of actual women in history and dilutes the usefulness of his otherwise helpful article.

Chaucer's apologia in defense of his use of profanity in *The Canterbury Tales* records an elaborate shrugging off of responsibility similar to Jean's appeal to the auctores. Although Chaucer says he uses foul language only because some of his speakers do, his practice also moves toward a more modern sense of mimesis and taste. Chaucer's and Jean de Meun's disclaimers come from opposite ends of the spectrum, of course, while sharing a superficially similar formulation: Chaucer disavows responsibility (and authority) by saying he is only recording actual speech; Jean disavows it by asserting that he is following august authorities from the hallowed, scripted past. It is perhaps instructive of the fundamental connection between literary misogyny and the authority of the auctores that the character Chaucer uses in *The Canterbury Tales* to critique authority most explicitly is the Wife of Bath: "Experience, though noon auctoritee / Were in this world, is right ynogh for me." She reasons by directly counterposing authority and experience. Even more explicitly, of course, she attacks the named tradition of misogyny, aggressively and literally going to the source and ripping pages out of the misogynist compilation of the clerk Jankyn, her last husband. As she reasons:

> Who peyntede the leon, tel me who?
> By God! if wommen hadde writen stories,
> As clerkes han withinne hire oratories,
> They wolde han writen of men moore wikkedness
> Than al the mark of Adam may redresse.
> Wife of Bath's Prologue, ll. 692–96

As mesmerizing as such an authentic-sounding voice may seem, however, it is necessary to realize that the wife here only opens up the possibility of an experientially based literature; Chaucer already interdicts such a discourse, as different and original as it might be. Indeed, the most important thing that the Wife of Bath can teach us is that the discursive slot in the literary system which allows for greatest resistance to authority has already been labeled "female writer" by Chaucer. When Dame Alisoun imagines the possibility of different stories that would narrate female points of view, Chaucer himself imagines through her the possibility of a literature based on the decorum of actual, individual, nonscripted experience. By further

35

labeling this radically new discursive place the "female-author position," he of course culturally undermines it. So too, not surprisingly, Alisoun is a figure who uses many full-blown, dirty words, made all the more wonderfully vulgar by her fake French euphemisms: she is a character, however, whose speech Chaucer claims he merely records.[39] The discursive position of the female objector to misogyny—and more fundamentally to the masculinist system of auctores which misogyny so paradigmatically mimics in its excess—would appear to exist as a possibility already authorized by the literary system. At least so it seems from Chaucer's characterization of the Wife of Bath.[40]

It is important for us to remember that the "experience" Chaucer posits as the opposite of authority in the Wife of Bath's opening remark is itself no less discursively formed than any literary text. Teresa de Lauretis has usefully argued that personal experience is the complicated process by which subjectivity is constructed and that gender is a fundamentally important part of that social construct: "a complex of meaning effects, habits, dispositions, associations, and perceptions resulting from the semiotic interaction of self and outer world."[41]

Christine's practice as an actual woman writer fulfills fewer misogynist expectations than Chaucer suggests would be the case through the person of an Alisoun who bases her authority on "experience"

[39] In defense of his vulgarity, Chaucer also appeals to the highest authority: "Crist spake hymself ful brode in hooly writ / And wel ye woot no vileynye is it" (Gen. Prol., 741–42). For a discussion of the relationship between canon-formation and "grammaticalness" or the relationship between divergent standards of correctness often registered as a difference between spoken and written language, a relationship that has bearing on the problem of Christine's objections to vulgar language, see John Guillory, "Canonical and Non-Canonical: A Critique of the Current Debate," *ELH* (1987), 483–527.

[40] The connections that are historically possible between Chaucer and Christine are alluring to contemplate—he could well have known of her, as her son was in attendance on the Earl of Salisbury from 1397–1400. Moreover, Henry IV invited her to his court immediately upon his accession, an invitation she declined. Willard, *Christine de Pizan*, pp. 164–65.

[41] Teresa de Lauretis, *Technologies of Gender: Essays on Theory, Film, and Fiction* (Bloomington: Indiana University Press, 1987), p. 18. De Lauretis further explains that "the constellation or configuration of meaning effects which I call experience shifts and is reformed continually, for each subject, with her or his continuous engagement in social reality, a reality that includes—and for women centrally—the social relations of gender" (p. 18).

only. Susan Schibanoff has interestingly argued that the Wife of Bath starts out as a better reader of misogynist tradition than Christine was, at least at first, because she is an "aural" reader, with no concept of the fixed, written text and is therefore freer to revise. Alisoun does not stop at burning books; her approach to misogyny is a full frontal attack. In contrast, Christine had to teach herself how to read "as a woman." Captured at first by male methods of allegorical reading, which inform her fixed interpretations in the *Epistre Othéa*, in the *Cité des dames* she learns to read with the strength derived from an "aural" tradition.[42] This is a useful distinction; in the hybrid text of the *Cité*, Christine represents her activities as a complicated amalgam of compilator's written practice and author's responsibility to both a lived experience and an oral tradition of communal female speakers. In a sense, Christine the compilator claims the traditional authority of her notable male *auctores* and the sibylline prophetic authority of her august female speakers, while simultaneously claiming the "science" allowed both by her experience as a "natural" woman and by her conversation with other women. Because Christine also associates this "naturalness" with the female body and would seem therefore to base her authority in part on a biological essentialism, it is important to realize what Diana Fuss finds so useful about Gayatri Spivak's defense of essentialism: "when put into practice by the dispossessed themselves, essentialism can be powerfully displacing and disruptive" (p. 32). This is the effect Chaucer notices and Christine deploys.

Christine's hybrid authority—copying the authors but revising according to "experience"—produces a compilation of stories extracted from authors as diverse as Boccaccio in his *Decameron* and Vincent of Beauvais who wrote saints' legends, stories that are radically, if subtly, rewritten and then put into an elaborate allegorical frame whereby they are told by three separate female figures of authority. Minnis suggests that, in contrast to Gower, "a compiler who tried to present himself as an author," Chaucer "was an author who hid behind the 'shield and defense' of the compiler" (p. 210). In this strategy, Christine is far more like Gower. Also like Gower in the

---

[42]Susan Schibanoff, "Taking the Gold Out of Egypt: The Art of Reading as a Woman," in *Gender and Reading: Essays on Readers, Texts, and Contexts*, ed. Elizabeth A. Flynn and Patrocino P. Schweikart (Baltimore: Johns Hopkins University Press, 1986), pp. 83–106.

Vox Clamatis, she claims a prophetic authority for the text dictated to her by the three personifications for whom she is mere scribe.[43] In the process Christine, however, makes herself into her own monumental figure of authority—strong enough to be herself an *auctor.*

In order to situate Christine's practice as specifically as we can within the tradition of authorial possibilities which she inherits as a medieval writer, we should consider her responses to her own auctores' claims to a compilator's humble irresponsibility. It is a striking fact that the compiler's excuse, so to speak, functions in yet another of Christine's *auctores* in the context of another definitely misogynist passage. The texts of misogyny carry embedded within them the twin parts of the tradition of "excuse"—both the appeal to auctores (as in Jean de Meun) and the newer more "verisimilar," mimetic excuse, that the writer simply copies what actual people actually say. Thus, in the *Decameron* (to which Christine refers in the *Cité*), Boccaccio also uses the "compilator's excuse" to underline, paradoxically, his own peculiarly original achievement in vernacular literature. "I could only transcribe the stories as they were actually told, which means that if the ladies who told them had told them better, I should have written them better. But even if one could assume that I was the inventor [l'inventore] as well as the scribe [lo scrittore] of these stories (which was not the case), I still insist that I would not feel ashamed if some fell short of perfection, for there is no craftsman other than God whose work is whole and faultless in every respect."[44]

There are doubtless many reasons for such a persistent misogynistic context to the compilator's apology. The fundamental denial to women of access to the institutions where the written tradition of the auctores was preserved (in its monastic, institutionalized scriptedness) would have made the mention of women a convenient boundary marker for any transgression over the line of traditional authority (a device Boccaccio uses in creating the *Decameron,* a very different generic undertaking from, for instance, *The Genealogy of the Gods*).[45] Chaucer's Wife of Bath marks the same boundary when

---

[43]For Gower as prophet, see Minnis, *Medieval Theory of Authorship,* p. 177.
[44]Cited in ibid. p. 205.
[45]Willard, *Christine de Pizan,* p. 45, reasons that Christine may have at first functioned as a scribe herself, just as other women copyists and illuminators were working in the newly energetic book trade of the time. Christine appears to have organized her

she assumes clerks and women do not get along: "Therfore no wom-man of no clerk is preysed" (l. 706). Any writer working in the vulgate, writing the mother tongue (such as Jean, Boccaccio, or Chau-cer), specifically not writing in Latin (and even, as with Boccaccio's *De mulieribus claris*, sometimes then too), might feel particularly compelled to make a disclaimer about the position of his text in relationship to social arenas labeled marginal to canonical authority by the presence of women.[46] The reference to women and their presumed hostility to the text (a reference thus presuming also their familiarity with it) rather precisely locates the work on the map of literary authority. His address of women in the *Decameron* ironically claims an "originality" that would otherwise be impossible to em-phasize without appealing to the limitations of his derogated female sources (who are here hardly "authorities"). It is not to be supposed that Boccaccio's first audience for the *De mulieribus claris* was women; rather, written in Latin, the text is aimed at a principally male audience. Its purpose is not to praise women but to spur men on to humanist achievements by goading them with the examples of heroic pagan women.[47]

Of course, these writers all knew actual women would be in their audiences and might have real objections to make. But the misogy-nist comment in the negative references to women would have func-tioned far more fundamentally as a code for signaling an unorthodox textual status and an experimental generic category to their male

own workshop and was accustomed to overseeing the production of manuscripts that became elaborate presentation copies to patrons such as the ducs de Berry and Bur-gundy and Queen Isabeau of Bavaria. Sandra L. Hindman, *Christine de Pizan's "Epistre Othéa": Painting and Politics at the Court of Charles VI* (Toronto: Pontifical Institute of Mediaeval Studies, 1986), p. 13, argues that Christine is France's first woman "publisher" as well as her first woman of letters and suggests that she was deeply engaged in all phases of book production, specifically providing her illuminators with detailed programs for the cycles of miniatures in manuscripts of her works (pp. 77–89).

[46]In the controversy over the *Roman de la rose*, Pierre Col, one of Christine's more persistent opponents, makes clear through his anachronism the association of women with the vernacular: "Ovide, quant il escript *L'Art d'amours*, il escript en latin, lequel n'entendent fammes" (Hicks, *Débat sur la "Rose,"* p. 105). "When Ovid wrote the *Art of Love*, he wrote in Latin, which women did not understand" (Baird and Kane, p. 108). The *De mulieribus claris* is a special instance of this case. See below, pp. 99–100.

[47]Giovanni Boccaccio, *De mulieribus claris*, ed. Vittorio Zaccaria, vol. 10, *Tutte le opere di Giovanni Boccaccio*, ed. Vittore Branca ([Milan]: Mondadori, 1967).

readers (that is, original work): the texts of social entertainment are to be judged differently from works of a more serious genre. Whatever its ultimate function in the literary system, however, it is important to realize that the misogyny of these disclaimers of intentional authority is ubiquitously present in the tradition Christine inherits. And her response to them is crucial to our understanding of the process of authority she constructs in the *Cité des dames*. But first it forms the basis of her attack on the *Roman de la rose*.

"The querelle de la *Rose*"

Christine specifically attacks the *Rose*'s defense of itself against misogyny; she refuses to accept the argument that the poem presents not the author's own opinions but the opinions of his characters. Because she does recognize the necessity of decorum for a given character's language, Christine objects to using vulgar terms for the sexual parts of the human body not only because such terms denigrate the proper and natural function of sexuality, but more importantly because such language is most inappropriate to a character such as Lady Reason (Hicks, pp. 13–14). In this she doubles up the argument from decorum; Lady Reason must not use vulgar terms both because of her literary status and also because of her social "gender": "trop traicte deshonnestment en aucunes pars . . . ou personnage que il claime Raison, laquelle nomme les secréz membres plainement par nom" (Hicks, p. 13); "he speaks too dishonorably in many parts . . . when he speaks through the character he calls Reason, who names the secret members plainly by name" (Baird and Kane, p. 48). Real women don't use such language. The problem arises because, in telling the story of Saturn's castration by Jupiter, Jean de Meun makes his Lady Reason use the slang term for testicles—"coilles"—for which "balls" might be a current slang translation.[48] This pivotal moment became a favorite one for later fifteenth-century illuminations of manuscripts of the *Rose*, and not merely, one assumes, because the moment was reasonably scandalous. The

[48]De Lorris and De Meun, *Le roman de la rose*, 1:5507.

7. Jupiter castrating Saturn, *Roman de la rose*, Ms. Douce 194, f. 76v. Oxford, Bodleian Library

illuminations are usually as explicit as Jean's very explicit language (Figure 7).[49]

---

[49]The miniature is from a manuscript in the Bodleian Library, Oxford; it was done in the late fifteenth century for Louise of Savoy and the count of Angoulême, parents of Francis I and his sister, Marguerite de Navarre, the author of the *Heptameron*. For a peculiarly full illustration of the whole story, showing both the birth of Venus from the dismembered genitals and the castrated body, see John V. Fleming, *The "Roman de la Rose": A Study in Allegory and Iconography* (Princeton: Princeton University Press, 1969), Fig. 33. The Valencia Ms. that Fleming prints may have been illuminated by one of the miniaturists Christine used, possibly causing her—so Charity Canon Willard suggests—greater consternation about the vulgarity of the text. See Willard, *Christine de Pizan*, pp. 229–30, n. 24.

Although a miniature provides no sure check on textual interpretation (visual evidence can be as easily misinterpreted as texts)
the two were assumed to be coherently readable together. Jean Gerson assumes they work in concert when, for instance, he questions:
"Mais qui plus art et enflemme ces ames que paroles dissolues et que
luxuryeuses escriptues et paintures?" (Hicks, p. 68); "But what burns
and inflames these souls more than dissolute words and libidinous
writings and paintings?" (my translation).

Christine's critique of Jean has drawn much criticism over the
centuries, but her objection to the language of the castration story
pinpoints her strongest move against Jean in the *Cité des dames*—as
well as her remarkable swerve away from the authority of her second
major auctor in the *Cité*, Boccaccio, whose *De mulieribus claris* is a
major source. As we will see, her rewrite of her auctores goes straight
to the heart of a castration anxiety that may be said to be the originary moment for the misogyny in the texts of both the *Rose* and the *De
claris*.[50] Reason's impolite language in Jean's text causes the lover to
dismiss Lady Reason as a figure of authority and to reject her kind of
love: the lover specifically asks for "quelque cortaise parole" (some
courteous word). Thus Jean anticipates the kind of response that
readers like Christine will have and makes it part of his text. The
rejection of Reason because of her crude word, however, motivates
the rest of the plot: in rejecting Reason, the lover turns to all the
other dramatis personae of the poem. A number of other attempts are
made in the *Rose* to explicate the story of Saturn's loss of his genitals;
one may say, without much exaggeration, that Jean's text is obsessed
with getting the story and its implications of idolatry understood
aright.[51]

[50]When Lady Reason explains that Ovid turned to writing attacks on women only
after he had been punished for his political and sexual transgressions by being "dif-
fourmez de ses membres" (i.e., castrated), Christine appears to point to this origin
(*Cité* p. 648; Richards, p. 21). The argument about Ovid was, of course, conventional,
but in the context of the *Cité*'s rejection of the whole misogynist tradition, Christine
anticipates a series of modern feminist critiques of Freudian theories about the oedipal
complex and female sexuality. See, in particular, Hélène Cixous, "The Laugh of the
Medusa," *Signs* 1 (1976), 875–93, reprinted in *The "Signs" Reader: Woman, Gender,
and Scholarship*, ed. Elizabeth Abel and Emily K. Abel (Chicago: University of Chicago Press, 1983), pp. 279–97. Luce Irigaray, *Speculum of the Other Woman*, trans.
Gillian Gill (Ithaca: Cornell University Press, 1985).

[51]For further discussion of the perhaps defensible tactic Jean de Meun uses and his
revision of his precursors, see my "Allegory, Allegoresis, and the Deallegorization of

Christine finds none of the story amusing or important, but she also objects with equal vehemence to the use of euphemistic language in talking about sexual intercourse, language that, she argues, is just as inflammatory as the vulgar and direct terms.

Il les nomme par mos poetiques entendables dix fois plus atisans et plus penetratis et plus delicteus a ceulx qui y sont enclins que se il les nommast par leurs propres nons. (Hicks, p. 125)

He names them by poetic but nonetheless explicit words which are a hundred times more enticing and more alluring and more sensual to those who are inclined in that way, than if he had named them by their proper names. (Baird and Kane, pp. 124–25)

Christine's critique of Jean de Meun's vulgarity speaks directly to the poem's own consideration of the proper relation between textual word and allegorical referent, although she chooses to recast her critique in terms of the postlapsarian moral responsibilities of literature.[52] Even more importantly, however, her moral concerns over the sexual stylistics of Jean's poem feed into her objections against the defamation of women throughout the text. Jean's defenders attempted to counter the criticisms of misogyny by using an appeal both to authorities and to the mimetic method of drama: it was decorous for certain characters to speak profanely and to refer to women derisively. Christine's answer is to say:

Tu respons . . . que maistre Jehan de Meung en son livre introduisy personnages, et fait chascun parler selonc ce que luy appartient. Et vraiement je te confesse bien que selonc le gieu que on vuelt jouer il convient instrumens propres, mais la voulanté dou jouer les appreste

---

Language: The *Roman de la rose,* the *De planctu naturae,* and the *Parlement of Foules,*" in *Allegory, Myth, and Symbol,* ed. Morton Bloomfield (Cambridge: Harvard University Press, 1981), pp. 163–86.

[52]In a way that recalls Samuel Johnson, in this instance Christine as critic is wrong but for the right reasons. She correctly understood, I think, that the argument about terminology was one of Jean's own central points of concern, as it had been for his major precursor, Alain. Christine mistakes, however, the philosophical seriousness of Jean's critique of the allegorical emptiness of euphemism and his thoroughgoing questions about the referentiality of language itself. She is right in pointing to referentiality as the problem, but wrong in dismissing Jean's motives as only vulgar misogyny.

telz come il luy fault. Touteffois certainnement, ne te desplaise, il failli de bien introduire ses personnnages de commettre a aucuns autre chose que leur office. (Hicks, p. 132)

You respond . . . that Master Jean de Meun introduced characters into his book, and made each one speak fittingly, according to what pertained to him. I readily admit that the proper equipment is necessary for any particular game, but the will of the player manipulates such equipment to his own purpose. And it is clearly true (may it not displease you) that he was at fault in attributing to some of his characters functions which do not properly belong to them. (Baird and Kane, p. 130)[53]

Christine's refusal to accept the compilator's excuse, here dressed out as the fidelity with which the verisimilar copier treats his "real" models, not only rejects claims of irresponsibility, it implicitly undermines Jean's appeal to the foundation of a scripted tradition of auctores. In both cases, Christine sees Jean pursuing his own purposes, for which he should be held responsible as author. For Christine to criticize misogyny is thus to criticize, at least in part, the assumptions upon which the appeal to the authority of auctores is based.

Chaucer's decision to model Dame Alisoun on La Vielle from the *Roman de la rose*, a character against whom Christine lodges particular complaints, reveals perhaps that he and Jean both had noses for a most alluring interstice within the literary system. Such an unruly woman has traditionally offered men a means for criticizing established authority—the Old Woman offers a similarly bawdy and outrageous freedom to Jean de Meun, whereby he reorganizes the tenor of Guillaume's courtly tone. So too men often masquerade as unruly women whenever they comedically (or seriously) wish to

[53]See also: "Et la laidure qui la est recordee des femmes, dient pluseurs en lui excusant que c'est le Jaloux qui parle, a voirement fait ainsi comme Dieu parla par la bouche Jeremie" (Hicks, *Débat sur la "Rose,"* p. 15); "And the ugliness about women which is there recorded, many say in excusing him that it is the Jealous Husband who speaks, just as God speaks through the mouth of Jeremiah" (my translation). Jean Gerson's position is articulated at greater length and in terms of legal statute: "Aucun escripra libelles diffamatoires d'une personne, soit de petit estat ou non—soit neis mauvaise—, et soit par personnaige: les drois jugent ung tel estre a pugnir et infame" (Hicks, *Débat sur la "Rose,"* p. 72); "If someone writes notorious books and, by means of introduced characters, defames some person, whether of low or noble or illegitimate birth the law holds such a writer to be wicked and deserving of punishment" (Baird and Kane, p. 80).

evade the rules of the system.[54] The radical potentialities of the Wife of Bath, of course, are partly undermined by Chaucer's ultimate dismissal of her unhappy and tragic case: she is, as Robert Hanning has recently pointed out, a creation made of "recycled components from various literary traditions of anti-feminism."[55] This origin provides something of a systemic limit: "Try as she (and Chaucer) might," Lee Patterson observes, "she remains confined within the prison house of masculine language; she brilliantly rearranges and deforms her authorities to enable them to disclose new areas of experience, but she remains dependent on them for her voice."[56] Christine's own objections to the misogynist tradition and the system of authorities it emblematizes are, not surprisingly, rather different from Chaucer's habitation of a potential discursive position through the character of the Wife of Bath, though the difference is not necessarily that Alisoun is a textual creature and Christine a real human being. If Dame Alisoun is made a victim of the literary system she attacks, then Christine takes care to manipulate it as fully as possible, authorizing her own practice in rewriting a tradition of literature and redefining women as they naturally are. Instead of confronting misogyny's essentialism head on, she redeploys it for her own purposes. All that was implicit about proper literary practice in the quarrel about the *Rose*, Christine makes absolutely explicit in the *Livre de la cité des dames*, where she describes in detail the workings of the misogynist tradition of auctores.

The Attack on Misogyny in the *Livre de la cité des dames:* Part I, Sections 1–14

Christine's attack on misogyny begins with the subtly unorthodox opening scene of her *Cité des dames*. Because her underlying genre is

[54]For a classic discussion of the political uses of the unruly woman in early modern France, see Natalie Zemon Davis, "Woman on Top," in her *Society and Culture in Early Modern France* (Stanford: Stanford University Press, 1977).

[55]Robert W. Hanning, "'I Shal Finde it in a Maner Glose': Versions of Textual Harassment in Medieval Literature," in *Medieval Texts and Contemporary Readers,* ed. Finke and Schichtman, p. 48.

[56]Lee Patterson, "'For the Wyves love of Bathe': Feminine Rhetoric and Poetic Resolution in the *Roman de la Rose* and the *Canterbury Tales*," *Speculum* 58 (1983), 682.

the allegorical dream vision, she has access to the power of a form that bases its authority on a foundation fundamentally different from the merely citational. The dream vision allows, in essence, a scope for "originality" that offers potential oracular authority for a character *Piers Plowman,* for example, calls, with uncomfortable suspicion, "Imaginatyf."[57] Since the *Roman de la rose* itself begins as an allegorical dream quest, it is clear how orthodox the form has become when Christine takes it up. By literalizing its elements, however, Christine gives her dream vision a fascinatingly different twist.

Surrounded by books, Christine sits in her study. Her opening situation locates her, then, at the privileged position for authorizing any text; she inhabits a space crowded with the accoutrements of scripted authority (Figure 8).

Christine's position within the framework of this kind of authority, however, is complicated by the very self-consciousness her gender causes at this traditional site of medieval authority. The first sentence of the text establishes her claim to occupy such a space:

Selonc la maniere que j'ay en usaige, et a quoy est disposé le excercice de ma vie: c'est assavoir en la frequentacion d'estude de lettres, un jour come je fusse seant en ma celle avironne de plusiers volumes de diverses matieres, mon entendement a celle heure aucques travaillié *de reccuillir la pesenteur des sentences de divers aucteurs* par moy longue estudiés, dreçay mon visaige enssus du livre, deliberant pour celle fois laissier em pais choses soubtilles et m'esbatre et regarder aucune joyeuseté des dist des pouettes. (p. 616; emphasis added)

One day as I was sitting alone in my study surrounded by books on all kinds of subjects, devoting myself to literary studies, my usual habit, my mind dwelt at length on the *weighty opinions of various authors* whom I had studied for a long time. I looked up from my book, having decided to leave such subtle questions in peace and to relax by reading some light poetry. (p. 31)

In this opening, Christine establishes her credentials as a compilator

---

[57]*Piers Plowman,* Passus XII; for a discussion of the highly articulated medieval assumptions about different categories of dreams, see Constance B. Hieatt, *The Realism of Medieval Dream Visions: The Poetic Exploitation of the Dream-Experience in Chaucer and His Contemporaries* (The Hague: Mouton, 1967), chap. 2.

8. Christine and Reason, Droitture, and Justice, the incipit to the *Cité des dames*, Ms. 4431, f. 290r. London, British Library, by permission

(with "reccuillir," to gather) of the opinions of aucteurs, one for whom poetry is no longer a métier as it had formerly been, but a mere diversion. By accident, however, the "petit livret" (small booklet) she fishes out from under the volumes, turns out to be not a book of poetry, but an anti-feminist tirade by Mathéolus. Intending to read it because she has erroneously heard that it speaks of "la reverence des femmes," she is interrupted before she can begin.[58]

Her mother calls her to supper. She puts the book down to go eat and does not resume reading the text of Mathéolus until the next day.

It is impossible to overstress the radical intrusion into the traditional reading scene such an interruption poses. We may sense just how radical it is if we compare this opening to that used by Christine's chosen precursor and ask: what if Dante had interrupted the

[58]Curnow, *"Cité des Dames,"* p. 128, comments that the book could have been a manuscript that bound both the *Lamentations* of Mathélous and the translator's reply to it, the *Libre de Leesce* by Jean Le Fèvre de Ressons.

first canto of the *Commedia* to go to supper?[59] Such a comparison is not merely arbitrary. In the absolutely orthodox reading scene of *Le chemin de long estude*, Christine herself had nodded off over Boethius's *Consolation of Philosophy* and had dreamed she was led by the Cumaean sibyl on a great journey through the land of knowledge. In this text, Christine specifically compares her journey to Dante's and with equal specificity signals Dante's celebration of the particular authority Virgil holds for him. After the sibyl quotes Dante, she says to Christine the dreamer:

> Or cognois a celle parole
> Que ne fu nice ne frivole
> Que le vaillant poete Dant,
> Qui a long estude ot la dent,
> Estoit en ce chemin entrez,
> Quant Virgille y fu encontrez
> Qui le mena parmy enfer,
> Ou plus durs liens vit que fer.

> Now you know those words—
> Neither stupid nor silly—
> Which the valiant poet Dante
> (Who had been hungry for long study)
> Said at the start of the road
> When Virgil met him there
> And took him down to hell,
> Where he saw chains far harder than iron.[60]

As Dante follows Virgil's authority in the *Commedia*, so Christine follows Dante's, taking the title of her own poem from the words "longo studio" ("long estude") of his salutation to Virgil.

At the close of Christine's *Chemin*, the allegory ends; yet just

---

[59]Or, to take a more domestic opening, in the initial scene of Guillaume de Lorris's part of the *Roman de la rose*, the dreamer is already within the dream when he walks out into the opening landscape, while sewing up his sleeve with some thread, thereby indicating how fashionably dressed he is (with long, dragging sleeves). The sleeve basting, a domestic detail that allows some precedence for the calling to supper, is not, however, an interruption of the usual forward movement of the plot (and indeed, Guillaume's text, like Dante's, lacks a reading scene).

[60]*Le livre du chemin de long estude*, ed. Püschel, p. 49; ll. 1139–46; my translation.

before she wakes up, she thanks the sibyl for the many thousands of pleasures she has been given. At that moment her mother hammers at the door, commanding her to wake up, for it is late. Christine's mother thus ends the dream, providing an abrupt closure for a Dantean, sibylline journey, much like the raucous shrieking of the birds which wakes the dreaming Chaucer at the end of *The Parlement of Foules*. And just as the down-to-earth realism of those lower-class birds provides an opposition to the courtly love attitudes Chaucer considers in the *Parlement*, so too for Christine the noise of her mother's loud knocking puts a period to the inspirational, bookish authority represented by the sibyl. Two powerful female figures, opposed to each other in the sequence of their appearance.

One cannot help but suspect that the mother's interruption of the reading scene at the opening of the *Cité des dames* is a further variation on the set piece Christine had mastered in the *Chemin*. The call to supper is a calculated violation of the usually masculine scene of reading: it is the first signal of the problem of the author's gender, a problem that will become one of the subjects of the text. It is Christine's mother who calls her, and the interruption is for a meal; thus we have a double and profoundly resonant cultural signal of femaleness. Both the mothering and the feeding are not only culturally significant, they literalize the meaning of "authority" inherent in its etymological origins in the Latin word *augere*—to cause to grow, to increase.[61] Christine's mother will indeed return as an issue in the text, specifically because of her objection to Christine's being given a full education by her father. Juxtaposed to a male-authorized scripted tradition, Christine's mother stands in for the problem of an alternative mode of nonscripted female authority (authority to which she is initially opposed in the *Chemin*, when her interrupting call is not to feed, but to awaken her daughter). In the *Cité* the mother becomes a key element of the allegory's opening "threshold text."[62] The threshold text of this allegory posits the central problem of Christine's

[61]For a discussion of food as a cultural symbol for women throughout the Middle Ages, see Caroline Walker Bynum, *Holy Feast and Holy Fast: The Religious Significance of Food to Medieval Women* (Berkeley: University of California Press, 1987).

[62]For a discussion of the "threshold text" as a generic element in all narrative allegory, see my *Language of Allegory*, chap. 1. A threshold text is an initiating scene whose elements become features that the rest of the text comments on in the mode of a narrative exegesis.

book as *the problematic relationship between the scene of reading and the woman's traditional role of mothering and physical nurturance.*

The two (widowed) women, mother and daughter (the daughter also is a mother), thus represent the two elements of "female authority" which are at least initially opposed; the relationship between these elements will need to be worked out by the rest of the allegory. The reading and the supper are profoundly resonant representations of the tangled etymological history of the word "auctor"—and indeed, the term functions in the first section of the *Cité* much like the key terms of any narrative allegory, repeated in all various guises through all possible permutations and combinations. Part of such "play" with the term, begun silently with the call to supper, continues in Christine's explicit and carefully marshalled assault on the problem posed by a tradition of misogynist male auctores.[63] Only after this critique can she provide an exfoliation of specifically female authority which is closely related to the experience alluded to in her mother's bizarre interruption.

Upon her return to her study, Christine reads the book by Mathéolus. In a move that is typically self-protective, she makes clear that she comes across the book by accident. In just the same way, she had stressed that she did not originate the "Querelle de la *Rose*," but only entered into the conversation, as it were, by accident, from the position of the interested bystander. Innocently expecting to read a celebration of woman, Christine is instead assaulted by Mathéolus's virulent attack. Her first response is dismissal. The book is of "no authority" (nulle auttorité, p. 617). But it does, however, make her wonder about the misogynist tradition of the auctores itself:

ot engendré en moy nouvelle penssee qui fist naistre en mon couraige grant admiracion, penssant quelle puet estre la cause, ne dont ce peut venir, que tant de divers hommes, clercs et autres, ont esté, et sont, sy enclins a dire de bouche et en leur traittiez et escrips tant de diableries et de vituperes de femmes et de leurs condicions. Et non mie seulement un ou deux cestuy Matheolus, qui entre les livres n'a aucune reputacion et qui traitte en maniere de trufferie, mais generaument aucques en tous

---

[63]For a discussion of play with the syllable "tre" in the opening section of William Langland's *Piers Plowman*, see my *Language of Allegory*, pp. 58–63.

traittiez philosophes, pouettes, tous orateurs desquelz les noms seroit longue chose. (pp. 617–18)

it made me wonder how it happened that so many different men—and learned men among them—have been and are so inclined to express both in speaking and in their treatises and writings so many wicked insults about women and their behavior. Not only one or two and not even just this Mathéolus (for this book had a bad name anyway and was intended as a satire) but, more generally, judging from the treatises of all philosophers and poets and from all the orators whose names would make a long list. (pp. 3–4; revised)

At first Christine attempts to answer this tradition herself, pitting her knowledge of her own character and conduct as a natural woman, "comme femme naturelle" (p. 618)—as well as her experience of the private and innermost thoughts of other women of all classes—against the testimony of so many notable men. Yet soon she confesses this experiential authority is no match for the tradition. Hardly can she pick up a volume on moral matters, "qui qu'en soit l'otteur" (no matter who the author), but she finds a chapter that blames women. Stunned into lethargy, she feels inundated by the tradition: "me venoyent audevant moult *grant foyson de autteurs* ad ce propos que je ramentevoye en moy meismes l'un aprés l'autre, comme se fust une fontaine resourdant" (p. 619; emphasis added). "Like a gushing fountain, a *series of authorities* whom I recalled one after another, came to mind, along with their opinions on this topic" (pp. 4–5). Ultimately convinced against her own better judgment, relying more on the views of others than on what she herself has felt and known, she laments:

Helas! Dieux, pourquoy ne me faiz tu naistre au monde en masculin sexe, a celle fin que mes inclinacions fussent toutes a te mieulx servir et que je ne errasse en riens et fusse de si grant parfeccion comme homme masle ce dit estre? (p. 621)

Alas, God, why did You not let me be born in the world as a man, so that all my inclinations would be to serve You better, and so that I would not stray in anything and would be as perfect as a man is said to be? (p. 5)

In despair, she considers herself most unfortunate because God has made her inhabit a female body in this world: "me tennoye tres malcontente de ce qu'en corps feminin m'ot fait Dieux estre au monde" (p. 621).

After this lament—as if the only antidote to the authority of this misogynistic scripted tradition is something that would exculpate her physical presence in a female body—the allegorical vision begins. The vision itself does not, however, start before Christine further specifies the exact physical position in which she sits in her chair.

> En celle dollente penssee ainsi que j'estoye, la *teste* baissiee comme personne honteuse, les *yeulx* plains de larmes, tenant ma *main* soubz ma *joe acoudee* sur le pommel de ma chayere, soubdainement sus mon giron vy descendre un ray de liumiere. (pp. 621–22; emphasis added)

> So occupied with these painful thoughts, my *head* bowed like someone shameful, my *eyes* filled with tears, holding my *hand* under my *cheek* with my *elbow* on the pommel of my chair, I suddenly saw a ray of light fall on my lap, as though it were the sun. (p. 6; revised)[64]

Given the fact that this detailed description of her melancholic position follows directly upon Christine's lament about her "corps feminin," the specific mention of body parts is striking. In an earlier text, the *Mutacion de Fortune,* Christine had written that Fortune changed her into a man so that she could take the helm of her foundering ship, but in the *Cité,* this masquerade is distinctly disallowed.[65] The problematic relationship between the experience of the physical body and the bookish tradition may be seen in a miniature in a Flemish translation of the *Cité des dames* (Figure 9). Here it is Cornificia who sits dejected in her study, surrounded by books, her hand on her cheek, elbow on arm rest. The knife on the desk beneath

[64]Richards translates "joe" as "armrest," which is, of course, possible. I think, however, that the main burden of Christine's list of body parts in this description would tend to make the "joe" a human cheek rather than the side-part of an armchair. For "joe" as "joue," specifically as "cheek," see A. J. Greimas, *Dictionnaire de l'ancien français* (Paris: Librairie Larousse, 1968). See also Fig. 9, where the posture of Cornificia copies the posture of Christine.

[65]*Le livre de la mutacion de Fortune,* ed. Suzanne Solente, 4 vols. (Paris: Editions A. & J. Picard, 1957), 1.51–53. See Willard, *Christine de Pizan,* p. 108, for a discussion of the transformation in the *Mutacion.*

9. Cornificia in her study, *De lof der vrouwen*, Ms. Add. 20698, f. 70r. London, British Library, by permission

the woman's left hand, a knife used for correcting scribal errors, points to the books on the shelf to the left. Such a detail may suggest that the illuminator understood quite well Christine's argument about the need to correct the written tradition.[66]

[66]I am indebted to Eugene Vance for this interesting reading of the detail of the knife. While the portrait is not of Christine, this miniature may indeed be an attempt by the artist, the "Dresden Master," to represent Christine in her distinctive posture. In a

Yet we miss the point if we assume that Christine intends so thoroughgoing a revision to mean eradication. Chaucer's Wife of Bath is deaf; her deafness was caused, so we are told, when her fifth husband, the clerk Jankyn, hit her on the side of the head after she ripped some pages out of his misogynist book. Alisoun's deafness speaks with a wonderful economy to the underlying and problematic orality of a female tradition that is necessarily opposed to the clerkly scripted tradition: the mutual violence, however, seems to promise no possibility for hearing the other side. Christine's position is very different from that of Chaucer's Wife: ensconced in a study, she is mistress of a scribal tradition she can correct, rather than merely destroy.[67]

Although, as Curnow points out, Christine's physical stance in the opening scene implies "the traditional position of reflection and melancholy" (p. 1039), the ray of light reaching her lap immediately qualifies this impression. There is a hint in this posture that Christine is subtly recalling the well-established tradition of the Annunciation to organize this moment of female inspiration. Mary is usually depicted seated, with a book open, and she often appears troubled by the angel's terrifying and confusing news.[68] When Christine finally accepts the charge laid on her by the three ladies in the apparition, she explicitly quotes Mary: "Voici votre chambriere preste d'obeir. Or commandez, je obeyray, et soit fait de moy selonc voz parolles" (p. 639). "Behold your handmaiden ready to serve. Command and I will obey and may it be unto me according to your words"

---

manuscript notable for its many different illuminators, the opening scenes of the text are by another hand; the portrait of Cornificia in her study would have been a good point for the Dresden Master to try to execute the scene that opens the text with Christine in her study. For the Dresden Master, see Bodo Brinkman, "Der meister des Dresdener gebetbuchs und sein kreis: Leben und werk eines burgeundischcen buchmakers zwischen Utretcht, Brügge, und Amiens" (Diss., Free University, Berlin, 1990).

[67]In the process of course, Christine, like any protagonist of an allegorical vision, is healed of her first dejection. According to Paul Piehler, *The Visionary Landscape: A Study in Medieval Allegory* (London: Edward Arnold, 1971), p. 19, "Medieval visionary allegory offers its readers participation in a process of psychic redemption closely resembling, though wider in scope than, modern psychotherapy. The process typically includes the phases of crisis, confession, comprehension and transformation."

[68]That such a possibility is present, if only as a potential undermeaning to the posture, seems far more likely in light of Christine's distinct representation of Mary in part III, where the entry of Christ's mother into the city as its first citizen is heralded with the angel's *Ave Maria*. See below, pp. 238–39.

(pp. 16–17). Worried that she does not have sufficient physical strength in her feeble female body to build the city, Christine even so accepts the charge in words that recall the peculiar strength of the female body to do the impossible. Also crucial to Christine's purpose in recalling the Annunciation is the further emphasis that hers is a *waking* vision—a vision like Dante's, not like the dreamer's in the *Roman de la rose*, who first falls asleep.[69]

It is not an angel, nor an ancient poet, who greets Christine, but three women. They have arrived not merely to console but also to chastise her for having given up in self-doubt her "certaine science," in favor of a plurality of "oppinions estranges." She resembles, they tell her, the fool in the story who was dressed in women's clothes while he slept: because those who were making fun of him repeatedly told him he was a woman, he "cru myeulx leurs faulx diz que la certaineté de son estre" (p. 623); believed their false testimony more readily than the certainty of his own identity (p. 6). Through this story, the text explicitly redeploys an essentialism that now works to undermine the authority of males, who have no certain basis for their (derogatory) knowledge about women.

The first of these splendid women holds a mirror that has special properties: anyone who looks into it will achieve clear self knowledge. She argues at once that all the misogynist claims that have so swayed Christine to feel self-disgust for her femaleness have turned her away from her selfhood. "Comment, belle fille, qu'est ton scens devenu? . . . Or te reviens a toy meismes, reprens ton scens et plus ne ta trouble pour telz fanffelues" (pp. 623–25). "Fair daughter, have you lost all sense? . . . Come back to yourself, recover your senses, and do not trouble yourself anymore over such absurdities" (Richards, pp. 7–8). Such an insistence is a metonymic reference to the alternative authority of "experience" that Christine introduces to de-authorize written misogynist tradition, in the process re-creating writing to suit her own purposes: sandwiched in between the two references to "scens" is a list of male authorities ranging from Aristotle to the authors of the *Roman de la rose*—an entire tradition Reason advises her to read antiphrastically. The three figures of authority in the *Cité des dames* themselves come out of books, while the very building of

---

[69]At the appearance of the light, Christine responds "as if wakened from sleep." Richards, *City of Ladies*, p. 260, stresses this particular wakefulness and the scene's echoes of Dante and Boethius.

the city is the writing of the *book* of the city of ladies. Lady Reason is herself one of the most traditional characters out of allegory, borrowed with pointed specificity from the *Roman de la rose,* if not even more particularly from Jean de Meun's auctor, Alain de Lille. Reason speaks with the full authority of tradition against the auctores. First, she cites a few authorities to show that it is possible to resist authority. In the process she demonstrates that Christine is at home in such a scripted tradition and has indeed given further consideration to the problem of the auctores since the "querelle de la *Rose.* "

> si comme tu meismes l'as veu ou livre de *Methaphisique,* la ou Aristotle redargue et reprent leur oppinions et recite semblablement de Platon et d'autres. Et notes, derechief, se saint Augustin et autres dotteurs de l'Eglise ont point repris meismement Aristote en certaines pars, tout soit il dit le prince des phillosophes. (p. 623)

> Notice how these same philosophers contradict and criticize one another, just as you have seen in the *Metaphysics* were Aristotle takes their opinions to task and speaks similarly of Plato and other philosophers. And note, moreover, how even Saint Augustine and the Doctors of the Church have criticized Aristotle in certain passages, although he is known as the prince of philosophers. (p. 7)

Second, Reason makes a traditional argument for strong allegorical reading—an argument that, given its echo of Jean's precursor text, Alain de Lille's *De planctu naturae,* may be an attempt to undermine Jean's power by appealing to his precursor text, one with prior and therefore greater authority.[70] She explains that it is possible to read against the obvious literal meanings of poets: often they mean the contrary of what their words openly say.

> Et les puet on prendre par *la rigle de grammaire qui se nomme antifrasis* qui s'entant, si come tu sces, si come on diroit tel est mauvais, c'est a dire que il est bon, et aussi a l'opposite. (p. 624; emphasis added)

> One can interpret them according to the *grammatical figure of anti-*

[70]For a discussion of this most fundamental of moves against an influential precursor, see Harold Bloom, *The Anxiety of Influence* (New York: Oxford University Press, 1973).

phrasis, which means, as you know, that if you call something bad, in fact, it is good, and also vice versa. (p. 7; emphasis added)

Just such an argument was used by Lady Nature in Alain de Lille's *De planctu,* part of which text Jean de Meun simply translated for one of Reason's praises of love in the *Roman de la rose.* Because Jean Gerson, Christine's colleague in the attack on the *Rose,* knew Jean de Meun's indebtedness to Alain quite well, it may be that Christine refers to the argument in Alain's allegory with her Latin tag.[71] In Alain's text, Lady Nature complains about unnatural sexuality in terms of grammar: *per antiphrasim,* Cupid corrupts the proper relationship between language and appropriate, "natural" sexuality. The metaphor of the grammar of Venus that Lady Nature uses in a bizarre cover for her sexual terms (subject and predicate do not go together correctly, masculine and feminine genders do not work appropriately). Lady Nature is able, however, to discuss sexual matters without using dirty words—and so the possible reference to Alain in Christine's discussion of antiphrasis would cohere with her argument against Jean's ribaldry.

Immediately following the argument about oppositional reading, Lady Reason criticizes the *Roman de la rose;* this poem is her real target, Mathéolus being a mere straw man:

Et la vituperacion que dit, non mie seullement luy mais d'autres et meesement le *Rommant de la Rose,* ou plus grant foy est adjoustee pour cause de l'auctorité de l'auteur, de l'ordre de mariage qui est saint estat digne et de Dieu ordoné, c'est chose clere prouvee par l'experience qu le contra est vray. (p. 624)

---

[71]Gerson writes against the *Rose:* "Vray est que cette ficcion poetique fut corrumpuement estraitte due grant Alain, en son livre qu'il fait *De la plainte Nature;* car aussy tres grant partie de tout ce que fait nostre Fol Amoureulx n'est presques fors translacion des dis d'autruy" (Hicks, *Débat sur la "Rose,"* p. 80). "It is true that this poetic fiction was abstracted from Alanus' great book, *The Complaint of Nature*—but corruptly . . . indeed the greatest part of our Foolish Lover's book is almost completely a translation of the writings of other authors" (Baird and Kane, p. 86). Gerson defends his authority to attack the *Rose* on the basis of his knowledge of Jean's auctores: "Remember, I first drank long ago in my youth at all, or almost all, those fountains from which the writings of your author have poured forth translated, like little streams" (Baird and Kane, p. 151). For a discussion of Alain's arguments about allegorical reading, see my "Allegory and Allegoresis."

As for the attack against the estate of marriage—which is a holy estate, worthy and ordained by God—made not only by Mathéolus but also by others and even by the *Romance of the Rose* where greater credibility is averred because of the authority of its author, it is evident and proven by experience that the contrary of the evil which they posit and claim to be found in this estate . . . is true. (p. 7)

Because of the greater authority of Jean de Meun, the *Roman de la rose* is more dangerous than Mathéolus's book. Reason next argues that no matter what you have seen in writing ("quoyque tu en ayes veu en script"), you will never see with your own eyes ("que oncques nul de tes yeux n'en veis") what the misogynists claim, with so many discolored lies ("si sont mençonges trop mal coulourees") (p. 625). The three ladies have therefore chosen Christine to construct a for-tified city as a place of refuge from misogynist attack; women have for too long remained, like an open field, without a hedge—indeed, much like the rose, so ill-protected at the center of the garden in the *Roman de la rose*: "descloses comme champ sans haye" (p. 629); "exposed like a field without a surrounding hedge" (p. 10). Christine has been chosen to construct this city specifically because of her long and continual study—"Pour la grant amour que tu as a l'inquisicion de choses vrayes par long et continual estude" (p. 628). Lady Reason here comes close to citing one of Christine's own titles, *Le chemin de long estude*. Then, just before this august personage announces her name, she prophesies to Christine: "Mais je te prophetise, come vraye sebille" (p. 631). "But I prophesy to you, as a true sibyl" (p. 11), that the city she builds will never be taken or fail, like the Amazon kingdom. Only now does she finally name herself: "Je sui nommee dame Raison; or avises donques si es en bon conduit. Si ne t'en dis plus a cest foiz" (p. 633); "I am called Lady Reason; you see that you are in good hands. For the time being then, I will say no more" (p. 12).

With Lady Reason's announcement of her identity, Christine is rewriting the famous moment of interview between Amant and Raison in the *Roman de la rose*. She rewrites it specifically by recast-ing her meeting with Reason in terms of Dante's protestation in his first interview with Virgil. "Io non Enëa, io non Paulo sono" (Inf., II.31–32); ("I am not Aeneas or Paul"). Christine interprets Dante's self-doubt with a reference to the doubting Saint Thomas: "Je ne suis mie saint Thomas l'apostre qui au roy d'Inde par grace divine fist ou

ciel riche palais" (p. 638). "I am not Saint Thomas the Apostle, who
through divine grace built a rich palace in Heaven for the king of
India" (p. 15).

Christine then introduces the other two female figures of authority
who will answer the arguments made by the misogynist characters
in the *Rose*. After each of the three guides introduces herself (and
after Justice, the third, addresses Christine directly), Reason returns
to her agenda of educating Christine about the tradition of *auctores*.

> "Or sus fille. Sans plus attendre allons au champ des escriptures: la sera
> fondee la Cités des Dames en pays plain et fertille. . . . Prens la pioche de
> ton entendement et fouys fort a faiz grant fosse tout partout ou tu verras
> les traces de ma ligne, et je t'ayderay a porter hors la terre a mes propres
> espaules." (p. 639)

> "Get up, daughter! Without waiting any longer, let us go to the Field of
> Letters. There the City of Ladies will be founded on a flat and fertile
> plain . . . Take the pick of your understanding and dig and clear out a
> ditch wherever you see the marks of my ruler, and I will help you carry
> away the earth on my own shoulders." (p. 16)

Earlier Christine had feared she would be unable to build the city
because of her "foible corps femenin." Here Reason helps to haul
away the weighty detritus of tradition on her own shoulders. In the
same way, all three figures of authority have promised to "deliver"
material for the building of the city. So Reason explains: "te *livrerons*
assex matiere plus forte et plus durable que marbre" (p. 639, emphasis added)—we will deliver enough material, stronger and more
durable than marble. Such transmittal of matter grounds the text's
architectural metaphor in a polysemy generically basic to allegory.
The physicality of the weight of misogynist "dirt"—its heavy pound-
age—is matched by the punning fact that such weight comes in
books. So too, the delivery of Reason's narrative material allows the
simultaneous building of the city and the writing of the *Livre de la
cité*. The incipit miniature is, in a sense, a picture of this pun. It
suggestively parallels the scattered books and bricks (see Figure 8).

Similarly, in the economy of allegorical metaphor, the clearing of
the Field of Letters represents the readjustment of the canon to allow
for the insertion of the *Cité* as a corrective answer to the tradition of

medieval misogyny. The first basketful of dirt to be removed is produced by Christine's asking if it is because of nature that the tradition of auctores is misogynist:

> Je vous pry, dites moy pourquoy ce est, et dont vient la cause, que tant de divers otteurs on parlé contre elle en leur livres, puisque je sens de vous desja que c'est a tort: ou se Nature les y encline, ou se par hayen le font. (p. 640)

> But please tell me why and for what reason different authors have spoken against women in their books, since I already know from you that this is wrong; tell me if Nature makes man so inclined or whether they do it out of hatred. (p. 16)

Reason answers her, "Fille, pour toy donner voye d'entrer plus en parfont, je porteray hors cest premiere hotes" (p. 640); "Daughter, to give you a way of entering into the question more deeply, I will carry away this first basketful of dirt" (p. 16). Reason explains that while it is not natural for men to hate women, there are, indeed, many and diverse causes of misogyny, which have resulted in women being blamed by "les autteurs en leurs livres" (p. 641), "those authors in those books" (p. 17). Some do so with a good intention—in order to warn men away from bad women or from their own lustful interests—but even these men are not to be excused, for their attacks are harmful, as Christine has already shown in her other writings: "et ces poins tu toy meisnes assez bien touchié autre part en dictiez" (p. 642).

Significantly, Christine's habit of referring to other places in her corpus which touch the same issues establishes Christine herself as one of the authorities to whom Reason can appeal. Even more important, with a profound and resonant wittiness, Reason vows to Christine that all who have attacked women "ce ne vint onques de moy"— "have never originated with me, Reason" and that all who subscribed to misogyny "have failed totally and will continue to fail" (p. 18); "tres grandement faillirent, et faillent, tous ceulx qui les ensuivent" (p. 643). By the authoritative word of Lady Reason herself, to defame (diffamer) women is branded irrational. The man who does it goes against reason and nature and is destined for failure; "il fait contre raison et contre nature" (p. 646). Christine has taken Jean's figure of authority and by literalizing the feminine gender of Reason, has made his Lady Reason speak against his own unreasonable project. Reason explains to Christine: "Si gittes hors ses ordes pierres broçonneuses et noires de ton ouvrage, car ja ne seront mises ou bel ediffice de ta cité" (p. 643). "So now throw aside these black, dirty, and uneven stones from your work, for they will never be fitted into the fair edifice of your City" (p. 18). The rubble of misogynist opinion must be cleared away before the city can be built. Another illumination by the Dresden Master from the Flemish translation makes the procedure of Christine's metaphor clear: Reason and Christine bend to their work, Christine following the marks of Reason as she continues to dig. The caption explains: "Cy dit comment Christine fouyssoit en terre: qui est a entendre les questions que elle faisoit a Rayson, et comment Rayson luy respondoit" (p. 647). "Here Christine tells how she dug in the ground, by which should be understood the questions which she put to Reason, and How Reason replied to her" (pp. 20–21; Figure 10).

If, as Lady Reason explains, some men are moved to attack women out of the defects of their own bodies, out of jealousy, and out of a delight in slander for its own sake, others turn to misogyny as part of a literary tradition:

Autres, pour monstrer que ils ont biaucoup veu d'escriptures, se fondent sur ce qu'ilz ont trouvé en livres et dient aprés les autres et aleguent les autteurs. (p. 643)

Others, in order to show they have read many authors, base their own writings on what they have found in books and repeat what other writers have said and cite different authors. (p. 18)

As Bloch has suggested, the citational mode of misogyny has all the power of a self-perpetuating canon; Reason denounces those who slander women for a variety of personal reasons, but leaves for last her answer to those who attack women simply in order to write. Just before analyzing the system of auctores, however, she lambasts a book titled *De philosophia* (saying, significantly, that she has forgotten the author's name) and proves that it should be called *Philosofolie* (love of folly)—the strained pun here alerting us to the more subtle and successful wordplay elsewhere throughout the text, as in the play upon "livrer." Ultimately, Christine's most scathing crit-

10. Christine and Reason clearing the Field of Letters of misogynist opinion, *De lof der vrouwen*, Ms. Add. 20698, f. 17. London, British Library, by permission

icism is reserved for those who do not even deserve to be called authors; they merely desire to meddle in writing:

> Et si comme il n'est si digne ouvraige, tant soit fait de bon maistre, que aucuns n'ayent voulu, et veullent, contrefaire, sont maint qui se veullent mesler de dicter. Et leur semble que ilz ne pueent mesprendre, puisque autres ont dit en livres ce qu ilz veullent dire, et come ce

medire; j'en sçay. Aucuns d'iceulx se veullent entremettre de faire parler en faisant dittiez de eaue sans sel, telz comme quelz, ou balades sans sentement, parlant des meurs des femmes ou des princes ou d'autre gent, et eulx mesmes ne se scevent pas congnoistre ne corriger leurs chetilz meurs et inclinacions. Mais les simples gens qui sont ingnorens comme eulx dient que c'est le mieulx fait du monde. (pp. 646–47)

And just as there has never been any work so worthy, so skilled in the craftsman who made it, that there were not people who wanted, and want, to counterfeit it, there are many who wish to get involved in writing poetry. They believe they cannot go wrong, since others have written in books what they take the situation to be, or rather, *mis*-take the situation—as well I know! Some of them undertake to express themselves by writing poems of water without salt, such as these, or ballads without feeling, discussing the behavior of women or of princes or of other people while they themselves do not know how to recognize or to correct their own servile conduct and inclinations. But simple people, as ignorant as they are, declare that such writing is the best in the world. (p. 20)

A tradition of mindless citation, misogyny is one among many discourses that can easily lead to empty imitation. The ground for any literary endeavor would need to be cleared of such detritus. Misogyny stands as the paradigm of bad writing; as Bloch suggests, it is a discourse peculiarly marked by the mere citation of borrowed authority.

The problem presented by the *named* authors—that is, those who are in fact "authors" (because only an auctor has a name)—requires more specific comment from Reason. But so too, the need to correct and clean up the ground of discourse is the same. Hence, Christine's next question, couched in an evaluation of the relative merits of Ovid and Virgil (Virgil is better), concerns Ovid's motivations for writing against women. Reason's answer, perhaps unfairly *ad hominem*, stages a dramatic confrontation between male and female bodies, specifically in terms of the defects Ovid pointed out in women but that Reason attributes to the defectiveness of his male body. According to Reason, Ovid wrote against women only after he had become impotent when he was punished for sexual excess by castration.[72] No longer able to enjoy women as before, Ovid became a misogynist.

---

[72]Christine's source for this traditional argument is Jean Le Fèvre's *Livre Leesce.*

More difficult to dismiss than Ovid's work is a book Reason is quick to deny could have been written by Aristotle; the text is notable because of the warning that no woman should read it since it contains statements about the female body which any woman, simply by the experience of her own body, would know to be lies. By such a juxtaposition of texts, Christine posits an abyss of difference between a female knowledge grounded in experience of the female body and a male knowledge grounded in fears of castration. Coming in such close proximity to her discussion of Ovid's punishment by castration for previous sexual excess, her insistence that women could easily correct men's mistaken sense of female anatomy suggests not so much her essentialist bias (knowledge of one's own body as an irreducible ground) as her assumption that male attitudes toward sexual difference are inflected by this specific fear. (Christine had borne and reared two sons.)

By far the most authoritative answer to the Aristotelian doctrine that woman's body is somehow incomplete and imperfect, something of which Nature herself is ashamed, is Reason's recourse to the text of Genesis, the greatest possible "Christian" authority, to answer pagan Aristotle. Reason's argument here also reveals the wittiness of the twists Christine is able to put into the normal hierarchies of authority. Reason asks: Is Nature a greater mistress than her master (God) from whom she takes her "auttorité"? God formed the body of a woman from one of man's ribs, signifying clearly that she should "stand at his side like a companion and not lie at his feet like a slave" (p. 23)—"elle devoit estre coste luy comme compaigne et nom mie a ses piez come serve" (p. 651); Furthermore, "elle fu fourmee a l'image de Dieu"—she was formed in the image of God. Preferring thus what is in fact the priestly version of the creation story, Christine has Reason attempt to accommodate the differences between the two versions: the creation of man in the image of God is specifically the creation of the soul. Woman's body, having been made from the body of man, was made from the noblest substance that had ever been created.

Reason's argument about the perfection of the female body has great typological reach across history—and doubtless Christine's interpretation of Genesis is effectively formulated in terms of her Mariolatry. Thus, although Cicero may have said that a man should never serve a woman, who can be happier—Reason wonders—than the man who serves the Virgin, who is herself above all the angels? When a pagan author such as Cato says, "Had it not been for women, man would converse with Gods," Christian wittiness can offer an answer. Indeed, Cato said truer than he thought ("il dist plus vray que il ne cuidoit" [p. 653]): had it not been for Mary and the incarnation of the savior within her female body, then men would indeed be conversing with the pagan gods—who are, after all, merely demons from hell. And furthermore: "Or puez tu veoir la folie de celluy on tint a saige: car par achoison de femme, homme raigne avec Dieu" (p. 652). "You can now see the foolishness of the man who is considered wise, because, thanks to a woman, man reigns with God" (p. 24). If human nature fell through Eve, it was elevated far higher by Mary. Thus Reason crushes a pagan proverb with salvation history.

Perhaps more pertinently, Reason practices what she has already preached to Christine, reading misogynist authority by *antiphrasis*—that is, by an ironizing method of interpretation which makes the pagan philosophers say the opposite of what they appear to have meant. The same Cato compared women to roses with thorns. Reason can only agree: "Derechief, dist plus vray qu'il ne cuida ycelluy Chaton" (p. 652): the thorns on these roses are a womanly fear of sinning, of doing evil. Thus women take careful guard of themselves. Such interpretation by antiphrasis, wittily turning the intended meaning against itself, provides more than a rhetorical troping of the proverb, for it suggests that hidden within pagan philosophy is something more than pagan Cato could understand. Reason's anti-misogynist argument subtly insinuates that there is a hidden otherness to pagan wisdom.

Under the tutelage of a second figure of authority, "Droitture" in the second section of the *Cité*, these subtler interpretations will blossom forth into far larger claims for prophetic pagan female authority. For her part, Reason remains in the first section in the realm of the reasonable, the grammatical and rhetorical, and continues to correct misogynist arguments by using well-known texts and current history. Reason takes the derogatory Latin proverb—that God made women to weep, talk, and sew—and turns it into high praise. By weeping did women earn Christ's miracles, just as St. Augustine's mother prayed him into conversion with her tears. So too, Christ chose to let the miracle of his resurrection be announced by women: "se langaige de femme eust esté tant reprouvable et de si petite auttorité, comme aucuns veullent dire, Nostre Seigneur Jhesu Crist n'eust jamais daigné vouloir que si digne mistere que fu celluy de sa tres glorieuse resurreccion fust premierement annoncié par femme" (pp. 659–60). "If women's language had been so blameworthy and of such small authority, as some men argue, our Lord Jesus Christ would never have deigned to wish that so worthy a mystery as His most gracious resurrection be first announced by a woman" (p. 28). In sum, the Latin proverb errs greatly. "Si est grant mauvaistié de rendre en reprouche aux femmes ce que leur doit tourner a tres grant gré, honneur et loz" (p. 663). "It is a great wickedness to reproach women for what should redound to their great credit, honor, and praise" (p. 30).

There remains one final scripted tradition with which Reason must deal before she begins the actual construction of the city. It has appeared intermittently through the biblical illustrations Reason gives of the good speech of women: the Canaanite woman and the Samaritan woman, who both serve God well with their language, are each outside the law. The first is "d'estrange loy" (p. 661); the second is "n'estoit de ta loy" (p. 662). These phrases mean that they are both gentile, but the use of the term "loi" (law) to refer to religion, while of course perfectly orthodox, begins to put pressure on the term and to call into question its own legitimacy.

Not surprisingly, Christine at this juncture asks Reason why women do not serve in courts of law or normally take on the responsibilities of government. Reason answers with what appears at first glance to be a very conservative defense of the division of labor, but on closer scrutiny becomes a defense of difference, one that authorizes a peculiarly female set of potencies that provide for reciprocity with men. Men and women are called to different tasks so that they may aid and comfort one another, "aidier et conforter l'un l'autre" (p. 665). Why send three people to do the job that can be done by two? Why have women do what men are already doing when men have, moreover, the physical strength necessary for enforcing the law? In the last analysis, Reason takes care to make clear that women are as fully capable of understanding and practicing the law as men. "Mais se aucuns vouloyent dire que femmes n'ayent entendment souffissant pour apprendre les loys, le contraire est magnifeste par preuve de experience" (p. 666). "But if anyone maintained that women do not possess enough understanding to learn the laws, the opposite is obvious from the proof afforded by experience" (p. 32). Denizen of the law courts in which she successfully sued for her widow's rights, Christine is surprisingly acquiescent in accepting the traditional exclusion of women from the practice of law. Even if the law did not at that time have the power and prestige it later gained as a profession, it offered real agency that Christine distinctly disallows women. Thus while she directly argues that women can—and do—govern, she makes an exception for the law. It is not for women.

One must ask what the purpose of this regressive tactic could be? Christine opposes to the mere written statutes of men a greater power than that of the law, which she dismisses as lacking in integrity. The important point is that women are not merely capable of the law, they are capable of this far greater science: Reason promises to tell stories of great women philosophers who "aprises de trop plus soubtilles sciences et plus haultes que ne sont lois escriptes et establissemens d'ommes" (p. 666); "have mastered fields far more complicated, subtle, and lofty than written laws and man-made institutions" (p. 32). Women's true talents lie elsewhere than in the study or mere enforcement of law, far beyond whatever had an origin in the written, which is here associated with masculine enterprises. As a brief first example of women's mastery of the law when necessary, Reason narrates the story of Nicolle, empress of Ethiopia, who instituted new laws for her country, bringing her people to proper manners and civilization: "Elle meismes institua loys tres droitturieres pour gouvernor son peupple" (p. 667). "She herself instituted laws of far-reaching justice for governing her people" (p. 33). Christine has added to her source in Boccaccio this heavy emphasis on Nicolle's law-giving authority, insisting that women have originary power with respect to the law.[73] The regressive-sounding prescription against women in law is there not so much to limit them as to prepare for the problematic issue of writing, a problem that will be taken up directly in part II. There an aptly named "Droitture" narrates stories about the ten sibyls, prophetesses who represent female knowledge far more powerful than the enforcement of mere written rules.

---

[73]Boccaccio, *De mulieribus claris*, pp. 184–85.

Having hauled off the detritus of misogynist opinion on her own shoulders—arguing, analyzing, and interpreting its claims to authority out of existence—Reason is finally ready to throw down the first stone in the fully excavated field. The first story is a shock. With it, Christine de Pizan seriously begins not only to revise her auctores, but to rewrite history.

Chapter 2

Rewriting Tradition: The Authority
of Female Subjectivity

Woman is never far from the "mother" (I do not mean the role but the "mother" as no-name and as source of goods). There is always at least a little good mother milk left in her. She writes with white ink.
—Luce Irigaray

Semiramis: Part I, Section 15

Semiramis was not only a great warrior queen, she was also the conqueror and rebuilder of the city of Babylon and therefore a most appropriate subject for this book of the *city* of ladies. Her story is the first "pierre" placed as the foundation stone in the wall of the City itself; it is thus both the foundation stone of the city and the initiating structure in the architecture of Christine's text.[1] Reason tells her, "Sy prens la truelle de ta plume et t'aprestes de fort maçonner et ouvrer par grant diligence. Car voycy une grande et large pierre que je vueil qui soit la premier assise ou fondement de ta cité" (p. 676). "Take the trowel of your pen and ready yourself to lay down bricks and labor diligently, for you can see here a great and large stone

[1]This architectural metaphor and its use of "stones" may resonate with textual reference to the punning on Peter's name—Pierre—the first stone upon which Christ built his church. The same pun underlies *Piers Plowman:* "Petrus, id est Christus." If this verbal play animates Christine's metaphor, it gives special weight to Psalms 118.22 (quoted in Matthew 21.42), "The stone which the builders rejected is become the headstone of the building," as a way of viewing Semiramis's exclusion from legitimate tradition. The use of the stones to construct a city, not a church, reveals Christine's early civic humanism as well as a strong anti-clerical bent, seen directly in her explicit criticism of the imperial hierarchy after the Donation of Constantine (*Cité*, p. 898; Richards, p. 169).

69

which I want to be the first placed as the foundation of your City"
(p. 38; revised).

There are problems with choosing Semiramis as the initial story.
The first is that Christine thereby quite strangely bases her city
on one of the most scandalous foundations in the field of letters:
mother/son incest. Semiramis's fame as a warrior and city builder
was surpassed only by her notoriety for having committed incest
with her son Ninus. To select her as the first stone bespeaks, then, a
resolute refusal from the outset to honor the originary set of anx-
ieties culturally associated with this most fundamental of all taboos.
Christine's refusal has, as we shall see, its specific coherence with
the problematic question of the written law that immediately precedes the narration of the legend of Semiramis. It coheres as well
with Christine's earlier refusal to grant any excuse to the story of
Saturn's castration in the *Roman de la rose*. More fundamentally,
however, her resistance to the underlying cultural force of the taboo
may also have some important theoretical implications for the underlying anthropology of female authority (in any period).

In telling her story, humanist Christine follows her explicit auctor
quite closely, indeed copying Boccaccio's *De mulieribus claris* nearly
word for word. But before we consider just how specifically and to
what effect she revises Boccaccio, it will be useful to consider the
appearance of Semiramis in Christine's primary model, the *Commedia*. Dante's treatment of Semiramis will both exemplify the
queen's position in cultural history generally and also indicate what
Boccaccio had to work with in his inheritance.

In the second circle of hell, Dante and Virgil come upon the lustful, whirled by the black winds of desire, among whom Virgil immediately identifies Semiramis and Dido. Semiramis is summed up in a
single line that is justly famous: it was she who made lust licit in her
law; "che libito fe licito in sua legge" (Inf., V.57). Dido killed herself, but, more to the point here, for love of Aeneas she lustfully
broke faith with the ashes of her husband Sichaeus. Semiramis's and
Dido's presence at the outset of the journey serve as a warning to
Dante's reader of the dangers there are in reading. The question is a
complicated one, but engages issues of reader involvement that we
know were also important to Christine. In Semiramis and Dido (and
in Francesca), Dante exemplifies the kind of reading he hopes his
readers will *not* perform with his text: Arthurian romance led Francesca astray, just as Virgil's Dido had led St. Augustine astray. Thus

Dante warns against the power that literature has to do ill and offers the hope that his poem, following Virgil, will have a different outcome.

Dante's two queens, one of Babylon and one of Carthage, represent as well a complex history of the city, which is also a complicated and deeply interwoven literary history. In this twin civic and literary background lie the possible causes for Christine's deeply scandalous selection of Semiramis as the foundation stone for her imagined city. As Giuseppe Mazzotta has explained, the middle term between the Rome of Virgil and the Rome of Dante is Augustine's *Civitas Dei*.[2] So too, Christine named her own *Cité des dames* after Augustine's *City of God:* in the *Cité* she calls him specifically "mon seigneur St. Augustin" (p. 659), and, like Dante, Augustine is one of her central auctores. Not surprisingly, her selection of Semiramis as the first story is profoundly determined by her relationship to the tradition of the city left her by Augustine and Dante. In the second circle of hell, Dante and Virgil confront, in the figures of Semiramis and Dido, representatives of two versions of the city which are opposed to the imperial legitimacy of Rome. By celebrating Rome, Dante of course radically revised Augustine. Augustine had written in *The City of God* against the pagan authority of Roman Virgil, making of Rome a version of the *civitas diaboli;* that dead and lustful city was typified by the biblical Babylon and opposed to the new Jerusalem, the proper civitas dei. Interestingly, Augustine's embodiment of civitas dei in the church that he himself served places it not far from Carthage— that is, the city that in Virgil's *Aeneid* stands as the antithesis of Rome. Dante reorganized Augustine's opposition between worldly Rome and heavenly Jerusalem, making Florence the demonic Babylon and reserving for an idealized imperial Rome a politically necessary place in the creation of the civitas dei. Resting on Rome's imperial laws, the pax romana had been, and continued to be, according to Dante, necessary for the creation of a true city where the church could serve God. Dante's sense of the central importance of Rome depended, as Joan Ferrante argues, on its law—a law distinctly different from Semiramis's libidinous *legge*.[3]

Dante most obviously signals his own rewrite of Augustine's re-

[2]Giuseppe Mazzotta, *Dante, Poet of the Desert: History and Allegory in the Divine Comedy* (Princeton: Princeton University Press, 1979), pp. 160–75.

[3]Joan Ferrante, *The Political Vision of the Divine Comedy* (Princeton: Princeton University Press, 1984), pp. 47–52.

write of Virgil by placing the Roman poet himself within the poem. But he also marks it by having Virgil confront the representative of Carthage, that other African city he had so tragically opposed to Rome in his epic. Augustine confessed that in his youth, a rebel to God's love, he had read Virgil and wept for the death of Dido, an African queen, *quia se occidit ab amore*, she who had died for love. "You I did not love," he confesses to God. "Against you I committed fornication . . . but this was not what I wept for: I wept for dead Dido 'who by the sword pursued a way extreme,' meanwhile myself following a more extreme way."[4] If, as Giuseppe Mazzotta argues, Dante differs from the youthful Augustine by being able to distinguish between Dido and Aeneas, condemning Dido's passion but condoning Aeneas's transcendence of it, then Christine differs further, for she overturns Dante's distinction. She pursues what would seem to be a preconversion Augustinian reading of Dido's story and in the second section of the *Cité des dames*, has her second figure of authority, Droitture, narrate the Carthaginian queen's tragic end in a grouping that includes stories of other women who have been constant in love.[5] A description of Dido's building of her city—including the details of her escape from her evil brother and the clever trick with the bull hide—finds a logical place in the first section of the *Cité* when Reason tells her story, along with Semiramis's and those of other city-builders. Christine's radically different version of the private part of Dido's life as an example of perfect constancy, however, will be useful for sensing the tone in which Christine can so directly contradict Dante's judgment on the queen's character. Droitture explains:

Mais selonc ce que l'experience ce monstra, moult fu plus grande l'amour de Dido vers Eneas que celle de luy vers elle: car nonobstant que il luy eust la foy baillee que jamais autre femme que elle ne prendroit et qu'a tousjours mais sien seroit, il s'en parti après ce que elle l'ot tout reffait et enrichi d'avoir et d'aise, ses nefs refraischies, reffaictes et ordonnees, plain de tresor et de biens, come celle qui n'avoit espargné

4Cited by Mazzotta, *Dante, Poet of the Desert*, p. 168n.
5Richards translates "Droitture" as Rectitude; Lady "Rightness" might be closer to the original and lacks the pompous tone of "Rectitude." But as "Rightness" is not colloquial, I have preferred to leave the name in the French.

l'avoir la ou le cuer estoit mis. S'en ala sans congié prendre de nuit en recellee traytreusement, sans le sceu d'elle; et ainsi paya son hoste. (pp. 930–31)

Dido's love for Aeneas was far greater than his love for her, for even after he had given her his pledge never to take any other woman and to be hers forever, he left her even though she had restored and enriched him with property and ease, his ships refreshed, repaired, and placed in order, filled with treasure and wealth, like a woman who had spared no expense where her heart was involved. He departed at night, secretly and treacherously, without farewells and without her knowledge. This was how he repaid his hostess. (p. 189)

Christine's subtle resistance to the tradition of opposed cities she inherited from Augustine and Dante persists all along the line of its various deployments; she reorganizes it and marshalls its resonance to empower a quite specific rewriting of her carefully selected precursors as she creates her own city. If Dido is condemned by Dante to the second circle of hell for unfaithfulness, Christine faults Aeneas for a similar infidelity. For Christine as well, there are two cities, as in Augustine's *City of God*—the Amazonian empire that failed to last, not because it was evil but because it was overpowered politically, and the city Christine is writing, her book of the city. For Christine, both Dido and Semiramis are city builders first and foremost. What Augustine and Dante condemn, Christine celebrates. If Babylon and Carthage are illicit because of their female builders, if they are opposed to the true Jerusalem or to Rome, for Christine they become original sites for an alternate tradition of civilization, and Athens, Rome, Carthage, even Paris (to which women brought the bones of its patron saint St. Denis) are shown to have been nurtured by women.

As a point of origin, lodged in the *Commedia*'s first architectural feature, eternally damned to the second circle, Dante's Semiramis stands for a law opposed to the one that decrees the architecture of hell down which Virgil and Dante scramble in the *Inferno*. Christine takes the illicit "legge" (law) Dante associates with Semiramis and gives to it her own legitimacy, making it provide the foundation— literally so, in terms of her own architectural metaphor—for an alternate tradition of female authority. Yet if the model provided by Dante's dismissal of Semiramis's "legge" helped lead Christine to place her *first*, it is Christine's rewrite of Boccaccio which provides the details of her narrative. A careful scrutiny of Boccaccio's text will reveal how specifically Christine revises him and how radically different her version of women's history thereby becomes.

According to Boccaccio, Semiramis was a glorious and ancient queen of the Assyrians who, on the death of her husband Ninus, masqueraded as her young son and took over the rule of the realm, leading the army to great victories. Having proved herself, she revealed her true identity, causing great wonder, Boccaccio says, that a mere woman could accomplish so much. In her own person she not only maintained her husband's empire, but added to it Ethiopia and India. She restored the city of Babylon and rebuilt its walls with ramparts, Boccaccio stresses, of great size: "restauravit murisque ex cocto latere harena pice ac bitumine compactis, altitudine atque grossitie et circuitu longissimo admirandis." "She surrounded it with walls of marvelous height, thickness and length, made of baked bricks cemented with sand, pitch, and tar."[6] Boccaccio takes care to relate one particular incident when Semiramis, who was having her hair braided, was interrupted by the news that Babylon had rebelled. Vowing to wear her other braid undone until she had subdued the city, she soon vanquished it and brought it to good order. A bronze statue was erected in Babylon of a woman with her hair braided on one side and loose on another, a reminder of Semiramis's brave deed.

The four-part incipit miniature in a manuscript of the French translation of the *De claris*, the *Cleres et nobles femmes*, a miniature probably done by Laurent de Premierfait in 1401, reveals the importance of Semiramis's story (and the centrality of the braiding scene) in the fourteenth-century French reading of the text. The episode of the messenger's arrival while Semiramis is having her hair braided is represented in the lower left quadrant, just beneath the author portrait in the upper left quadrant (Figure 11).[7]

---

[6]Giovanni Boccaccio, *De mulieribus claris*, ed. Vittorio Zaccaria, vol. 10, *Tutte le opere di Giovanni Boccaccio*, ed. Vittore Branca, ([Milan]: Mondadori, 1967), p. 34; hereafter cited in the text. The translation is from *Concerning Famous Women*, trans. Guido A. Guarino (New Brunswick: Rutgers University Press, 1963), p. 5; hereafter cited in the text.

[7]The only text of the *Cité* to have any of its internal stories illustrated, the late fifth-century Flemish translation *De lof der wrouwen* (Ms. Add. 20698 in the British Library, f. 41) also illuminates this moment, for it is a signal event in Christine's version of the story as it is in Boccaccio's. See Figure 14.

11. The incipit to the *Des cleres femmes*, Ms. Royal 20 C V, f. 1r. London British Library, by permission

By contrast, the usual illumination of the same moment in manuscripts of the French translation of Boccaccio's text emphasizes the infamous side of Semiramis's story. Boccaccio makes clear the terrifying sexual ambiguity her incest causes.

> But with one wicked sin this woman stained all these accomplishments . . . which are not only praiseworthy for a woman but would be marvelous even for a vigorous man. It is believed that this unhappy woman, constantly burning with carnal desire, gave herself to many men. Among her lovers, and this is something more beastly than human, was her own son Ninus, a very handsome young man. As if he had changed his sex with his mother, Ninus rotted away idly in bed, while she sweated in arms against her enemies. (p. 6)[8]

A representative illumination of this aspect of Semiramis's story reveals the distinctly uncomfortable position in which his mother's martial power places the young son Ninus (Figure 12).

Boccaccio's figurative sense of Ninus's exchange of sex with his mother implies an emasculation that the illumination also hints at in Ninus' posture: the truncated hand, stuffed (protectively?) into the young boy's placket in the general area of the genitals all too clearly answers the menace of the queen's remarkably large sword. Doubtless the sword is meant to represent Semiramis's great martial courage and achievements, but juxtaposed with the figure of Ninus, it points to the young man's effeminization (his unworn armor hangs on a rack above him). By depicting Semiramis's sword as bisecting the head of the one of the armed soldiers standing behind her, the miniaturist may be implying that her martial prowess menaces more than Ninus.

"Oh," Boccaccio laments, "what a wicked thing this is! For this pestilence flies about not only when things are quiet, but even among the fatiguing cares of kings and bloody battles, and, most monstrous, while one is in sorrow and exile. Making no distinction of time, it

[8]Ceterum hec omnia, nedum in femina, sed in quocunque viro strenuou, mirabilia atque laudabilia et perpetua memoria celebranda, una obscena mulier fedavit illecebra. Nam cum, inter ceteras, quasi assidua libidinis prurigine, ureretur infelix, plurium miscuisse se concubitui creditum est; et inter mechos, bestiale quid potius quam humanum, filius Ninias numeratur, unus prestantissime forme iuvenis, qui, uti mutasset cum matre sexum, in thalamis marcebat ocio, ubi hec adversus hostes sudabat in armis (Boccaccio, *De mulieribus claris*, p. 36).

12. Semiramis and Ninus, *Des cleres femmes*, Ms. Royal 20 C V, f. 8v. London, British Library, by permission

goes about, gradually seizes the minds of the unwary and drags them to the edge of the abyss" (p. 6). In order to cover her crime, Boccaccio's Semiramis decreed "that notorious law" (legem . . . insignem) which allowed her subjects to do what they pleased in sexual matters. On the other hand, he tells us that, according to some, Semiramis invented chastity belts. Boccaccio explains that others record how the queen came to a bad end, for one reason or another: "Either because he could not bear seeing his mother with many other lovers, or because he thought her dishonor brought him shame, or perhaps because he feared that children might be born to succeed to the throne, Ninus killed the wicked queen in anger" (p. 7). Ninus's distinctly overdetermined matricide opens up possible questions about the connection between the legend of Semiramis and the first story Boccaccio tells concerning Eve, the mother of us all. More important, Boccaccio's humanist uncertainty about Ninus's motives underscores the problematic nature of textual transmission. Because the authorities disagree, he offers many endings for Semiramis's story.[9]

Christine's Semiramis is more of a city builder than Boccaccio's— in her text, the first empire was a dual achievement of the elder Ninus and Semiramis together; she, no less than her husband, campaigned in arms, "qui semblablement comme luy chevauchoit en arms" (p. 677). Upon her husband's death, the *Cité*'s Semiramis does not cross-dress, but simply continues in her role of ruler and conqueror, adding Ethiopia and India to her domains and fortifying Babylon. Christine retells the episode of the queen's response to rebellion (the revolt of another kingdom, *not* the city of Babylon, which remained loyal) with the incident of the undone braid commemorated in a statue, this time a bronze richly gilt. Then, where Boccaccio begins his descant on incest, Christine quietly acknowledges: "Bien est vray que plusiers luy donnent blasme—et a bon droit luy fust donné se de nostre loy eust esté—de ce que elle prist a mary un filz qu'elle avoit eu de Ninus son seigneur" (p. 680). "It is quite true that many people reproach her—and if she had lived under our law, rightfully so—because she took as husband a son she had had with Ninus her lord" (p. 40). Where Boccaccio spends time speculating about Ninus's possible motives in killing his mother, Christine points out the possible reasons Semiramis may have had for taking her son as husband. First, she wanted no other crowned lady in the realm, and this would have happened if her son had married; second, no other

[9]For a discussion of Christine's and Boccaccio's different relation to textual tradition, see Liliane Dulac, "Semiramis ou la veuve héroique," *Mélanges de philologie romane offerts à Charles Camproux* (Montpellier: C.E.O. Montpellier, 1978), pp. 315–43.

man, except her son, was worthy to have her as a wife. What troubles Christine most is that "de ceste erreur, que trop fu grande, ycelle noble dame fait aucunement a excuser" (p. 680). "But this error, which was very great, this noble lady did nothing at all to excuse" (p. 40). Why? Because "adonc n'estoit encore point de loy escripte"; "there was still no written law" (p. 40). Indeed, then, Christine reasons, everyone lived according to the law of Nature, where all people were allowed to do whatever came into their hearts without sinning.[10]

In Boccaccio Semiramis decrees a law; Christine's queen lives before any such thing exists. That this law that the queen predates is a *written* law, is, I think, significant. It subtly recalls all of the previous conversations between Christine and Reason about the written authorities of the misogynist tradition that Christine finds so daunting in the generic reading scene of her allegory. Her correction of such a written tradition is of a piece with her revision of Boccaccio's legal detail: by means of the speaking presence in the text of a visionary female figure of authority who persistently says she speaks prophetically, a figure whose textual gender is made more literal by its coherence with the author's own, Christine strives to establish her specific, female authority on alternative grounds to a merely scripted textual tradition. So too Christine suppresses Boccaccio's humanist concerns about the divergent versions of the legend offered by different textual transmissions at the same time as she suppresses mention of Semiramis's death at the hands of her son. Different versions are more problematic for a written tradition that ideally passes on a fixed text than for the kind of oral culture Christine associates with Semiramis. In the oral-aural mode Susan Schibanoff ascribes to such transgressive readers as Chaucer's Wife of Bath, for example, the multiplicity of versions is not a problem. The process of "structural amnesia" in the constant retellings of oral culture work

[10]See Augustine, *The City of God*, trans. Marcus Dodds, (New York: Random House, 1950), 15.498. According to Augustine, incest was allowed in antediluvian ages. See also Marc Shell, *The End of Kinship: "Measure for Measure," Incest, and the Ideal of Universal Siblinghood* (Stanford: Stanford University Press, 1988), p. 30, for further authorization in support of Christine's reasoning: "For Noah's family after the Flood, as for Adam's family after the Fall, incest was allowable to ensure the survival of the human species. Neither incest nor fornication, by both of which the human species may increase and multiply, were yet infractions of the divine law. They became so only later in biblical history."

to "slough off" irrelevant elements and to harmonize traditions to "serve the needs of the present experience" (Schibanoff, p. 89). Christine mimics such a style of reading in her recasting of Boccaccio's story, silently sloughing off the irrelevantly tragic end to Semiramis's story.

We do not need to invoke much theoretical apparatus to see the priority that Christine grants oral experience in her story of Semiramis. In order for us to understand the significance of her stance, however, it is helpful to remember that Jacques Derrida's discussion of the "violence" that writing is presumed to do to an oral society focuses on a scene that shows little girls divulging to Claude Lévi-Strauss the secret names of the tribe.[11] In the anthropologist's seduction (he is both seducing and being seduced by the little girls) and the girls' betrayal (they are betraying the tribe and being betrayed by their confidant), the scene genders the violence of writing as a transaction between a dominant male and prepubescent females. By introducing the whole technological apparatus of long-distance, non–face-to-face communications, writing deprivileges a communal sphere of face-to-face oral communications at which women, denied literacy, are forced to excel. Chaucer makes the Wife of Bath deaf as a punishment for destroying the page of a book; Semiramis lives before the written law. Female authority in both instances is opposed to the written.

It is crucial to realize, however, that Christine's practice of privileging the preliterate is aimed at bringing previously unscripted sciences—essentializing, aural, experiential—into textuality; her practice is not to oppose scriptedness per se. Her own authority in the *Cité* is indeed markedly textual. Reason is constantly reminding Christine (and the reader) of what she has written in her prior texts, so that Christine's own corpus of texts forms part of the authorities to which Reason, Droitture, and Justice appeal (Richards, p. 43). Christine's "corpus" in this sense has a double-natured existence: both her "corps feminin" and the body of her collected works. Still, the ultimate claim of female authority is to a nonscripted, prophetic mode, grounded in a realm of discourse that is made to stand as far outside the textual as anything within a text can get.

In a sense, Christine's emphasis on a prior, unscripted freedom that

[11]For a discussion of this moment in Lévi-Strauss's text, see Jacques Derrida, *Of Grammatology*, trans. Gayatri Spivak (Baltimore: Johns Hopkins University Press, 1976), pp. 101–40.

would authorize mother/son incest as being acceptable and even honorable is of a piece with her criticism of Jean de Meun's vulgar terms for body parts and also his euphemism in describing the act of sexual intercourse: the relationship between written and oral language becomes most crucial in naming the parts of the body. While her two auctores founded their texts in stories that underscore the originary problem of castration anxiety, her objections—overt against Jean and implicit against Boccaccio—react not only to their terms but to the fundamental importance of the problem.[12] One does not need to invoke Freud to see the peculiar emotional burdens revealed by manuscript illuminations of the two oedipal scenes in Jean's and Boccaccio's male-authored texts. Christine's city is built with a foundation stone (the story of Semiramis) and written in the language of an allegory that refuses to recognize the peculiar terror of castration anxiety as being primary, or even finally very significant.

Christine's practice differs from a male tradition that locates its origin in fears about the male body. While the two misogynist texts against which she writes based their discourse in narrative events that underscore the original oedipal anxiety, she quite neatly revises the importance of the issue by saying that, for women, castration anxiety simply does not apply. Since such a summary of her argument courts a biologism that may confuse the issue, however, it might be more helpful to state the problem in terms that allow us to understand what, specifically, the dismissal of the taboo against mother/son incest achieves for Christine as an author. Anthropology can supply some terms to explain the active good to be gained by such a scandalous move on Christine's part.

In her now classic article "The Traffic in Women: Notes on the

---

[12]Contemporary poststructuralist French feminist theory argues for a similar critique of the fundamental importance of castration anxiety. For example, Hélène Cixous confronts Freud's argument about the Medusa directly: "Too bad for them [men] if they fall apart upon discovering that women aren't men, or that the mother doesn't have one [a penis]. But isn't this fear convenient for them? Wouldn't the worst be, is the worst, in truth, that women aren't castrated, that they have only to stop listening to the Sirens . . . for history to change its meaning. You only have to look at the Medusa straight on to see her. And she's not deadly. She's beautiful and she's laughing." From "The Laugh of the Medusa," *Signs* 1 (1976), 875–93, reprinted in *The "Signs" Reader: Women, Gender, and Scholarship,* ed. Elizabeth Abel and Emily K. Abel (Chicago: University of Chicago Press, 1983), p. 289. Christine also argues that the Medusa is simply an extremely beautiful woman.

Political Economy of Sex," Marxist anthropologist Gayle Rubin explains the social subordination of women in terms of the double action of the single decree: first, following Lévi-Strauss, Rubin argues that the incest taboo at the social level enjoins exogamy, or marriage out of the immediate family; that is, it encourages the traffic in women, whereby men trade women among themselves in the founding act of civilization, thereby rendering asymmetrical a male's right in himself and a female's lack of a right in herself.[13] He trades her; she is traded. And second, the incest taboo works through the familial process of the oedipal complex to create differently gendered—and heterosexually desiring—others, the male possessed of the phallus, its power passable to another male through a female, the female a passive conduit for that power, unable to have it herself. Whether or not Rubin's persuasively capacious yet neat Marxian analysis of both Lévi-Strauss's description of kinship and Lacan's argument about the oedipal complex is correct in all its details, her location of the social dominance of men over women at the point of the incest taboo may help us to understand Christine's unusual thematic transgression of this taboo at the outset of building her city.

According to Christine de Pizan's commentary on the story of Semiramis, the incest taboo is not natural, but cultural. In this opinion, she appears to anticipate a modern structuralist, if not post-structuralist, anthropology.[14] As Rubin explains them, kinship systems underwritten by the taboo

---

[13]Gayle Rubin, "The Traffic in Women: Notes on the 'Political Economy' of Sex," in *Toward an Anthropology of Women*, ed. Rayna Reiter (New York: Monthly Review Press, 1975), pp. 157–210.

[14]Claude Lévi-Strauss, *The Elementary Structures of Kinship* (Boston: Beacon Press, 1969); this is, of course, one of Lévi-Strauss's main themes: "The incest prohibition is at once on the threshold of culture, in culture, and in one sense, as we shall try to show, culture itself" (p. 12). Rubin objects to some of the implications of this evaluation of the identity of the taboo and of culture: "Since [Lévi-Strauss] argues that the incest taboo and the result of its application constitute the origin of culture, it can be deduced that the [oppression of women] occurred with the origin of culture, and is a prerequisite of culture" (p. 176). Rubin instead argues for the need to understand the function of a fully analyzed "sex/gender system" within the "imperatives of social systems"; she maintains that the fundamental taboo is not against too intimate contact between family members but an interdiction against any active female desire (p. 182). For a discussion of the asymmetry between father/daughter and mother/son incest, where father/daughter incest is far more prevalent because it is fostered by the power arrangements of patriarchy, see Judith Herman and Lisa Hirschman, "Father-Daughter Incest," in Abel and Abel, *The "Signs" Reader*, pp. 257–78. The authors also discuss possible reasons as to why women so seldom commit incest.

do not merely exchange women. They exchange sexual access, genea-
logical statuses, lineage names and ancestors, right and *people*—men,
women, and children—in concrete systems of social relationships.
These relationships always include certain rights for men, others for
women. "Exchange of women" is a shorthand for expressing that the
social relations of a kinship system specify that men have certain rights
in their female kin, and that women do not have the same rights either
to themselves or to their male kin. In this sense, the exchange of women
is a profound perception of a system in which women do not have full
rights to themselves. (p. 177)

It appears that in order to imagine the building of the city of
ladies—itself the textual construction of literary authority for
women—one needed to rewrite the first "written" law that confined
women to a nonpublic, non-self-owning silence, a law that assigned
to women the status of signs, not makers of signs. In the case of
Semiramis, a female is granted a choice of sexual partner that runs
counter to the prevailing social norm. The movement of the traffic is
thereby stalled, so to speak, at the place where the woman speaks her
own active desire (both sexual and political) and takes an unusual
"right" in herself. Boccaccio's Semiramis takes many lovers; her
incest with her son is only the worst case of a very transgressively
active sexuality. The law his Semiramis decrees allows total libidinous freedom. There are, presumably, no interdicted categories of
sexual union. Christine's Semiramis honorably marries her son, enacting a pointedly transgressive sexual desire.

Rubin argues that the incest taboo organizes not only all sorts of
social categories, but most fundamentally, female desire. It is the
very activity of that desire which is the primary tabooed social fact—
an actively desiring woman is more difficult to trade at will. Rules for
female behavior all follow the general need to produce objects of
exchange rather than subjects who actively do trading. Not the least
of the rules is an interdiction against public speech, or any other kind
of social (or literary) "authority."

Significantly, the transgression of the taboo on autonomously active female desire may be most clearly marked (in female texts, like
the *Cité des dames*) by the female's desire for the tabooed male
family member. A merely energetic sexual desire is not itself tabooed
(though it may be condemned): the twist comes when the female also
transgresses that part of the taboo aimed directly at the male subject,
who is not to desire his own females. Semiramis is the most startling

case imaginable because she transgresses the taboo against active female desire, specifically by transgressing the taboo against sexual contact between mother and son. Assuming absolute rights in herself, Semiramis chooses her own partner actively; she chooses her own son because no one else is worthy of her. At the place of halt, at a boundary line of licitness, this female is not traded out by another male, but turns inward to a nonexogamous arena over which she has total control and claims a subjectivity for herself: here the discursive space for the female opens unimpeded by any limit. As a rhetorical tactic, the move is shocking and brilliant.

Insofar as Semiramis can be described in male terms, she becomes less threatening; thus Boccaccio's emphasis on her transvestism relieves some of the threat (Christine most specifically suppresses such transvestism). Yet one of the key elements in the queen's legend insists upon her gender: the braiding of her hair genders her martial prowess just as specifically as her incest with her son genders her active sexual desire. (She does not merely desire exogamous men, as men would desire exogamous women.) In each version, the narrative makes her previously masculine power specifically female: her vow of revenge is troped by a feminine hair-do (and turned into a piece of monumental art) and her active desire is marked female by a transgression of the most fundamental law of all. Figure 13, which is an enlargement of part of Figure 11, and Figure 14, a line drawing from the Flemish translation, both clearly show Semiramis in her private domestic space, a space gendered female by the cosmetic care of her coiffure. In both cases, the illuminators mark the threshold of the space literally, with the messenger kneeling to deliver the message just inside the doorway. Each picture represents prominently within it the fact of the threshold.

For the male authors, Semiramis stands as an instance of the primal scandal of female shame. For Christine, Semiramis feels no shame; she must therefore exist prior to what Christine specifically terms a scripted, male-authored law. She is free to do whatever she wants: she is free to act, autonomously. Semiramis thus represents a freedom which is unscripted and unbound by law at its most radical, originary foundation. Her story is placed first in the building of the city because it also unmoors motherhood, and the power of procreation, from its engagement in the traffic in women. That maternal authority, first represented in Christine's text by her own mother's interruption of the reading scene, is in Semiramis's legendary trans-

13. Detail of the incipit to the *Des cleres femmes*, Ms. Royal 20 C V, f. 1r.
London, British Library, by permission

gressiveness made honorable. By such a peculiar validation, Christine begins to heal the essential scandal of motherhood itself.

The Body of the Mother: Part I, Sections 16–26

The threshold text of Christine's allegory states the basic problem
of female authority as one of relationship between (*a*) the authority of

14. Semiramis receiving news of the rebellion of Babylon, *De lof der vrouwen*, Ms. Add. 20698, f. 41. London, British Library, by permission

a scripted tradition of named male authors whose potency is witnessed by books and (*b*) the "authority" of the anonymous mother whose power is located in (but is not represented by) the culturally problematic female body. After placing the first stone of Semiramis, Reason continues to raise the foundation of the city of ladies by addressing the problem of mother/child, and in particular, mother/son relations. While there is of course a larger cultural reason for taking up the situation of motherhood specifically in mother/son terms (males are dominant in the culture and a female will find her power more reliably authorized in relationship to a male than to a female child), there was also a specific and local political context that made this emphasis an important one for Christine de Pizan. From the very outset of the *Cité*, Christine has counseled a wise, prudent, and active approach to regency on the part of a number of widowed female rulers: thus Queen Fredegonde exercises power for her infant son and Queen Blanche of Castile governs well during her son's minority. It should come as no surprise that throughout the period in which Christine was writing the *Cité*, she was busily attempting to persuade Isabeau of Bavaria, queen of France, whose husband the king was intermittently insane, to throw her efforts behind making a peaceful rapprochement between warring ducal factions: in particular, the party of the duke of Burgundy, the king's uncle, and that of the duke of Orléans, the king's younger, illegitimate brother. (Some scholars assume Isabeau and Orléans were having an affair, which would, of course, have been incestuous.) In 1405, the year of the completion of the *Cité*, Isabeau switched allegiances from Burgundy to the illegitimate Orléans. That summer the queen was involved in an attempt to kidnap the dauphin and get him away from Paris. On October 5, 1405, Christine wrote a letter to Isabeau which is a practical education in how to rule as regent, adducing the same models that we find in the *Cité*.[15] The early emphasis on the power relationships between mother and son in the *Cité* may have much to do with Christine's increasingly desperate attempts to counsel the French ruling elite, and particularly Isabeau of Bavaria to keep the peace.[16]

The next group of stories Christine has Reason tell are all about various warrior queens, beginning with an initial set of Amazon rulers. It is perhaps odd that Amazons should be a means for discussing mother/son relations because, as all the sources agree, they were notorious for killing off all their male children in order to maintain their single-sex kingdom. Christine explains, however, that in fact they did not kill their sons, but rather sent their male children to the boys' fathers to be raised, feeling no loss of maternal responsibility thereby. This odd Amazonian maternality gets put to rather strange

[15]See "The *Livre de la Cité des Dames* of Christine de Pisan: A Critical Edition," ed. Maureen Curnow, 2 vols. (Ph.D. diss., Vanderbilt University, 1975), pp. 55–58.

[16]For a close analysis of the two different political programs of the illuminations of the *Epistre Othéa*, one dedicated to Isabeau and the other to the duke of Berry, see the brilliant study by Sandra L. Hindman, *Christine de Pizan's "Epistre Othéa": Painting and Politics at the Court of Charles V* (Toronto: Pontifical Institute of Mediaeval Studies, 1986).

and sadistic use in the story of Queen Thamiris, and it is possible that Christine uses the myth as a means of legitimizing female violence through an appeal to the prerogative of a mother to protect her children. Notable for having defeated the great Cyrus, king of Persia and onetime conqueror of "Babylon and much of the world" (p. 42) through a clever ambush, the Amazon queen Thamiris capped her victory over Cyrus by hideously murdering and then dismembering him. In Christine's version, Thamiris has him beheaded and then orders his severed head to be put in a bucket full of his own soldiers' blood (p. 43), so that it can drink fully of blood—after which it so constantly thirsted. Herein Christine follows Boccaccio; the dismemberment scene (Figure 15) is illustrated in Christine's earlier version of the story in the *Epistre Othéa*. Thamiris's grisly revenge is occasioned, Christine explains, "out of anger over the death of one of her beloved sons, whom she had sent to Cyrus" (again the interpretation follows Boccaccio). And so in this first story told of an individual Amazon queen, Christine restages the cultural threat of the male-murdering Amazons, but relocates that dismembering power as a means of protecting, rather than destroying, the mother's son. Thamiris, moreover, specifically dramatizes her power as an object-lesson display: Cyrus is forced to watch his barons being decapitated. The shift in the power of the castrating mother, from threatening the child to protecting him, also authorizes maternal anger by allying it to the "legitimate" politics of conquest. What is important to realize is that Christine emphasizes the Amazonian anger not merely as self-protective (Thamiris attacks only when it is clear that Cyrus is readying an assault on her kingdom), but as maternal—using Boccaccio's detail, but underscoring the new Amazonian practice of grisly violence as a means of intimidating the adult male who would threaten the (far younger) son.

Like those of the Amazons, all of the stories told to build the foundations of Christine's city are about women characterized by great physical strength: they are narrated specifically to answer the question Christine had asked Reason about Aristotle's arguments that women are unhappily possessed of "le corps foible" (p. 673). While the tales about warrior queens ably demonstrate that the female body has the strength to achieve the deeds of a man, Christine is equally concerned, as we have seen, to rechannel the real fears this

15. Thamiris viewing Cyrus's head in a bucket of blood, *Mutacion de Fortune*, Ms. Harley 4431, f. 121v. London, British Library, by permission

potent body causes into an acceptance of the rightful power of the mother. In order to balance the power, she narrates stories not only about mothers decapitating powerful men, but also provides a long and moving version of the heroic death of the Amazon Penthesilea, who was killed in service to the ideal of the dead Hector, self-sacrificing hero of Troy.[17] Devoted to Hector, Penthesilea arrives in Troy after he has been slain; she worships at his tomb, and then goes out to do battle, where she wounds Achilles' son, Pyrrhus, who vows revenge. Following Pyrrhus's prior order, his soldiers surround the Amazon princess and, attacking her en masse, shear off a large quarter of her helmet. "Pyrrhus was there, and seeing her bare head with its blond hair, dealt her such a great blow that he split open her head and brain. So died the brave Penthesilea" (p. 51).[18]

By providing a female decapitation to match that of Cyrus, Christine's text balances the dismemberment of bodies. Penthesilea's corpse is taken ceremoniously back to the Amazonian kingdom. Christine then dates the warrior's dynasty to the time of Alexander, suggesting that readers can synchronize the lesser-known, eight-hundred-year history of the Amazons with the better-known history of Greek and Trojan conquests. The decapitated bodies of Cyrus and Penthesilea are the connecting links between the two disparate histories. They rehearse, as it were, the vulnerabilities of female to male and male to female as they are staged by the mythology that speaks most directly about male terror, not merely of female anatomy but

[17]Hector had figured as the young boy who receives Othéa's instruction in the *Epistre Othéa*; Trojan mythology was, of course, central to the French monarchy, who derived themselves from the wandering Trojans. See Hindman, *Epistre Othéa*, pp. 50–55.

[18]Because no other source readily available to him features the death of an Amazon by decapitation (neither Virgil, Homer, nor other post-Homeric poets such as Quintus Smyrnaeus), Edmund Spenser may be remembering this moment in *Faerie Queene* V, the book of Justice, when he has Britomart decapitate the Amazon queen Radigund. He may also have been inspired to take her peculiar name from a saint because of the third section of the *Cité*, narrated by Justice. Spenser could have known Christine's detail of decapitation from the 1521 translation of the *Boke of the Cyte of Ladies* (London: Pepwell, 1521); reprinted in *Distaves and Dames, Renaissance Treatises For and About Women*, ed. Diane Bornstein (New York, Scholar's Facsimiles, 1978), H,iiii, 3ᵛ: "Then Pyrus when he saw ye heed bare by which her yelowe heer appered gave her so grete a stroke yt he cleft iun sondre ye heed and the brayne. And thus ended the worshypfull Pantassylle of whom it was grete losse to the Troyans and grete sorowe to all her countre which made gete sorowe and lamentacyon for never syth there reygned none such upon the Amozones."

also of female autonomy. By providing dismemberments of both male and female bodies, Christine locates the body as the problematic site of Amazonian mythography, and not simply because of the decapitations. The Amazons were, of course, equally famous for their self-mutilation. Legendary for cutting off a breast to be better warriors, these mythic female figures dramatize in a direct way the process by which society uses the body to represent its own organization. In this process, as anthropologist Mary Douglas has argued, the body provides a potent source of symbols for representing social arrangements:

> The body is a model which can stand for any bounded system. Its boundaries can represent any boundaries which are threatened or precarious. The body is a complex structure. The functions of its different parts and their relation afford a source of symbols for other complex structures. We cannot possibly interpret rituals concerning excreta, breast milk, saliva and the rest unless we are prepared to see in the body a symbol of society, and to see the powers and dangers credited to the social structure reproduced in small on the human body.[19]

Such an understanding of the symbolic function of the body—and by extension myths about the body—may help us to understand what the narratives about Amazonian mutilation were intended to accomplish. Of course, Amazonian society is only an imaginative construct, but the disposition of the body is thereby all the more immediately a carrier of pure social meaning.

Culturally, females have seldom engaged in war. The Amazonian myth suggests that were women to transgress this social boundary, the transgression would need a major mark on the body to signal the change in social role. A change from female nurturance by the breast to a self-inflicted wound would mark the transformation most efficiently. Douglas's argument may also help make more sense of Christine's inclusion of an otherwise oddly specific indication: according to Christine, lower-class Amazons removed the right breast (the better to use a bow), while the Amazon nobility removed the left breast (the better to carry a shield). In a sense Christine pursues the logic of body symbolism, rendering the martial female body more

---

[19]Mary Douglas, *Purity and Danger: An Analysis of the Concepts of Pollution and Taboo* (1966; rpt. London: Arc Paperbacks, 1984), p. 115.

familiar by inscribing the contemporary social-class code upon it. This is not to domesticate the mythically strange body, but to allow it a recognizable social function, so that it displays signs of class difference. Such a pronounced emphasis on the body in the Amazon kingdom emphasizes the corporeality subtending the temporal city vulnerable to history and to male power. Christine will use the dismembered bodies of the saints in part III to populate her city; the saints' bodies, however, become texts—legends—as well as transtemporal corporeal presences. They can outlast time. She thus rewrites the dismemberment of the mythic Amazons in the martyrology of the last section.

Stories of Zenobia and Artemisia continue Christine's legitimation of female martial power as an outgrowth of mothering. Like the French princess Fredegonde, who carried her infant son into battle at the head of his armies (her story is narrated next), these two ancient warrior-queen regents exercise female political authority as part and parcel of their more legitimate motherhood, governing in the place of their young children. But inserted into the sequence of their legends is the bizarre story of Lilia, mother of Theodoric, a Christian of Constantinople. For this tale, Christine goes to an entirely different source from the ones she has been consistently using (either Boccaccio or the *Histoire ancienne*). From the *Grande chroniques de france*, she takes Lilia's story, which is very different from those of warriors like Zenobia and Artemisia, because Lilia was never personally present in battle. Why, then, is her history grouped with those of Semiramis, the Amazons, and the warrior-queen regents? Because, while her relationship to battle is quite mediated, her relationship to her son Theodoric is anything but sexually indirect. We hear that when Lilia wanted to inspire her cowardly son to return to battle in defense of Rome and found words to no avail, she shamed him by showing him her womb:

adonc la dame, surprise de grant courroux, leva sa robe par devant et luy dist: "Vrayement, biaux filz, tu n'as ou fouyr se tu ne retournes derechief ou ventre dont tu yssis." Adonc fu Tierris si honteux que il laissa la fuyte, rassembla sa gent et retourna en la bataille. (p. 712)

the lady, overcome with great anger, lifted up the front of her dress and said to him, "Truly, dear son, you have nowhere to flee unless you return to the womb from which you came." Then Theodoric was so ashamed that he abandoned his flight, regrouped his troops, and returned to the battle. (p. 58)

Reason explains that Theodoric won his battle, saving all Italy. Yet "it seems," she argues, "that the honor of this victory should be credited to the mother rather than the son" (p. 59). As in the case of Semiramis, the claim for female authority is made at the crucial nexus of relations between mother and son, specifically as those relations speak to the response of male shame when confronted by the female body. Christine does not analyze this story in detail, but has Reason simply explain that the greater honor should go to the mother. But in what did Lilia's greater courage or knowledge consist? Does she show her genitals as sign of her own powerful female sexuality that gave birth to him? Is he shamed by their sight because her recourse to this display proves he is not a man? Is he terrified of the emasculation they might threaten? Whatever the necessarily speculative answers to such questions may be, the important thing to realize is that Christine's interpretation insists upon the mother's heroism: the victory is hers because she showed courage in her brave recognition of her son's cowardice, in her wisdom about what act would make him return to battle, and in her ability to perform that act.

It is hardly surprising that Lilia's is not one of the stories Boccaccio chose to narrate. As his condemnation of Semiramis hints, he would have had trouble praising this kind of exercise of the powers of motherhood. Indeed, even in his version of Zenobia's story, to take only one example, he insists upon the final impotence of that famous warrior queen's power. Thus, in a conclusion that Christine suppresses entirely, Boccaccio ends Zenobia's story at the point when she is ultimately conquered by the emperor Aurelian and taken back to Rome in the sort of triumph Cleopatra notoriously avoided. Boccaccio's Zenobia finishes her days quietly, a private Roman woman. As Constance Jordan sums it up:

This defeat [of Zenobia] culminates in what appears to be a symbolic adjustment of status: "The triumph over, conspicuous for its prizes and treasures, Zenobia lived in private among the other Roman women to the end of her days." The statement effectively calls into question this queen's extraordinary abilities, suggesting that if they have not actually been misdirected, they are at least capable of considerable redirection. In the end Zenobia is no different from a decent Roman matron.[20]

Christine suppresses all mention of the Roman triumph in her story and so allows Zenobia to end her life as a ruling queen. Such a change is part of the pattern of her revisions of Boccaccio. Similarly, she had modified her sources for the *Epistre Othéa:* as Christine Reno puts it, her rewrites are "far from being random" but are instead "quite deliberate changes made in the spirit of feminism."[21] We may perhaps less anachronistically say that in the *Livre de la cité des dames,* Christine consistently corrects whatever defamation of women she finds in her various *auctores.*

Although she suppresses any reference to the city of Rome in the story of Zenobia, Rome does press its claims in the two stories with which Christine concludes her grouping of vignettes that completes the foundations of her city. The final two narratives portray Camilla, the Volscian virgin who fought against Aeneas, and Cloelia, a Roman virgin whose heroism concerns a city seen as far less powerful than Boccaccio's Rome. The Camilla story is, of course, a Roman version of the Penthesilea legend, variant for two reasons. First, Camilla loves and serves her father absolutely; such filial piety is furthermore emphatically stressed in Christine's version of her story. Second, she fights for Turnus and therefore against the Trojan Aeneas's marriage with Lavinia. Camilla dies fighting heroically, but she dies waging war against the founding of Rome. She shows absolute loyalty to her father, vowing never to marry, thereby refusing to be traded out in the politics of the period and at the same time maintaining an intimate bond with her father. As told in the *Cité,* the story seems to analyze into its component parts acceptably domestic father/daughter relations as distinct from the power of the patriarchy to dispose of its subjects at will. The virgin Camilla fights against the doubly marked

[20]Constance Jordan, "Boccaccio's In-Famous Women: Gender and Civic Virtue in the *De mulieribus claris,*" in *Ambiguous Realities: Women in the Middle Ages and Renaissance,* ed. Carole Levin and Jeanie Watson (Detroit: Wayne State University Press, 1987), pp. 37–38.

[21]Christine Reno, "Feminist Aspects of Christine de Pizan's 'Epistre d'Othéa à Hector,'" *Studi Francesi* 70 (1980), 271–76.

dynastic traffic in women which cemented the founding of Rome in Italy: promised to Turnus, Lavinia must be traded instead to Aeneas. Camilla, having herself refused to be given in marriage, fights for the right of the more endogamous Turnus against the stranger Aeneas.

So too, in some of its implications the last story in this section of the *Cité* also appears to point to the problematic power the city of Rome exercised in its female trading practices and in its questionable determination to protect its female inhabitants. The maiden Cloelia never participated in war or battle; she was sent as a guarantee of various treaties Rome had made with an enemy king. Finally, bored with being a hostage, Cloelia escaped, taking with her a number of her young companions: "she considered it dishonorable for the city of Rome that so many noble virgins were being held as prisoners" (p. 62). Even though she had never ridden before in her life, she used a horse she found in a pasture to ferry her companions one by one over a river, until they were all safe; she thus returned all of the hostage young women back to their parents in Rome. This amusing vignette of girlish heroism is something of a surprise after the martial super-heroics of characters like Babylonian Semiramis and Palmyrian Zenobia. As an answering antiphon to Semiramis's story, however, the brief narrative of Cloelia may serve a number of purposes. It labels as "Roman" the girlish passivity into which Cloelia was raised; it also labels as "Roman" the trading of female hostages to hostile enemies as guarantees that imperial Rome can be forced to keep its word. Finally, it also demonstrates how physically brave even such a girlish maiden can be—riding a horse for the first time— and how courageously capable she is of setting her own moral value on her city's honor, in defiance not only of her own captivity but also, presumably, of the Roman statesmen who had traded her as hostage.[22] It is with this final reassurance about the "weak" female body, given to her nonmartially trained female readers, that Christine concludes her foundation building. On the stones of these women of courage, her city can now be raised.

---

[22]The Great Schism, with one pope in Rome and another French-supported one in Avignon, lasted from 1378 to 1409 and detracted from the authority of the city of Rome as well as the papacy. This is the local political context for Christine's anti-Roman tendencies in the *Cité*. Imperial Rome, of course, is the great enemy during the persecution of the martyrs, the material of part III of the *Cité*.

The Walls of the City, the Body of the Text: Part I,
Sections 26–48

At a point of extreme architectural (and structural) juncture—the change from the constitution of the city's foundation to the construction of its walls (a right-angle turn, so to speak)—Christine has Reason move from telling stories about women who are martial heroes to narrating legends about women who are textual adepts. Their authority derives not from the strength of their bodies, nor from their moral characters, but from their facility with script. Reason later explains to Christine that there are two kinds of prudence: "one is the gift of God thanks to the influence of Nature" and "the other is acquired through long study" (p. 87). For Christine, the second is by far the more valuable, for natural prudence (common sense, really) dies with the person who possesses it, while acquired learning "lasts forever for those who have it, because of their fame, and it is useful for many people insofar as it can be taught to others and recorded in books" (p. 88). Most appropriately, then, at the outset of this section of the text, with its long roll call of female artists, poets, scholars, and seers, Christine announces the name of her own major auctor, Boccaccio, citing him for the first time when narrating the story of the learned Cornificia—although she has, of course, copied him through a large number of narratives already: "De laquelle chose Bocace l'Italien, qui fu grant pouette, en louant ceste femme dist en son livre" (p. 724); "The Italian Boccaccio, who was a great poet, discusses this fact in his work and at the same time praises this woman" (p. 65).

It is significant that just after naming Boccaccio as her auctor, Christine retells his story of the Roman woman Proba. Proba is a particularly fascinating context for an acknowledgment of an auctor, for she was famous for a peculiar kind of composition which pays great respect to the auctores: Proba had rewritten the stories of scripture by using the verses of Virgil. As Christine explains, "in one part she would take several entire verses unchanged and in another borrow small snatches of verse, and, through marvelous craftsmanship and conceptual subtlety" she was able to narrate the Bible, from Creation to the Apostles, in Virgil's poetry (p. 66). As Boccaccio describes the effect of such pastiche-work: "ut huius compositi ignarus homo prophetam pariter et evangelistam facile credat fuisse Virgilium" (p. 394); "this composition made it easy for an ignorant man to believe that Virgil had been both prophet and evangelist" (p. 231).

Constance Jordan criticizes Boccaccio's praise of Proba for implying that women were incapable of "original" work: "Proba's poetic function is limited to re-presenting what male poets have written and does not extend to changing the canon" (p. 30). While Jordan is certainly correct to point out that in general Boccaccio is very nervous about his illustrious women's accomplishments and consistently colors his "praise" with a "condemnation of the woman's audacity in venturing into a world reserved for men" (p. 27), the model that Proba provides is very close to Boccaccio's own practice as compilator, especially in a text like the *De claris*. His assessment of Proba's achievements is in complicated ways bound up with his sense of his own autonomous authority and may carry more complex baggage than a mere cultural dismissal of the "other." As we have seen in his preface to the *Decameron*, Boccaccio associates his ambivalence about the problematic originality of his writing with the problem of women; there his misogyny allows him ironically to claim an originality that would undermine his compilator's authority in other, more serious, works such as the *Genealogy of the Gods*.[23] Proba's own practice in its canonical orthodoxy—a classical style for a biblical subject matter—proleptically and particularly stages the very problem the Renaissance would find so tricky to solve: how to tell a Christian story in a pagan form. Suffice it to say that Christine was at least one fifteenth-century compilator who noticed the significance of Proba's achievement, if not for Boccaccio's problematic relationship to his *auctores*, then for her own relationship to him.

There is, indeed, an even further twist to Christine's naming of Boccaccio at this point. In the prologue to the *De claris*, he rests his claim to humanist originality (and his difference specifically from Petrarch, whom he names) on the distinction between the oft-told

---

[23]Thomas Hyde, "Boccaccio: The Mythographer at Sea" (unpublished paper) has argued that the voyage plot of the *Genealogy* "seems to image the absence of authority in his fictive material . . . the reckless ingathering of sources" which causes Boccaccio concern about his authorial legitimacy.

tales of saints' lives and the fact that the merits of *pagan* women "have not been published in any special work up to now and have not been set forth by anyone" (p. xxxix).[24] Furthermore, he does not include any Christian women in his text, on the grounds that pagan and Christian women cannot be compared equally:

> excepta matre prima, his omnibus fere gentilibus nullas ex sacris mulieribus hebreis chistianisque miscuisse; non enim satis bene conveniunt, nec equo incedere videntur gradu. (p. 26)

> with the exception of our first mother, I have neglected to include Hebrew and Christian women among these pagans. But this was done because it seemed they could not very well be placed side by side, nor did they strive for the same goal. (p. xxxviii)

Yet Proba, of course, was a Christian, and as such is an instance whereby Boccaccio breaks his own rule.

Christine's inclusion of a martyrology in the third section of the *Cité* goes directly against Boccaccio's authoritative pronouncements about the propriety of discussing the virtues of pagan and Christian women together. By acknowledging Boccaccio in the context of one of the few stories he does in fact narrate about a Christian woman, Christine shows herself to be remarkably attentive to any worries he might have about his own authority.[25] Since the story is about Proba, a woman who in her poetic practice successfully bridged the abyss Boccaccio insisted was not negotiable between biblical and pagan standards for female virtue, Christine revises him at just the point where he bases his own greatest claim for originality. Thus Boccaccio dismisses the text of Christian women with tongue-in-cheek praise for their authors:

> Moreover, not only do Christian women, resplendent in the true, eternal light, live on, illustrious in their deserved immortality, but we know that their virginity, purity, saintliness, and invincible firmness in over-

---

[24]"nullo in hoc editor volumine speciali . . . et a nemine demonstrata, describere, quasi aliquale reddituri premium" (Boccaccio, *De mulieribus claris*, p. 28).

[25]I am indebted to Richards's note for first suggesting this line of reasoning: "Proba's treatment of Virgil exemplifies in part Christine's relationship to Boccaccio, whom she rewrites and Christianizes" (p. 262).

coming carnal desire and the punishments of tyrants have been described in special books, as their merits required, by pious men, outstanding for their knowledge of sacred literature and for their venerable greatness. The merits of pagan women, on the other hand, have not been set forth by anyone, as I have already pointed out. I have, therefore begun to describe them in order to give them some reward. (p. xxxix)[26]

In the next stories, the problem of originality itself surfaces. Reason tells these histories to Christine in order to demonstrate that women have been not only compilators, but original creators and discoverers of "new and unknown thing[s]." Among these creators are Carmentis and Ceres, the latter depicted here not as a goddess but in the euhemerist reasoning Christine probably learned from Boccaccio, as an exemplary woman. The life of Carmentis is doubly important for it considers both the problem of originality and of the lettered tradition. Carmentis founded the Latin alphabet. She was also the first to give laws to the people then living on the Palatine hill, that is, on the site where Rome was later to be built. The first foundation of law and letters at the physical origin of the future Rome was therefore created by a female authority that, moreover, owed its potency to prophetic inspiration: "Ceste noble dame sceut par inspiracion divine et par esperit de prophecie" (p. 736). By prophetic inspiration Carmentis knew that Rome would come into being. Thinking that it would not be fitting for so victorious a people to use a foreign nation's script of strange characters, she developed the Roman script. Orthographic wit makes the point clear: what Carmentis thereby avoided were "*karacters estranges et mendres d'autre pays*" (p. 737); "strange and inferior letters and characters of another country" (p. 72). In the same spirit of self-consciousness about the scriptedness of language and its place as a point of origin for proper names, Reason explains that Carmentis's own name comes from the Latin for "song." Further play on the word "ita" (meaning,

---

[26]"Preterea he, vera et indeficienti luce corusce, in meritam eternitatem non solum clarissime vivunt, sed earum virginitatem, castimoniam, sanctitatem, virtutem, et, in superandis tam concupiscentiis carnis quam suppliciis tiramnorum invictam constantiam, ipsarum meritis exigentibus, singulis voluminibus a piis hominibus, sacris literis et veneranda maiestate conspicuis, descriptas esse cognoscimus; ubi illarum merita, nullo in hoc edito volumine speciali—uti iam dictum est—et a nemine demonstrata, describere, quasi aliquale reddituri premium, inchoamus" (Boccaccio, *De mulieribus claris*, pp. 26, 28).

we are told, "yes") reveals the origin of the word "Italy." Such dense verbal play, using the unusual Kappa (K), for example, not only is generic to allegory, it connects law and letters with the site of a Rome, discovered by a female prophetic authority and therefore established by a previously overlooked female agency. Reason also points out the irony involved in Carmentis's invention of the tool by which men claim such great authority in learning:

> Or se taissent, or se taisent d'or en avant, les clers mesdisans de femmes, ceulx qui en ont parlé en blasme et qui en parlent en leurs livres et dittiez, et tous leurs complices et confors, et baissent les yeux de honte de ce que tant en ont osé dire a leurs diz, considerant la verité qui contredit a leur diz, voyant ceste noble dame Carmentis, laquelle par la haultesce de son entendement les a apris comme leur maistresce a l'escolle—ce ne pueent ilz nyer—la leçon de laquelle savoir se treuvent tant haultains et honnourez: c'est assavoir les nobles lettres du latin! (p. 751)

> Henceforth, let all writers be silent who speak badly of women, let all of them be silent—those who have attacked women and who still attack them in their books and poems, and all their accomplices and supporters too—let them lower their eyes, ashamed for having dared to speak so badly, in view of the truth which runs counter to their poems; this noble lady, Carmentis, through the profundity of her understanding taught them like a school-mistress—nor can they deny it—the lesson thanks to which they consider themselves so lofty and honored, that is, she taught them the Latin alphabet! (p. 80)

As a parallel to Carmentis's invention of the Latin alphabet, the story of Minerva follows next and emphasizes her invention of Greek script. To women are credited both of the classical languages and thus the literary cultures of Greece and Rome.

Although it does not involve a problem of textuality, a continuing emphasis on the founding of cities shows up even in Ceres's story. As the teacher of agriculture, she enabled people to live in urban, civilized centers: "Et ordena aucuns hommes es champs pour faire les labours, par lesquelz tant de villes et de cités sont reamplies et ceulz soustenus qui font les autres oeuvres necessaires a vivre" (p. 750). "By organizing certain men to perform field work, she made it possible for so many cities and towns to be populated and for their residents, who perform the other works necessary for life, to be supported" (p. 79).

Nor does Reason forget the immediately practical contribution of "women's work" to human civilization. She installs in the city Arachne, a great weaver who first taught the spinning of linen on a distaff: "Laquelle chose me semble a esté neccessaire au monde, quoyque l'exercite en soit par plusieurs hommes reprouché aux femmes" (p. 753). "It seems to me that this technique was quite necessary for the world, although many men have reproached women for practicing it" (p. 82). Such a positive valuation of women's work qua women's work is fundamentally integrated into Christine's overall anti-misogynist argument. She does not merely claim that women originated many technologies conventionally credited to men, she also praises the arts women are traditionally thought to have added to the world, specifically disagreeing with the poet Boccaccio and other authors—"Et nonobstant que aucuns autteurs, et meesmement celluy poette Bocace" (p. 754)—who have argued that mankind was better off in a prelapsarian paradise where clothes and cooking (the arts of a fallen civilization) were not necessary. We are told that no less of an authority than Christ himself paid great honor to the science Ceres invented when he decided to give himself to men and women under the species of bread.

Although Christine has made it clear in the story of Carmentis that Rome's laws were first established by a woman, a veritable basso profondo of (largely negative) Roman citations runs throughout the section about the building of the walls of the city of ladies. Reason reminds us that Minerva (Athena) and Isis, a Greek woman and an Egyptian woman, were both so important to human culture that the Romans were foolish enough to worship them as goddesses. Here as elsewhere Christine has it both ways; the fame of Minerva and Isis among Romans proves their worth *and* the Romans' pagan limitations. Roman women are prominently mentioned: a Roman painter and a Roman scholar are among the examples demonstrating female achievement in the arts. And finally, of the last four stories exemplifying prudence in women, three have to do with women connected to Rome: Gaia Cirilla (the wife of King Tarquin), Dido, and Lavinia, wife of Aeneas. Even in the fourth legend, Ops, the wife of Saturn, is described as someone worshipped as a goddess "even at the height of Rome's prosperity" (p. 96). Ops was, of course, also Saturn's sister; by concluding with her, Christine gives us a reprise of the theme of incest, as well as a possible reference to the full story of Saturn which Jean de Meun's Reason had so mishandled—for, of course, it was Ops's prudent, motherly care in that myth that spared her son Jupiter, so that he could live to castrate his father.

Gaia Cirilla, mother of the Tarquin who raped Lucretia, exemplifies housewifely care and foresight and initiates Christine's consideration of Roman matronship at a most problematic spot in that city's history. One cannot help but think that Christine meant her reader to be quite conscious of the unsavory parts of this famous story and to see her praise of the good Roman matron in an ironic light— especially when she explains that Roman brides were expected to answer "gaia," when they entered their groom's house for the first time, thereby to signal their desire to imitate Gaia Cirilla's paradigmatic housewifery. Because Christine tells Lucretia's story in two other separate places in the text of the *Cité* and so makes fully accessible to her reader the results of Gaia Cirilla's mothering of the rapist Tarquin, it is likely that she expected her reader to know the part of the story which conflicts so violently with descriptions of this mother's peacefulness. Even perfect matronly dutifulness does not protect one from the fundamental violence of Roman politics: thus Christine represents the episode of Tarquin's first sight of Lucretia in a quiet domestic setting, as she sits at the end of the day, in a plain gown, knitting, awaiting her husband's return. What inflames Tarquin with desire to rape her is not Lucretia's beauty, but her modestly dressed and paradigmatically dutiful fulfillment of the role of housewife exemplified by his mother.

As is to be expected in any text of female city-building, Dido's is the longest narrative in this subgrouping; it comes directly after the story of Tarquin's mother, and thus allows Christine to compare with Gaia the Carthaginian nonwife Dido, who is usually contrasted to the Roman wife, with her empire-sustaining virtue. In Christine's text, Dido exemplifies not a contrast but an extension of the same virtues as Gaia Cirilla. Hounded out of her native land by an avaricious brother, forced to flee like Aeneas to foreign shores, Dido founds the great city of Carthage. As she institutes its laws so that her people can live according the rule of law and justice, her fame for prudence grows. People begin to call her Dido, a name that is the equivalent of the Latin term *virago*—an honorific title meaning "the woman who has the strength and force of a man." Focusing on Dido's city-building, Reason analyzes that part of the queen's story illustrating the issue of the moment—prudence; she explicitly postpones the rest of Dido's story (Droitture's narration of the betrayal by Aeneas appears in the second section of the *Cité*), though of course all readers would have known that Dido, no less than Lucretia, suffered betrayal by a Roman man.

Like Dido, Ops is prudent. She outwits Saturn's attempts to kill all her male offspring and succeeds in saving Jupiter, Neptune, and Pluto—who, when grown, through their unusually great authority increase her reputation as the "mother of gods." Lavinia, wife of Aeneas, is descended from Saturn; since Ops is Saturn's wife and sister the two women are therefore necessarily part of the same family. Lavinia figures in the city-building section as the mother of Julius Silvius; through her prudence, she ruled the future site of Rome as regent for her son, while managing to keep the peace between Julius and Ascanias, Aeneas's older Trojan son. The contrast between the two stories of incestuous Ops and bartered-bride Lavinia may recall Semiramis's incest that stabilizes a discursive female power by halting the traffic in women. Ops mythically could not be traded and her incest, like antideluvian biblical incest, is necessary. Lavinia, however, is the traded woman par excellence: the whole war with the Trojans is occasioned because Lavinia's mother—in contrast to her father—wanted her to be married to her betrothed, Turnus. The Etruscan king, however, realizing that exogamy is necessary, instead traded his daughter out to the Trojans. The story of the founding of Rome makes its civilization originate in the giving of the gift of Lavinia to the stranger Aeneas, rather than to the familiar Turnus. Exogamy brings civilization while endogamy does not. Standing at the origin, Ops mythically manages by her prudence to rise above the oedipal chaos and to save her sons; Lavinia, by her prudence, manages to rise above the violence of her marriage trade and to make peace between potentially warring sons. Motherhood, complexly engaged in the violence of oedipal dramas as it is, is a power upon which to found cities, even Rome.

Chapter 3

Rewriting the City:
The Politics of Prophecy

> Women doubtless reproduce among themselves the strange gamut of
> forgotten body relationships with their mothers. Complicity in the
> unspoken, connivance of the inexpressible, of a wink, a tone of voice, a
> gesture, a tinge, a scent. . . . Not communication between individuals
> but connections between atoms, molecules, wisps of words, droplets
> of sentences. The community of women is a community of dolphins.
> —Julia Kristeva

The second section of the *Livre de la cité des dames*, narrated
by the unusual figure of Droitture, refocuses the central problem of
the relationship between a scripted and an unlettered female authority. As in the initial scene of reading interrupted by Christine's actual
mother, a bookish tradition continues to be both opposed to and
synthesized with an unscripted tradition of oral wisdom. Unlike
Justice and Reason, who are two of the four traditional daughters of
God, Droitture herself is unorthodox as a figure of authority. She is
not original with Christine, but is borrowed from a contemporary;
thus she does not have the authoritative stature that time would give
her.[1] The name Droitture means both "correctness" and "straightness" (rectitude) and also points to the judicial, the law (droit); I do
not translate this name because the French usefully keeps in play the
multiple notions of legality and straightness of rule, as represented
by Droitture's emblematic ruler. She builds the square buildings (the
walls are round, as in the incipit miniature). Here is the very arena be-

---

[1]She had first appeared in Phillippe de Mézière's *Songe du Vieil Pèlerin*, written in
1387. See Charity Canon Willard, *Christine de Pizan: Her Life and Works, A Biography* (New York: Persea Books), p. 137.

yond men's written laws which, Reason predicted, is the real sphere of female power. It thus falls to a punningly named Droitture to construct the city's buildings by narrating stories about women whose authority is peculiarly extralegal and therefore quite different from that of ruler queens or well-known poets.

The Authority of Sibylline Prophecy: Part II, Sections 1–6

Droitture opens her case for women's intellectual worth with legends of the ten sibyls. When she explains that the sibyls are prophetesses and that the word "sibyl" itself, a term of office, means "knowing the thinking of God," she glosses her definition of her own nature at the outset of the text. "Dieu magnifeste par moy a ses amis ses secres" (p. 633); "Through me, God manifests to His friends His secrets" (p. 13). In the same way, in the opening of the *Cité*, Reason had prophesied to Christine by claiming the authority of a true sibyl, "Mais je te prophetise, come vraye sebille" (p. 631), that the city of ladies she would be building would last longer than Troy, Thebes, or the Amazonian kingdom.

All three figures of authority function therefore in the same sibylline way in this text, manifesting by their appearance to Christine the previously secret, hidden wisdom of female power in the world, putting it into a textual form by helping to build simultaneously the city and the book (livre). Their shared role is further stressed by Droitture's repetition of Reason's earlier pun: "maçonnes fort a la trampe de ta plume, car assez de quoy te *livre*ray" (p. 786); "build strongly with your tempered pen, for I will *deliver* you enough material" (my translation). The simultaneous building of the city's structures and the narration of the stories of the sibyls is represented in the miniature at the opening of the second part of the *Cité des dames*. There a taller, crowned Droitture leads into the partially constructed city a group of variously dressed women, while a small figure raises another roof (Figure 16).

The second section of the *Cité* is not the first text in which Christine had written of the sibyls: the final episode of her very popular *Epistre Othéa*—that is, the hundredth letter to be sent by Othéa to

16. Droitture leading the sibyls into the city, *Cité des dames*, Ms. Harley
4431, f. 323. London, British Library, by permission

Hector—concerns the Cumaean sibyl's prophecy to Caesar Augustus of the coming of Christ. The terms in which this prophecy is couched there become most significant in relation to the *Cité*'s later consideration of imperial Roman legitimacy:

> Cesar augustus was emperour of rome & of al the world; &, for as myche as, in the tyme of hys empyre, pees was in al the werld so that he rewled pesebly in hys tyme, the lewed mysbelevyng people supposed that the pees had be bycause of hym but it was not, but for our lord jhesu that than was borne on the virgyne marye, & was then on erth; & as long as he leved on erth, pees contynued through-owt the erth; & so these mysbelevyng people aforseyd honoured hym; & then sybylle the prophetesse seyd to hym that he schold be-ware to be wurschypped in that wyse, & seyd ther was but on god that created & made all-thyng of noght.[2]

Rome, then, should understand that its famous success as an empire was due not to Augustus but to the son born of the Virgin Mary. The "texte" summarizes the point of the prophecy: by this message Hector, Othéa's disciple, is to realize that he should not disdain her writing, even though she is a woman. Just as the Cumaean sibyl taught Augustus, so Othéa can teach Hector. The last "texte," then, restages the problem of the gendering of authority throughout the *Epistre Othéa*, as a divinely inspired woman speaks in prophecy to, and instructs, an adolescent male.

> An hundred autorites j have to the sent,
> Wyche by myn aduyse thu schalt not dispyse.
> Prent hem in the mend in good intent,
> As thu wylt of prowes have the entrepryse.
> Augustus the emperour, for all hys conceyl wyse,
> Of a woman schall lerne his lyff to amend.
> Disdeygne not this pystle, thoug j to the
> it send.[3]

---

[2]James D. Gordon, ed., *The Epistle of Othéa to Hector; Harley MS 838* (Philadelphia: University of Pennsylvania Press, 1942), p. 145. There is no modern translation of the *Epistle Othéa* and no printed version of the French text.

[3]Gordon, *Epistle of Othéa*, p. 144. Compare Curt F. Buhler, ed., *The Epistle of Othéa*, trans. Stephen Scrope, Early English Text Society, vol. 264 (London: Oxford University Press, 1970), p. 120: "And because that Cesar Augustus, the which was prince of all

Sibylline prophecy thus corrects Rome's pagan arrogance in the *Othéa*, with an authority specifically gendered female. Figure 17 shows the sibyl revealing her vision of the mother-child dyad, which was the destined purpose of the founding of the Roman empire.

In the *Cité des dames*, Droitture's emphasis on the sibyls continues the subtle critique of Rome begun in section one by Reason and reinforced by her emphasis on an alternate tradition of female civilization with its very different set of cities, Carthage and Babylon. Most appropriately Christine takes her cue from Augustine, who refers in Book X of the *City of God* to the Cumaean sibyl's prophecy in Virgil's fourth eclogue: "It is of Him, too, that the most famous poet [Virgil] speaks, poetically indeed, since he applies it to the person of another. . . . For that he did not say this at the prompting of his own fancy, Virgil tells us in almost the last verse of that 4th Eclogue, when he says 'The last age predicted by the Cumaean sibyl has now arrived'; whence it plainly appears that this had been dictated by the Cumaean sibyl."[4] Augustine's privileging of the Cumaean sibyl's authority over that of Virgil makes even more pointed Christine's selection of her as psychopomp in the *Chemin de long estude* (1403), where she specifically serves for Christine the same purpose that Beatrice (not Virgil) had served for Dante in the *Commedia* (Figure 18). The sibyl shows Christine the organization of the heavens.

The substitution is particularly notable in the *Chemin* which Christine conspicuously names with a translation of Dante's phrase describing how he studied and loved his master, Virgil with long study—"il longo studio." (We consequently know exactly where Christine would insert her poetic name into the essentially Italianate

---

the worlde, lerned to knowe God and to beleve of a womman, to the purpos may be seide the auctorite that hermes seith: Be not ashamed to here trouthe & good teching of whom that euer seith it, for trouthe noblith him that pronounceth it." In the version of this prophecy found in the *Ovide moralisé*, ed. C. De Boer, *Verhandelingen de Knoniklijke Nederlandsche Akademie Van Wetenschappen, Afdeeling Letterkunde*, Nieuwe Reeks, 43 (1938), 38–44, the Cumaean sibyl announces the miraculous coming of Christ during the time of Caesar Augustus in terms of divinely incestuous family relations: "Que Dieu envoit son fil en terre / Pour son peuple sauve et querre. / Cil sera samblable à son pere, / Et sa fille sera sa mere" (XIV.1267–70). Augustus is treated to no vision, however.

[4]Augustine, *The City of God*, trans. Marcus Dodds (New York: Modern Library, 1950), 10.333.

17. The Cumaean sibyl showing the emperor Augustus the Virgin and Child, *Epistre Othéa*, Ms. Harley 4431, f. 141r. London, British Library, by permission

18. The Cumaean sibyl showing Christine the heavens, *Chemin de long estude*, Ms. Harley 4431, f. 189v. London, British Library, by permission

list of texts she constructs to be her tradition.) She also gives to the Cumaean sibyl the prophecy of her own future fame as an author:

> Que ton nom sera reluisant
> Apres-toy par longue memoire
> . . . .
> Je t'aim et vueil faire a savoir
> De mes secres une partie.

(I prophesy) that your name will be illuminated
after you by a long memory

. . . .

I love you and want you to know
some part of my secrets.[5]

Led by the sibyl, Christine is shown the fountain of Sapience in
which the nine muses bathe and is then taken on a journey through
the vast cosmography of learning, through all the categories of
knowledge on earth, in hell, and throughout heaven. Figure 19 shows
the sibyl revealing visions to Christine, just as she had to Augustus.

Borrowed from Virgil, who was—according to Augustine—then at
his most inspired, the Cumaean sibyl supplies Christine with a
panoramic allegorical vision that surveys all known means of authority. It is a vision ended only, as we have seen, when Christine is
awakened in the morning by her mother. Outside a legitimate textual tradition, but intersecting it at important nodal points, the
sibyls have thus consistently represented in Christine's oeuvre an
alternative tradition of orally based scripted authority, one associated
with the interrupting power of the mother.

According to Droitture in the *Cité des dames*, the special authority of the sibyls is due to their clarity in prophecy, because they use
no figures or obscure and secret words. More particularly, all of the
sibyls, like many of the exemplary heroic women in the first section,
are outside or beyond the usual law; Christine emphasizes that the
sibyls did not follow the law of the Jews: "Et toutesvoies furent elles
toutes payennes et non mie de la loy des Juyfs" (p. 788). Their extralegal position makes their wisdom about the coming of the Christian
savior all the more striking, for they foretold the future without
benefit of scriptural prophecy. In essence, sibylline prophecy proves
better than that of the Old Testament prophets. "Et meesmes de
l'advenement Jhesu Crist, qui de moult longtemps vint aprés, en
parlerent plus clerement et plus avant que ne firent, si qu'il est
trouvé, tous les prophettes" (pp. 787–788). "They even spoke more
clearly and farther in advance of the coming of Jesus Christ, who
came long afterward, than all the prophets did" (p. 100).

[5]*Le livre du chemin de long estude*, ed. Robert Puschel (Paris: H. LeSoudier, n.d.),
ll. 496–501; my translation.

19. The Cumaean sibyl showing Christine the Fountain of the Muses, *Chemin de long estude*, Ms. Ffr. 835, f. 5. Paris, Bibliothèque Nationale

Like Semiramis (and the non-Jewish Canaanite and Samaritan women), the sibyls belong to a nontextual, extralegal tradition Christine is excavating throughout the building of her city.[6] In the construction of this alternate tradition, the first story Droitture most appropriately narrates when she begins this section of the text concerns the sibyl Erythrea. Like Semiramis, Erythrea was born in Babylon; Christine takes special care in her first listing of all ten sibyls to

[6]For a survey of the sibyls in the Middle Ages, see Bernard McGinn, "*Teste David cum Sibylla:* The Significance of the Sibylline Tradition in the Middle Ages," in *Women of the Medieval World,* ed. Julius Kirshner and Suzanne F. Wemple (Oxford: Basil Blackwell, 1985), pp. 7–35.

cite Erythrea's Babylonian name, Eriphile, and to explain that it is different from her second name, which is taken from the Greek island where she wrote her books. This double origin for Eriphile's identity, indicated by her two names, emblematically suggests the double function of the sibyls in the second section of the *Cité*, both to authorize a nonscripted secret authority for women and to bring that authority into a tradition with its own textual development: "tant estoyent clers et entendibles et plains leurs diz et escrips" (p. 787). Born in a fundamentally illicit (or prelicit) Babylon, the sibyl Erythrea takes up a Greek position from which to write.

Christine gives to Erythrea the Greek phrase "Jesus Xristos theou uios soter" (Jesus Christ, son of God the savior) that Augustine had drawn as an elaborate acrostic from a sibylline prophecy, in Book XVIII, chapter 23, of *The City of God*. Of course, while Augustine makes no mention of the native city of the sibyl who speaks that prophecy, Christine does so, thereby making the previously denigrated Babylon an origin for sacred, prophetic knowledge about the future. Because Erythrea also prophesied the fall of Troy—a subject about which, Droitture says, "Homer wrote with so many lies"— Christine is able to set all the sibyls in general, not only Erythrea in particular, over against both Jewish and pagan textual traditions. The sibyls possess a tradition different from and prior to Old Testament and Homeric authority.[7] Of the sibyl Almathea, for example, Christine comments rather breezily, without mentioning Virgil by name that: "Auçunes ficcions dient qu'elle mena Eneas en enffer et le ramena" (p. 793). "Several fictions claim that she led Aeneas to Hell and back" (p. 103). Such stories are, however, mere "fictions"; Virgil must have got it wrong (Figures 20, 21).[8]

Appearing less as readers than as writers of books, the sibyls are presented in Boccaccio manuscripts entirely within a bookish frame, different from their representation without books in Christine's text. Yet however textual they necessarily are, their tradition from its inception was marked by a strongly provisional attitude toward the

[7]McGinn, *David cum Sibylla*, p. 35, writes: "These prophetesses were able to make a remarkable transition from paganism to Christianity largely because they were seen not only as foretelling the gloomy message of coming doom and the fate of kings, but also because they were reckoned the peers of the Jewish prophets."

[8]Earl Jeffrey Richards, trans., *The Book of the City of Ladies* (New York: Persea Books, 1982): "Christine relegates Virgil to the literary scrap-heap without even bothering to name him" (p. 263n.).

20. The sibyl Almathea, *Des cleres femmes*, Ms. Royal 20 C V, f. 38v. London, British Library, by permission

value of script and a concomitant reliance on the mystique of super clarity in a language that relies on play—as in the famous acrostic.[9]

[9]For the ambivalence of the sibyls' language in the *Cité des dames*, I am indebted to Roberta Davidson, "Suspicion and the Sibyl: Truth and Authority in *Le Livre de la Cité des Dames*," unpublished paper.

21. The sibyl Erythrea, *Des cleres femmes*, Ms. Royal 20 C V, f. 32v. London, British Library, by permission

Christine narrates the well-known story of Almathea's offer of nine books of prophecy to the Roman king Tarquin. Refused the price she asked, she burnt three of the books in his presence. The next day she came back, requesting the same amount and threatening to burn the rest of the books if he refused. This time he quickly paid her asking

price. "Si furent les livres bien gardez, et fu trouvé que ilz declairo-
yent entierement les faiz qui aux Rommains estoyent a avenir"
(p. 793). "These books were well preserved, and so it was discovered
that they declared in full the future of the Romans" (p. 103).

Droitture now asks Christine to consider the impact of such authority on her own sense of female worth: "Et tu, comme folle, te
tenoyes naguaires malcomptent d'estre du sexe de telz creatures,
penssant que Dieu l'eust si comme en reprobacion" (p. 794). "A short
while ago, like a fool, you considered yourself unlucky to be a member of the sex of such creatures, thinking that God held this sex in
reprobation" (p. 104). How foolish indeed to think ill of God's evaluation of women's insight, now shown to be remarkably high. So authoritative has the sibyl Almathea become that, Droitture points
out, Virgil himself has spoken of her: "De ceste sebille parla en vers
Virgille en son livre. Elle fina ses jours en Siche; et le tumbel d'elle fu
par longtemps monstré" (p. 794). "Virgil speaks in verse about this
sibyl in his book. She ended her days in Sicily and for a long time
afterward her tomb was shown to visitors" (p. 104). Having already
dismissed Virgil for his mistake about Almathea, Christine still cites
him as named auctor, but only when he shares his authority with the
prophetess. It is a way of saying that her tradition equals his, her
female authority matches his canonical status.

After the parade of the ten sibyls, Droitture logically moves on to
biblical prophetesses from both the Old and New Testaments, as well
as more recent figures from France's early history. As a building block
to the city, Deborah is depicted not as a judge but as a prophetess, the
law again being derogated in favor of prophecy; Elizabeth, who is
Mary's cousin and John the Baptist's mother, is also a prophetess:
"Assés d'autre femmes prophettes trouveras, se tu y prens garde, en la
loy des Juyfs, en celle des christiens comme inffinies, se come les
saintes plusieurs" (p. 795). "You will find many other women prophets in the Jewish religion, if you pay attention, and in the Christian
religion you will find almost an endless number, along with numerous saints" (p. 105). Christine quickly drops this line of Christian
prophetesses, who are themselves functioning within the new law,
and returns instead to the anticipation of this new law within the
"pagan" tradition. Thus, we are told the story of the moment when,
on a visit to Solomon's Jerusalem, the wise and learned queen of
Sheba prophesied that a plank she saw lying over a mud puddle would

become covered with precious gems from the treasuries of princes, gems honored by all: "Et dessus le fust de ceste planche mourra celluy par qui sera anientié la loy des Juyfs" (p. 797). "And he who will destroy the law of the Jews will die on the wood of this plank" (p. 106). Through the queen of Sheba, Christine is able to include in her survey of female prophecy yet another city, the city of Jerusalem, but a Jerusalem now emblematic of the destruction of a law, not the civic installation of one.

As if to underscore the notion of destruction, juxtaposed to Sheba's story is the tale of the Trojan prophetess Cassandra. Beaten by her father and her brothers for what they consider her crazed and false insistence on future doom, she continues (accurately) to prophesy that Troy shall fall. Implicit in this unusual conjunction of Sheba and Cassandra is a claim for female insight into the tragedy of history and the triumph—that out of the fall of Troy, out of Roman-Jewish politics, will come a new empire and a new "law." In a further historical extension of the notion of the *translatio empirii* (the westward movement of empire), Christine tells the story of Queen Bassine, wife of Childeric, fourth king of France, who interpreted her husband's visions of France's future, foreseeing a long line of rulers descending from him. Over and over again, Droitture's female prophets outline a revised history of imperial cities and civilizations: Babylon, Rome, Jerusalem, Troy, France. As Roberta Davidson sagely observes, the building of the city is "an act of deconstruction of the cities of men." Droitture has amply proved her case: "Sy puez clerement veoir, belle amie, comment Nostre Seigneur a magniffesté souvent au monde ses secrez par femmes" (p. 801). "Thus you can see clearly, dear friend, how our Lord has often revealed his secrets to the world through women" (p. 108).

Mother and Daughter: Part II, Sections 7–11

Droitture's next set of stories appears to bear very little relation to the preceding group of narratives about famous female prophets. Because this new grouping concludes the actual building of the city—with its addition the masonry parts are finally complete—it would be useful to understand just what connection, if any, this particular part has to the whole, as well as to the prior section on prophecy. Droitture tells all these stories in response to a question Christine asks in a seeming non sequitur after learning the value of the sibyls: why are parents disappointed when a daughter rather than a son is born? The juxtaposition of the domestic and familial consideration with high arguments for secret female prophetic authority—usually aimed at empire—is remarkably disjunct. So disjunct, indeed, that the rupture becomes an element of the text needing interpretation. As in all allegory, the text of the *Cité des dames* calls attention to its crucial passages. So too the articulation of the architectural metaphor is another blatant signal of the necessity for commentary. While the last tale Droitture mentions is the legend of the suffering Griselda, Christine does not narrate this famous story in detail here but explicitly postpones it to a later part of the text where its main tenet, a woman's patience in the face of her husband's cruel and capricious exercise of authority, may properly take its place. In contrast to the explicitly postponed tale of Griselda comes a different final story, narrated in detail to conclude the actual building of the external physical structures of the city. The last tale in a set of stories about daughters loyal to their fathers, this end-piece is Boccaccio's tale of a nameless Roman woman, a daughter who breast feeds in prison—not her father, as in conventional renditions—but her mother: "la . . . fille, qui assez de nouvel avoit eu un enffant, donnoit la tette a sa mere tant que tout luy avoit la mere tiré le laitt des mamelles. Et ainsi rendoit la fille a la mere en sa viellesce ce que avoit prise d'elle en son enffance" (p. 813). "The . . . daughter, who had recently had a child, would give her teat to her mother until the mother had taken all the milk from her breasts. In this way the daughter gave back to her mother in her old age what she had taken from her mother as an infant" (p. 115). What possible thematic relations could there be between the secret knowledge of God conveyed by prophetesses and the intimacy of such a filial connection?

The placement of this story as the last element of physical architecture in the *Cité* immediately recalls the story of Semiramis, the first stone flung down. In both tales there is an interestingly similar hierarchical switch in mother/child relations: in the final architectural feature, there is a daughter nursing a mother, which may be said to match (although not symmetrically) in its reversal of the normal mode of relations, the mother/son incest at the scandalous center of the first architectural feature, Semiramis. The problem of a mother's relationship with children of both genders then becomes the text's overarching question, posed, as it were, by the architecture itself. The echo effect of the architectural metaphor speaks to the immediate context in which the story about the loyal daughter is told—how are daughters different from sons? This doubling of textual signals—both the question as asked by Christine within the text and the bracketing of the story by the metaphor of city-building—insists upon the notion of sexual difference, that is, sexual difference as it concerns the relations daughters have with mothers and how they are very unlike the relations sons have with mothers. If incest is the controlling issue for the relationship between mother and son, then motherhood seems to be the issue controlling (at least at this point in the text) consideration of the relationship between mother and daughter.

A brief comparison between Christine's and Boccaccio's versions of this story will help to highlight the emphasis given to mother/daughter relations in Christine's recasting and to offer therefore some further legitimacy for understanding her emphasis on their difference from mother/son relations (Figure 22).

Boccaccio has shifted the parent nursed in this well-known tale from the aged father to the mother, but his version of the story stresses the way in which the daughter's breast-feeding of her mother may stand as emblem of how all children—both men and women—should treat their parents (both father and mother). The male author appropriates the daughter's capacity for nurturance and makes it metaphoric:

> Hec pietas non solum sancta, sed admirabilis fuit; nec tantum equanda, quinimo preferenda nature muneri, quo docemur parvulos natos lacte in firmiorem etatem deducere ac parentes morti subtrahere.
>
> Mirabiles ergo pietatis sunt vires; nam nedum feminea corda, que facile in compassionem trahuntur et lacrimas, sed non nunquam in efferata et adamantina, obstinatione durata, pentrat pectora.

> This filial devotion was not only holy but marvelous and is to be deemed superior to that gift by Nature by which we are taught to raise our small children to a stronger age with our milk and save our parents from death.

22. The Roman woman nursing her mother in prison, *Des cleres femmes*, Ms. Royal 20 C V, f. 102v. London, British Library, by permission

Marvelous is the power of devotion, for it not only pierces the hearts of women, who are easily moved to compassion and tears, but it sometimes pierces cruel, hardened, stony breasts.[10]

[10]Giovanni Boccaccio, *De mulieribus claris*, ed. Vittorio Zaccaria, vol. 10, *Tutte le opere di Giovanni Boccaccio*, ed. Vittore Branca ([Milan]: Mondadori, 1967), p. 264. The translation is from *Concerning Famous Women*, trans. Guido Guarino (New Brunswick, NJ: Rutgers University Press, 1963), p. 143.

Boccaccio makes such devotion emblematic of what *all* children feel toward their parents, although gender does not disappear as a differentiator; the cruel, hardened, and stony breasts also capable of producing a devoted and nurturing "milk" are, of course, implicitly male, because they are distinctly opposed to women's hearts. The implication is that the greater miracle of devotion is revealed in the case of the (male) stony hearts; women's hearts are easily moved to compassion anyhow. Less frequent and more difficult to attain, the cruel man's "milk" is therefore the more noteworthy. In contrast to Boccaccio's subtle argument for the greater value of male devotion, Christine insists that the story is specific to mothers and daughters and reveals a pure mother-daughter reciprocity. The daughter gives directly back to the mother the milk she received as an infant from her, something a male offspring simply cannot do physiologically. Such a physical limitation does not hamper Boccaccio's metaphorical appropriation of the milk; his praise of intergenerational reciprocity as enacted by the story of the Roman woman is finally generalized to include nameless good deeds by both sexes: "ut minus miremur si quid pium filii in parentes agamus, cum eo potius videamur vices redere et quod alias sumpsimus debita restitutione persolvere" (p. 264); "so that we children do some pious deed for our parents, since it seems rather that we are repaying our debt and returning with appropriate payment what we have received earlier" (p. 143).

Christine's alternative emphasis on the specifically gendered nature of the restitution, a mother's milk returned to a mother by a nursing daughter who is therefore herself necessarily a mother, calls into question the idiosyncrasy of this relationship and most importantly, its potentially very great difference from mother/son relations. What the story emphasizes in context is that the daughter can herself be a mother of her own child, a possibility empowering her to nourish her own mother.[11]

[11]Christiane Klapisch-Zuber, "Blood Parents and Milk Parents: Wet Nursing in Florence, 1300–1530," in *Women, Family, and Ritual in Renaissance Italy*, trans. Lydia C. Cochrane (Chicago: University of Chicago Press, 1987), pp. 132–64, argues that wet nursing was "men's business," that is, it was undertaken at the desire of the newborn child's father to resume sexual relations with the mother without endangering the life of his child, which would be the case should a new pregnancy cause her milk to dry up while she was nursing. Such findings suggest that at the time Christine's own assumptions would have been shaped, the widespread practice of wet-nursing reflected less on women's attitudes toward breast-feeding than on male control over this phase of female reproductive processes.

Since this section of Christine's text is explicitly and fundamentally concerned with sexual difference within the family, that is, with the different relations of males and females to their (male and female) parents, it will be useful at this point to borrow terms from contemporary theories about the creation of gender difference in order to analyze Christine's arguments. Nancy Chodorow's discussion in *The Reproduction of Mothering* of how the family creates differently gendered male and female children provides a way to describe how the stories about parent/daughter relationships which Christine narrates are aimed at articulating the difference between sons and daughters. Chodorow's account of the internal experience of the growing girl may also help to suggest why the architectural metaphor juxtaposes the mother/daughter stories next to narratives about prophecy. So too, by making a brief appeal to some French and American psychoanalytic theory, we may also outline some answers about what the female-to-female affective bond across generations may have in common with language that foretells the secret future.

Chodorow's thesis is an interesting aid for interpreting Christine's work because it focuses on the role of the mother who—socialized herself—socializes her children into their different gender roles. According to Chodorow, men and women experience mothering in radically different ways, and the effect of this difference reproduces the different social and psychological experiences that constitute the two genders. Infants of both sexes usually have their first relational experiences with a female, usually (but not always) their mother, who supplies their needs for warmth, food, and safety; at this period the infant makes no distinction between itself and its mother. As awareness dawns that the self is separate from the mother, the mother in response confirms that separate existence. At this point the process of becoming an individual separate from the mother grows more complicated for a girl than for a boy. Because the mother knows she shares her gender with the female child, she may not establish so sharp a separation from her daughter as from her son, who is more clearly a "differentiated other," different from her by virtue of his gender. The gender shared between mother and daughter blurs the lines of separation between them, while the difference in gender between mothers and sons helps to accentuate the son's far more complete sense of separateness. According to Chodorow, "this process entails a relational complexity in feminine self-definition and personality which is not characteristic of masculine self-definition or personality. . . . Because of their mothering by women, girls come to experience themselves as less separate than boys, as having more permeable ego boundaries. Girls come to define themselves more in relation to others. Their internalized object-relational structure becomes more complex."[12] The complex social activity of mothering is reproduced by means of the mother's behavior toward her daughter: "mothers normally identify more with daughters and experience them as less separate" (p. 109). Such an identification is not only prevalent in infancy, but continues throughout childhood and adolescence: the complex ties between mother and daughter are maintained. "The resurfacing and prevalence of preoedipal mother-daughter issues in adolescence (anxiety, intense and exclusive attachment, orality and food, maternal control of a daughter's body, primary identification) provide clinical verification of the claim that elements of the preoedipal mother-daughter relationship are maintained and prolonged in both maternal and filial psyche" (p. 109–110). In essence, according to Chodorow, "A girl does not simply identify with her mother or want to be like her mother. Rather mother and daughter maintain elements of their primary relationship which means they will feel alike in fundamental ways" (p. 110).[13]

Reflecting a similar perspective on gender difference, Christine argues that parents ought to rejoice at the birth of a girl child: far more than sons—and we then hear examples of many sons who were cruel or indifferent to their parents—daughters continue to remain loyal long after they are grown. Indeed, they can be relied upon to care for their elderly parents.

> si voit on communement les filles tenir plus grant compagnie a peres et a meres que les filz, et plus les visittent, confortent et gardent en leurs maladies et viellesce: la cause si est pour ce que les filz vont plus a vau le

---

[12]Nancy Chodorow, *The Reproduction of Mothering: Psychoanalysis and the Sociology of Gender* (Berkeley: University of California Press, 1978), p. 93.

[13]It is important to realize that the Western idea of the "individual" had roots deep in the classical and early Christian past. For a discussion of some of its origins in early Christian political resistance to imperial Roman rule and the high value placed on the family, sexuality, and civic humanism, see Elaine Pagels, *Adam, Eve, and the Serpent* (New York: Random House, 1988), p. 96. For an argument that places the development of the modern "subject" at the installation of the ideology of liberal humanism during the Renaissance, see Catherine Belsey, *The Subject of Tragedy: Identity and Difference in Renaissance Drama* (London: Methuen, 1985), especially the chapter "Autonomy."

monde et ça et la, et les filles sont plus *coyes,* si s'en tiennent plus pres. (p. 808; emphasis added)

One usually sees the daughters keep their fathers and mothers company more often than the sons, and the daughters visit them more, comfort them more and take care of them in sickness and old age more frequently. The reason is that the sons wander through the world in every direction, and the daughters are *calmer* and stay closer to home. (p. 112)

An entire chapter in the history of female virtue could be traced out in the ideological shift in the meaning of the word "coy" in English from a proper reticence and restraint to an enticing provocativeness. The translation here renders it "calm"; the French word also preserves the same sense in which Chaucer uses it of the Prioresse, denoting a shy quietness. It should not surprise us that Christine's observation of such effects should seem so "familiar"; they are themselves caused by remarkably persistent gendering practices within the family, which both re-create and reinforce social practices. If daughters remain closer to home, it is not only because of their socialization by their mothers, but also in part because society does not allow them to go far away, they are not given the specific wherewithal to travel, and they are thought to be at risk except when safely enclosed within a boundary of privacy. Indeed, fears of "permeability" dominate the policing of females at many social levels throughout many periods and cultures.[14]

More pointed than Christine's observation of the similar social effects resulting from the restriction of women, however, is her use of her own personal case as an example; thus Droitture reminds her:

[14]For a discussion of the need to "enclose" the female in the English Renaissance, for example, see Peter Stallybrass, "Patriarchal Territories: The Body Enclosed," in *Rewriting the Renaissance: The Discourses of Sexual Difference in Early Modern Europe,* ed. Margaret Ferguson, Maureen Quilligan, and Nancy Vickers (Chicago: University of Chicago Press, 1986), pp. 123–42. The location of structural instability at the margin, or boundary, of a system is a usual event in human society. Chodorow's notion of permeability may thus be another version of Mary Douglas's explanation of the "instability" haunting all social margins. "Psychological explanations cannot of their nature account for what is culturally distinctive. . . . Each culture has its own special risks and problems. To which particular bodily margins its beliefs attribute power depends on what situation the body is mirroring." Mary Douglas, *Purity and Danger: An Analysis of the Concepts of Pollution and Taboo,* (1966; rpt. London: Arc Paperbacks, 1984), pp. 121–22.

ainsi que de toy meismes le puez veoir: car, nonobstant que tes freres fussent tres naturelz et de grant amour et bons, ilz sont alez par le monde et tu suelle es demouree pour compagnie a ta bonne mere, qui luy est souverain reconfort en sa viellece. Et pour ce, en conclusion te dy que trop sont folz ceulx qui se troublent et marrissent quant filles leur naissent. (p. 808)

as you can see from your own experiences: for even though your brothers are quite normal, very loving and virtuous, they went out into the world and you alone remained to give your mother a little company, which is her greatest comfort in old age. For this reason, I tell you in conclusion that those who are troubled and upset when daughters are born to them are exceedingly foolish. (p. 113)

Chodorow's thesis is that women are reproduced as mothers by their mothers' specialized treatment of them, a treatment that insists on a sameness and intimacy. This intimate identification shapes the female-gendered child into someone who will "reproduce" the role of mothering, someone who shares an expectation that her life will be filled with connectedness and intimacy with children. Presumably no daughter could be more different from her uneducated Italian mother than the medieval woman who became France's first "professional" author. However, from the genre-breaking appearance of Christine's own historical mother, on the very first page of the text of the *Cité*, this maternal figure persistently recurs, each time marking the profound difference between Christine's allegory and any authored by a male. Indeed, Christine's point in the passage just quoted is about her difference from her brothers—who in all other ways shared her upbringing; their differing treatment of their mother is due to their different genders, the boys feeling free to leave and she presumably not feeling so, but remaining instead as a comfort to her mother's old age.

Why this fundamental question of gender difference in the treatment of the mother, specifically couched in terms of Christine's relationship to her own mother, should come up directly after her discussion of the tradition of mysterious and hidden knowledge passed on in extralegal and transtemporal ways by the sibyls is rather more complicated, and speculation about connections between the sibyl's sort of knowledge and the familial experience of being gendered female must remain tentative. We are forced by the genre, that is, the normal method of suggesting interpretation by parataxis, at least to consider the possibility of connection between these two issues. Chodorow, bolstered by some insights from French feminist psychoanalytic theory, may provide some clues.

In describing the effect the closeness of the mother/daughter bond has on the mental and emotional life of the daughter, Chodorow presents a psychic situation that is hospitable to a woman's identification with all female figures of authority. Chodorow explains the end result of the female child's very different negotiation of the oedipal phase: "there is a greater complexity in the feminine endopsychic object-world than in the masculine" (p. 167). Because "girls do not 'resolve' their oedipus complex to the same extent as do boys," sharing as they do a sense of sameness with their mothers, "they neither repress nor give up so absolutely their preoedipal and oedipal attachments to their mother, nor their oedipal attachment to their father. This means that girls grow up with more ongoing preoccupations with both internalized object-relationships and with external relationships as well" (p. 168). Adolescent girls then, experience the self, insofar as they experience such an entity, as "continuous with others": "their experience of self contains more flexible or permeable ego boundaries" (p. 169). Such a familial experience produces in the girl a character suitable to certain social behaviors:

> Women's roles are . . . based on what are seen as personal rather than "social" or "cultural" ties. The corollary to this is that women's roles typically tend to involve the exercise of influence in face-to-face, personal contexts rather than legitimized power in contexts which are categorical and defined by authority. Finally, women's roles, and the biological symbolism attached to them, share a concern with the crossing of boundaries: Women mediate between the social and cultural categories which men have defined; they bridge the gap and make transitions—especially in their role as socializer and mother—between nature and culture. (p. 180)

The denser complexity in a daughter's internal "relational world" may find textual representation in Christine de Pizan's diverse relationships to the vast number of female figures of authority which habitually populate allegory, especially as enacted in the opening scene, or threshold text, of this allegory. In order to get a shorthand sense of the multiple and shared nature of the mutual nurturance, we

pres les parolles
De la premiere
Dame qui Raison
estoit nommee

23. Justice leading the sibyls into the city, *Cité des dames*, Ms. Ffr. 1177, f. 45r. Paris, Bibliothèque Nationale

need only think of the incipit illumination to the opening of the *Cité des dames*, where Christine's study is crowded with three female figures of authority or the one in which the cluster of all ten sibyls enters the city of ladies (Figure 23).

The three figures of authority initially explain their functions in terms that specifically associate them with the sibyls: all of them prophesy, all possess a secret and female knowledge of the future, all support Christine in her bid for authority. So too, as we have seen, Christine appropriates the traditional wisdom of the sibyls to authorize her own bid for scripted authority, as she inserts herself into a *written* tradition. Taking the role of the female as a liminal boundary figure to a mythic extreme, the sibyls traditionally stand at thresholds mediating between nature and culture for both men and women. As we have seen, Almathea's leading of Aeneas to hell is a trip that, although deemed spurious by Christine, demonstrates the cultural function of sibylline boundary-crossing.

These three figures of authority also nurture the narrator in far more important ways that are immediately associated with Christine's biological mother, whose interruption of the reading scene anticipates the interruption of Christine's lamentations by the three figures. With all four "women" appearing, then, right at the outset of the text, Reason, Droitture, and Justice connect themselves to the pivotal figure of the biological mother; with great traditional authority they speak in terms of domestic intimacy to author Christine. Reason continually addresses her as "fair daughter" as well as "dear friend." In other words, these authorities "mother" the narrator as well as prophesy to her.

As virgins, the sibyls are not of course themselves mothers, but they are powerful female figures who are bound together in a tradition that, as an alternative to a masculine scripted legacy, speaks to the transtemporal generativity of female knowledge.[15] Furthermore

[15]In "Virginity as an Ideal in Christine de Pizan's *Cité des Dames*," Christine Reno argues that the basic ideal "Christine sets forth for all readers is virginity," *Ideals for Women in the Works of Christine de Pizan*, ed. Diane Bornstein (Detroit: Consortium for Medieval and Early Modern Studies, 1981), p. 81. She further specifies that the text demonstrates how women can gain "masculine rewards" by "foregoing their traditional roles as wives and mothers" (p. 83). While it is indeed true that Christine, in conformity to the ideals of her society, appears to value virginity more highly than motherhood, there is, as I have tried to point out, a continuous and subtle process in the text which associates female authority with mothering and female sexual activity, of both genital and more simply physical sorts (such as, for instance, nursing). For a discussion of the powerful presence of the mother in *Lavision Christine*, see Maureen Slattery Durley, "The Crowned Dame, Dame Opinion, and Dame Philosophy: The Female Characteristics of Three Ideals in Christine de Pizan's *Lavision Christine*," in Bornstein, *Ideals for Women*, pp. 29–50.

they are organized into no hierarchy but are members of an aggregate of women, who all share the same authority with the ten sibyls. We need only think again of Christine's model in Dante to sense his very different sequential arrangement of authorities. For Dante there are two psychopomps, Virgil and Beatrice, a male father/mother and also a female "mother"/lover, who together form a hierarchy—although it is a reversal of the normal gender hierarchy, the virginal, Christian Beatrice being of far great sanctity than pagan, male Virgil. They substitute for each other, but do not inhabit the poem simultaneously, as Christine's multiple female figures of authority do. In the same way, Christine departs from her earlier auctor Boethius when she provides herself with multiple female interlocutors. At the opening of the *Consolation of Philosophy*, Philosophy specifically drives the nine Muses off from their whorish attempt to console Boethius; his female figure of authority is carefully stripped of libidinous sexual power so that only her nurturing nature remains. Nor does Boethius even recognize who the august woman is: "My sight was so dimmed by tears that I could not tell who this woman of imperious authority might be."[16] In contrast, Christine has not forgotten who the three figures of authority are. She simply regrets her own physical body, having lost track of the value of her femaleness. Such a bifurcation of emphasis matches Chodorow's description of the difference between the more starkly contrasted and restricted dramatis personae in the endopsychic life of the boy whose negotiation of the oedipal phase leaves him with a fairly clear-cut psychic orientation: he "substitutes a general sexual orientation for the specific attachment to his mother (this attachment is composed of both the remainders of his infantile love and his newer sexualized and genitalized attachment)" and assumes an identification with his father and with it "the superiority of masculine identification and prerogatives over feminine" (p. 94). Whereas a male represses his specific

[16]Boethius, *The Consolation of Philosophy*, trans. Richard Green (Indianapolis: Bobbs-Merrill, 1962), p. 5. Philosophy addresses Boethius as a former nursling: "Are you not he who once was nourished by my milk and brought up on my food; who emerged from weakness to the strength of a virile soul? . . . Don't you recognize me?" (p. 6). Christine might be said to imitate this opening, but she literalizes it—not splitting the female figure into the sexually tantalizing sirens and the good mother, but into the actual biological mother who in fact nursed her (and still feeds her) and the three crowned figures of authority who lecture to her about female worth. Both sorts of figures remain complicatedly present to the discursive project of the *Cité*.

attachment to his mother and experiences a self that is entirely other from her, a female never experiences herself as absolutely different from the mother, because she shares her gender with her. Hence, while females cannot fully embrace the general contempt for the feminine sphere by which males become masculinized, a girl must necessarily experience some form of hostility toward her mother, from whom she must achieve separation.

One can see in Christine's representation of the sibyls the anti-rational but powerfully persuasive mystic-prophetic tradition of a specifically female knowledge, exercised face to face, a relational experience, situated at the liminal spaces of social boundaries—and thus both condemned and honored by society throughout the centuries in such contrary guises as the persecution of witches and the reverence for female saints. Sibylline knowledge may seem a far cry from a daughter's domestic loyalty and attentiveness to homebound elderly parents. Yet sequence in allegory always insists that the reader make thematic connections: the sequence presented by the *Cité* implies that such female sapiential style as that of the sibyls is related to the gendering of females as persons more loyally tied to their mothers—as Christine herself is. The sequence thus would seem to comment on the opening scene's positioning of the various figures, with Christine's mother located just outside the discursive space represented by the book-filled study, inhabited by the daughter who confronts the prophetic, august female figures within it. Prophecy and motherhood, the internal "complex ties" of relation between mother and daughter, are connected to a different, experientially based, secret female authority, obedient to no scripted law, although it may become expressed in script.

Allegory as a genre has always had the ability to project in personified form powerful endopsychic states and intrapsychic battles. In Christine's handling of her threshold text's representation of her various female figures of authority—not only Reason, Droitture, and Justice, but her own mother, located at the boundary of the site of vision—she restages the sort of endopsychic conflict Chodorow outlines. Most important, Christine allows the existence of her actual—and significantly, sometimes hostile—biological mother free entry onto the stage of discourse. The point is not so much that Christine has anticipated feminist theorists like Chodorow as that, in being one of the first female writers to articulate what is specifically gendered about the female experience of history—what is in fact gendered *differently* from males—she comes up with a description strikingly similar to that of a later female thinker considering the same issues.

Julia Kristeva is another theorist who, although sharing with Chodorow a basis in psychoanalytic theory, works from an entirely different tradition. Yet Kristeva also locates the pivotal moment of relation with the mother at the preoedipal stage of infant/mother symbiosis—a monad enveloped by something she calls the "chora." Comprised of the dynamic relation between two who are not yet distinguished from each other, the chora is "neither model nor copy," and it "precedes and underlies figuration and thus specularization." It is "analogous only to vocal or kinetic rhythm."[17] This chora is "semiotic," that is, it is a preverbal functional state preceding the "symbolic" phase of language use. However, it is itself involved in language by its early organization of the connections between the body, objects, family, and social structure—specifically through the ordering principle of the mother's body (p. 27). According to Kristeva, the semiotic "logically and chronologically precedes the establishment of the symbolic," that is, the child's ability to locate himself within the unreferential, arbitrary nature of language. The importance of the chora as a system of signs is that its ordering principle lies in the mother's body and voice; it thus installs at the "threshold of language" a maternal power capable of breaching the symbolic, usually by means of "poetic language" (p. 62), which in its musical rhythms has access to the powerful semiotic pulsions that underlie speech.

Unlike Chodorow, Kristeva does not distinguish between male and female children and their relationship to the semiotic chora. Existing prior to the differentiation of the subject, the chora is a site before sexual difference altogether. The gendering of different subjects is not Kristeva's main concern. But elsewhere she does concede that the special relation of women to the experience of the semiotic chora as mothers grants them a particular relationship to language among themselves: "Women doubtless reproduce among themselves the strange gamut of forgotten body relationships with their mothers.

---

[17]Julia Kristeva, *Revolution in Poetic Language*, trans. Margaret Waller (New York: Columbia University Press, 1984), p. 26.

Complicity in the unspoken, connivance of the inexpressible, of a wink, a tone of voice, a gesture, a tinge, a scent. . . . No communication between individuals but connections between atoms, molecules, wisps of words, droplets of sentences. The community of women is a community of dolphins."[18]

Although as theorists they differ in many essentials, Luce Irigaray shares with Kristeva this sense of a specifically different "female" language that somehow can communicate without recourse to ordinary grammar and syntax and that has the dolphin-like power of a fluidity that exceeds and evades containment within boundaries: "Woman's desire would not be expected to speak the same language as man's."[19] For Irigaray, "hers are contradictory words, somewhat mad from the standpoint of reason, inaudible for whoever listens to them with ready-made grids, with a fully elaborated code in hand. . . . One would have to listen with another ear, as if hearing *an 'other meaning' always in the process of weaving itself, of embracing itself with words, but also of getting rid of words in order not to become fixed, congealed in them"* (p. 29).

As attractively analogous as these descriptions of secret, communicating, virtually "allegorical" speech may be to the insistence in the text of the *Cité* on the secret and prophetic power of the speech of the sibylline figures of authority, it is important to realize that the magic babble of any maternally or uterine based speech makes serious sacrifices of intelligibility and sophistication in its effort to reclaim an authoritative difference from masculine language.[20] As we have seen, Christine does not, in fact, choose to locate her prophecy only within the realm of the spoken, but continually registers its inscription in the powerful discourse of a *named* tradition: Dante, Boccaccio, Augustine. The polysemous play with the word "livre" with which Reason and Droitture simultaneously describe city and text insists upon the bookishness of the project, but such polysemy is

---

[18]Julia Kristeva, "Stabat Mater," in *The Kristeva Reader*, ed. Toril Moi (New York: Columbia University Press, 1986), pp. 180–81.

[19]Luce Irigaray, *This Sex Which Is Not One*, trans. Catherine Porter (Ithaca: Cornell University Press, 1985), p. 25. See also particularly "The Mechanics of Fluids," pp. 106–18, and "Volume-Fluidity," pp. 227–42, in *Speculum of the Other Woman*, trans. Gillian Gill (Ithaca: Cornell University Press, 1985).

[20]Roberta Davidson argues in "Suspicion and the Sibyl" an unpublished paper, that Christine's sibyls are like Irigaray's "La Mysterique," a hysteric who is like a saint.

endemic—indeed generic—to all allegory, whatever the gender of its author.[21]

In a useful critique of Kristevan and Irigarian descriptions of feminine discourse, Kaja Silverman has interestingly observed that a usual error in discussions of the plenitude of the mother/infant couple is that the fantasy of wordless union usually envisioned is developed by putting the fully functioning adult mother *inside* the enveloping enclosure experienced by the child, thus stripping her of her adult discursive authority and endowing her with a magic language reminiscent of the semiosis of the nonspeaking infant. Of Kristeva's argument in particular Silverman asks: "Are we to understand the mother as somehow representing . . . forces . . . antipathetic to language and identity? The answer is apparently yes. What occurs here is [that] once again the child's discursive exteriority—its emergence from the maternal enclosure—can be established only by placing the mother herself inside that enclosure, by relegating her to the interior of the chora, or—what is the same thing—by stripping her of all linguistic capabilities."[22]

Silverman points out that Kristeva necessarily must disavow the "tutelary role the mother classically assumes" in a child's education via her role as "language teacher, commentator, storyteller" (p. 105). In contrast to Kristeva's repression of the mother's important relationship to language, Silverman refuses to relegate the mother/daughter bond purely or even mainly to the preoedipal phase, a site outside of language, even though to do otherwise is to insist that the bond also is marked by all the lacks attendant upon the oedipus complex: "insofar as the relationship of mother and daughter is understood to stand outside signification [in the preoedipal oneness before language and differentiation], it must also be understood to stand outside desire, and so to exercise little influence over psychic

---

[21]The polysemy generic to the form, as well as its typical privileging of female figures of authority, may have helped attract Christine to allegory as a favored genre. For the genre's use of wordplay, see my *The Language of Allegory: Defining the Genre* (Ithaca: Cornell University Press, 1979). For a demonstration of the seductiveness and real danger of seeing any polysemous use of language as participating in the nonunivocal character of "female" speech, see Joel Fineman, "The Turn of the Shrew," in *Shakespeare and the Question of Theory,* ed. Patricia Parker and Geoffrey Hartman (London: Methuen, 1985), pp. 138–59.

[22]Kaja Silverman, *The Acoustic Mirror: The Female Voice in Psychoanalysis and Cinema* (Indianapolis: Indiana University Press, 1988), p. 105.

life" (p. 123). What is finally not oedipal in the Freudian sense about the girl's "passion" for her mother, according to Kristeva, is that "her aspiration to occupy the place of the mother does not imply"—as Freud argued—"the latter's exclusion from her erotic economy, but the endless reversibility of their relative positions" (p. 153). Silverman very suggestively proposes that the third term in the triangle of desire necessarily constructed is not Freud's "troublesome rival," the father, but the baby whom the daughter wishes to bear her mother. "There is . . . another, more important third term here, one which plays a far more central place within the daughter's early libidinal economy than does the father. I refer, of course, to the child whom she both wishes to give to the mother and to receive from her" (p. 153).

The reversibility of the relations Silverman indicates here illuminates with peculiar intensity the pivotal story in the *Cité* of the Roman woman who nurses her mother—the capstone, as it were, in the construction of the physical city of ladies. Repaying a debt to her mother which she incurred as an infant, the daughter can "mother" her mother *because* she has recently given birth to her own child. Told as another way of demonstrating the value of daughterhood in the mother/daughter relation, which the story of Christine's loyalty to her own mother equally demonstrates, the Roman prison story is aimed at counteracting the culturally low value placed on female children. Silverman's account of the potency of the mother's voice for shaping the child's entry into language and the daughter's persistent (because self-identified) desire for that voice and for the mother—despite the mother's culturally de-authorized position in society—provides an analytic tool for understanding how Christine's sibylline tradition is offered as another means of recuperating the authority denied the language of the mother.

It is important in this context to realize that the *Cité's* assumption of an affinity between the complications of mother/daughter relations and the secret power of prophecy gains greater point with the recognition that there was a real professional prophet in Christine's actual family—one who made a living, so to speak, by foretelling the future—and that he was Christine's father, astrologer to Charles V. It was, moreover, her father who attempted to give Christine the education her mother specifically argued that she did not want Christine to have. Again, Christine tells us of this conflict directly in the *Cité des dames*. In part II, Droitture explains:

Ton pere, qui fu grant naturien et phillosophe, n'oppinoit pas que femmes vaulsissent pis par science apprendre, ains de ce qu'encline te veoit aux lettres, si que tu sces, grant plaisir y prenoit. Mais l'oppinion femenin de ta mere, qui te vouloit occupper en fillasses selonc l'usaige commun des femmes, fu cause de l'empeschement qu ne fus en ton enffance plus avant boutee es sciences et plus en parfont. (p. 875)

Your father, who was a great scientist and philosopher, did not believe that women were worth less by knowing science; rather as you know, he took great pleasure from seeing your inclination to learning. The feminine opinion of your mother, however, who wished to keep you busy with spinning and silly girlishness, following the common custom of women, was the major obstacle to your being more involved in the sciences. (p. 154)

Sheila Delany sees a great deal of understandable bitterness in this complaint against Christine's mother for her refusal to support her daughter's desire for an education in the masculine mode. Delany interestingly points out that in the earlier text of the *Mutacion de Fortune,* Christine had "effaced" her biological mother, substituting an allegorical personification of Lady Nature, while at the same time she "mythifies" her actual father as the possessor of two valuable jewels, a knowledge of health and of the future, which she as daughter is unable to inherit.[23] Although it is true that Christine specifically names this mother "dame Nature" and gives this figure far more power than any real, individual female person could have (she will not die until judgment day), it is also true that such a figure personifies the power of motherhood, of generation, of life and nurture, and thereby represents those functions that Christine's actual mother did in fact perform for her. Christine writes of this greater mother in terms of high praise:

> Ma mere, qui fu grant et lee
> Et plus preux que Panthasellee
> (Dieu proprement la compassa!),
> En tous cas, mon pere passa
> De sens, de puissance et de pris,
> Non obstant eust il moult appris,

---

[23]Sheila Delany, *Women Writers and Women in Literature, Medieval to Modern* (New York: Schocken Books, 1983), p. 193.

> Et fu royne couronnee,
> Tres adoncques qu'elle fut nee.
>
> My mother, who was large and generous,
> And more powerful than Penthesilea,
> (God suitably measured her),
> In any case, passed my father
> In sense, in power, and in value,
> Notwithstanding that he had more learning,
> And she was crowned royally
> As soon as she was born.[24]

In a sense, by describing her biological mother in these more generalized terms Christine portrays the historical human being *as* a biological mother. Far from effacing her—at least in her procreative role—she emphasizes the quintessential femaleness of her mother, a femaleness that in allegory easily translates into an abstraction, as we have seen, because of the traditionally female gender of figures of authority. What the *Cité* makes clear is the relative power of the two parents: the mother had the greater influence, at least in this case, to decide the daughter's education. The mother retained authority. The desires of Christine's mother for her held sway until Christine was herself a mother and a widow. In view of Christine's specific defense elsewhere of the importance of spinning, it is also unlikely that she intended entirely to disparage the female arts of cloth-making in her use of the contentious term "fillasses" to refer to the labor her mother insisted she take up instead of pursing studies in the masculine manner. Christine may indeed be effacing her actual historical mother's specific individuality in revenge for this effacement of her individual desires, but in figuring her mother as Mother Nature, she celebrates the female activity of generation she shares with that mother, an activity that mother insisted she share with her. It is a power so great as be divinely authorized. While it is true that Christine takes some characteristics of Dame Nature from the *Roman de la rose*, she again plays with the literalness of the gender of this mother figure—by calling attention to her own gender (the problematic subject of the first part of the *Mutacion*). Thus, although her

[24]*Le livre de la mutacion de Fortune*, ed. Susan Solente, 4 vols. (Paris: Editions A. & J. Picard, 1957), 1.338–46; my translation.

father wishes to have a son to be his heir ("tres grant voulenté d'avoir / Un filz masle, qui fust son hoir," ll. 381–82), her mother's wishes are more powerful:

> Mais il failli a son entente,
> Car ma mere, qui ot pouoir
> Trop lus que lui, si voult avoir
> Femelle a elle ressemblable,
> Si fus nee fille, sanz fable;
>
> (ll. 388–92)

> But he failed of his intent,
> Because my mother, who was more powerful
> Than he, wanted to have a
> Girl to resemble herself;
> Thus in truth I was born a girl.
>
> (my translation)

The change celebrated by the poem—the mutation of its title—is Christine's transformation from a woman inhabiting the traditional, customary role into one who can fulfill the role of a man—steering a ship, being economically independent.[25]

Far from being a dismissal of her mother—and more specifically, of feminine power in general—Christine's text acknowledges the very real gifts that her female education gave her, gifts figured in the form of a chapelet with eight jewels, far more various than the two gems

[25]Joel Blanchard, "L'entrée du poète dans le champ politique au XVe siècle," *Annales ESC* (1986), pp. 43–61, argues that the change of sex in the *Mutacion* represents the author turning her back on the personal lyric and looking toward universal history: "le changement définitif de sexe correspond à une orientation nouvelle de son imaginarie. . . . Cette mise en situation du poéte . . . est destinée à souligner l'origine et le statut nouveau de l'intellectual chargé de prendre compte des évènements" (p. 47). For further discussion that Christine explicitly rejects the metaphorical mutation in the *Cité*, see Kevin Brownlee, "Ovide et le moi poétique 'moderne' à la fin du moyen âge: Jean Froissart et Christine de Pizan," *Modernité au moyen âge: Le défi du passé*, ed. Brigitte Cazelles et Charles Méla (Geneva: Droz, 1989). See also Susan Schibanoff, "Taking the Gold Out of Egypt: The Art of Reading as a Woman," in *Gender and Reading: Essays on Readers, Texts, and Contexts*, ed. Elizabeth A. Flynn and Patrocino P. Schweikart (Baltimore: Johns Hopkins University Press, 1986), pp. 83–106. Schibanoff traces an evolution in Christine's ability to read "as a woman" from an earlier dependence on traditional masculine modes of authorization to a later female-focused independence.

she was unable to inherit from her father (although those two are described as more valuable). In yet another text, Christine realizes that she was only able to give herself a masculine education in the scripted tradition after both her father and her husband had died.[26] And as the very opening page of the text of the *Cité* makes clear, her own mother provided the domestic underpinning for her program of study. She cooked while Christine read. To suggest therefore, as Delany does, that Christine's real mother did not play a part in her "thinking back" is too partial a view of her figure as it recurs throughout Christine's work. What is striking is how fully incorporated into the texts her actual mother is. Delany most usefully explains, however, just what Christine did have to accomplish by writing herself into a tradition that had no prior female author to whose authority she could appeal.

> Christine had no mothers to think back through; no near contemporaries to use as models. Since she had only woman as object, written by men predominantly misogynistic, she must create mothers for herself: woman as mistress of discourse (the poets and scholars and rhetoricians), technique (the great sorceresses and inventors), and temporal rule (queens and military leaders). Because she must fabricate her mothers, Christine's work takes shape at a far more archaic level than that of a man confronting the sources. Her "anxiety of influence" cannot be about herself as writer only, because it is first about herself as woman. (p. 196)

The actual mother, the one she did not create for herself, is represented over and over in her texts, serving as her own boundary figure, opening a text (the *Cité*), or sealing it off in closure (*Chemin de long estude*). An archaic event is something that happens at the beginning (arché-beginning)—and it is at beginnings and endings that Christine most often confronts her mother. So too, her confrontation with her

---

[26]*Lavision-Christine,* ed. Sister Mary Louis Towner (Washington, D.C.: Catholic University of America, 1932), p. 175: Philosophy tells Christine that had she not been widowed, "occupacion de meisnage" (household occupation) would have kept her from her studies. Also in *Lavision,* pp. 173–74, Philosophy points out the good fortune Christine has had to have her mother with her, comforting her in her impatience with her misfortunes: "avec tout de si noble mere laisser vivre en ta compagnie en sa vieillece pleine de tant de vertu et quantes fois elle ta reconfortee et ramenee de test impaciences a cognoistre ton dieu."

male auctores is often "strong" in a Bloomian sense, because she goes to a moment prior to the precursor's, by situating Semiramis before the written law, so distinctly different from Boccaccio's making the Babylonian queen one who legislates perverse laws. Her rescripting of Boccaccio is in this sense literally "archaic"—just as her argument in the *Mutacion* that her "mother" was stronger than her father stems from the originary nature of the mother, that is, from Mother Nature herself.

Her own mother stands at the threshold margin of the text of the *Cité* and recurs throughout it—most specifically in that group of stories about mothers and daughters which completes the construction of the city—the last story itself focusing as we have seen, as intensely as possible on the bond of breast feeding which any infant shares with its mother, a bond that here can be reversed only by a daughter who has herself become a mother. The scene that ends the physical construction of Christine's city thus reverses the scene that opens her *text*, the reading scene in which her mother calls her to dinner. With such intricate maneuverings, the text of the *Cité des dames* organizes itself along allegory's usual lines, with the generic procedures involving complex reechoings, restatements, and reversed mirrorings of preceding moments in the text. No moment in any allegory is more complexly recalled than Christine's startling opening of the *Cité des dames*.

The First Citizens: Part II, Sections 12–16

After the city's external framing structures (its houses, towers, and turrets) are installed, Droitture moves on to explain the need to populate the city. Christine and she will seek inhabitants, for this city is a new realm of women—"nouvel royaume de Femenie"—far worthier than the Amazon kingdom before it, because, Droitture reasons, here it will not be necessary to go outside the realm in order to beget new generations. These residents are immortal. While biological reproduction is thus not necessary in the new textual city Christine constructs, we should not consequently assume that she intends to denigrate sexuality. It was not biology but war and a vulnerable position in history which brought to an end the Amazonian dynasty, which had in any case refused to become an empire. Christine's city has the special "proprieté" that it can never be taken away from its possessors—especially not by heroes such as Theseus, conqueror of Hippolyta.

Introduced as they are in distinction to the Amazons, who needed to procreate in order to repopulate, it is not surprising that the first "citoyennes" whose stories Christine narrates are all *wives,* that is, women who are defined solely in terms of their intimate domestic relations to men. Their social position contrasts as diametrically as possible with that of the unmarried Amazons, who lived separately from men. The citoyennes' stories are told, furthermore, specifically to answer the Theophrastian slander that women are so disloyal and spiteful to their husbands that men should not marry. Now that Reason has proved women capable of individual virtues (great physical strength, valor, prescience, learning, common sense), Droitture will prove them capable of relational virtues (great constancy, loyalty, chastity, love). Metaphorically housed by a structure completed through a legend of the mother/daughter bond, the process of populating the city will first take place through considerations of marriage which specifically rule out childbearing; in these tales, the wife's primary care is not for progeny but for spouse. At the time Christine wrote, the prime function of marriage was not mutual comfort or the alleviation of loneliness, but the bearing of dynastically legitimate children.[27] Yet with the stories narrated to install the first citizens within the city, the text thus takes up the companionate function of marriage. Christine's emphasis on marriage in which childbearing is secondary to companionship anticipates the emphasis of a much later social formation—the middle class of the seventeenth century; similar arguments are made, for instance, by John Milton's divorce tracts. Milton was considered very radical to

---

[27]Georges Duby, *The Knight, the Lady, and the Priest: The Making of Modern Marriage in Medieval France,* trans. Barbara Bray (New York: Pantheon, 1983), p. 30., outlines the early church argument that procreation justifies marriage. Questions of kinship and power continued to dominate the idea of marriage up through early modern France. See Jean Louis Flandrin, *Families in Former Times: Kinship, Household, and Sexuality in Early Modern France,* trans. Richard Southern (Cambridge: Cambridge University Press, 1979), p. 19. In fourteenth- through fifteenth-century Tuscany, the purpose of marriage was to increase lineage associations and the development of dynastic power. See Georges Duby, ed., *The History of Private Life,* vol. 2, trans. Arthur Goldhammer (Cambridge: Harvard University Press, 1988), p. 162.

argue in mid-seventeenth century that the prime end of marriage was not a sexual function of any sort, but a "fit conversation" between a husband and a wife. In her attempt to find terms for her remarkably early articulation of the ideals of a "companionate" marriage, Christine hits upon the methods later English Protestant theorists will also try: she introduces notions of formerly aristocratic masculine friendship into the bourgeois relations between husband and wife.[28] In a sense, the best way of proving the loyalty of wives would be to make the middle class woman share the most privileged of male bonds, that of military comrades in arms, and this is what Christine does: the first stories are all about women who campaigned with their husbands in the field. The friendship between husband and wife thus borrows the cachet attached to masculine battlefield bonding.

The first wife, Hypsicratea, is a special case: she not only fought beside her husband while cross-dressed, she also proved herself more loyal than any of his male cohorts. While they deserted him in defeat, she stayed:

> Et lui, qui de tous ses amis estoit delaissié et relainqui ne plus n'avoit esperance, estoit reconforté par sa bonne femme . . . elle luy faisoit si oublier que souvent il disoit que il n'estoit point homme exillé, ains luy sembloit que il fust tres deliccieusement en son palais avec sa loyalle espouse. (pp. 823–24)

> Though abandoned and deserted by all his friends, with all hope gone, he was comforted by his good wife . . . she made him forget so that often he would say that he was not an exile, but that it seemed to him that he were at his leisure in his palace with his loyal spouse. (p. 122)

Where Boccaccio compares Hypsicratea's solace of her husband to the joy of their nuptial night and praises her soft femininity, Christine insists on the uplifting quality of her loyal conversation and the sense of release from exile she was able to cultivate. This internal homely detail about the palace—a change from Boccaccio's emphasis on sexual solace—echoes the domestic placement of the story:

[28]Duby, in *Knight, Lady, Priest*, p. 31, points out that the church included "amicitia" as one of the values of marriage. So too, Edmund Spenser has his dynastically central lovers Britomart and Artegall, first meet (and battle) in the Book of "Friendship," Book IV of *The Faerie Queene* (1596).

the first noble "palace" of the city is a structure specifically designated for Hypsicratea. She is installed in her palace because she managed to make her husband think he was back in his. Her imagined domesticity is thus supported by her martial prowess and comradely loyalty.

An initial emphasis on warrior queens in the first grouping of "citoyennes" recalls the first stone in the edifice of the city, the pivotal legend of Semiramis. Like her, the first two citizens here are noted for their martial ferocity; unlike her, of course, they do not engage in incest. They have no children. That difference may help to indicate the function of the frame inserted at this point in the text, with the completion of the physical structures. In contrast to the construction of the architectural elements of the city, particularly the walls, via the stories about foundational motherhood in part I, the remainder of part II will be given over to narrations not about women driven by the mother bond (a tie which, as we saw, motivated even the Amazon stories), but women seen specifically in their relations to men. The stories that are not about loyal wives concern virtuous women in some problematic relation to the power of men (women who are either raped or seduced and abandoned). We see how the articulations of the metaphor of city construction allow Christine to impose a further network of framing devices, beyond the three-part structure of the text itself. Here, the switch from the city's physical structure to its human inhabitants echoes an emphasis on the less foundational connection of collateral female-to-male relations as contrasted to the basic bond of motherhood. Marriage, essentially a political and a social connection, comes within the category of a similarly political grouping—citizenship.

Just as Christine and Boccaccio differ in their portraits of Semiramis, so she also diverges from him in the tonal emphasis she givès the next portrait, that of the heroic empress Triaria. Whereas Boccaccio praises Triaria for her valor, he also finds her quite suspect. Although he has no direct evidence with which to charge her, lack of information does not stop him from suggesting (under the guise of humanist lament at the loss of the details of her story) that her martial exploits hint at potentially darker powers:

Et si tanto cum impetu se tulit hec in arma nocturna mulier, quis credet eam hoc tantum facinore fuisse conspicuam, cum non consueverint seu exitiose sint seu celebres, sole mortalium pectora subire virtutes? (p. 392)

And if this woman had carried arms with such violence in the night, who would believe she was famous only for this deed since virtues—and vices—do not dwell singly, within the breast of mortals? (p. 27)

For her part, Christine vitally misrepresents Boccaccio's suspicious praise of Triaria's valor, as if it were a fundamental celebration of marriage: "ce dit Bocace, la grant amour qu'elle avoit a son mary, en approuvant le lian de mariage que autres veullent tant reprouchier" (p. 825); "the great love which she had for her husband, as Boccaccio himself noted, approving the marriage bond which others want to attack" (p. 123).

The next three citizens to enter the city all demonstrate a wife's loyalty to her husband, but do so in ways that increasingly drive toward the margin of abjection which marks the cultural boundary of fear about the body's limits. Thus Artemisia, Argia, and Agrippina not only share the same initial letter of the alphabet, they also demonstrate their wifely affection in similar ways, by enacting increasingly dramatic transgressions of the boundary between life and death. Just as Semiramis transgressed the proper boundary of incest—of the necessary distinctions between mother and child— these first good wives are situated at another boundary, that between life and death. As we will see in the third section of the *Cité*, this boundary is a traditionally privileged place for female activity; women have conventionally been given the work of caring for the dead adult body as well as for the living infant one. Artemisia is, of course, most famous for her care of the dead. She constructed one of the seven wonders of the world, the Mausoleum in honor of her dead husband Mausolus; both Boccaccio and Christine duly narrate the fabulous erection of this temple, with Christine suppressing the detail that Artemisia died before it was completed, so that in her version Artemisia's fame coincides with the monument's. In both versions of the story, however, Artemisia creates yet another monument for her husband's corpse, the vessel of her own body. So great is Artemisia's grief at Mausolus's loss that the only manner of mourning which satisfies her is to entomb bit by bit her husband's ashes in her own body by ceremoniously eating them. Both Christine and

Boccaccio find in this behavior admirable evidence of her love, and both point out that Artemisia's actions are parallel: the Mausoleum and her tomb-body are equal achievements as appropriate sepulchers for her husband.

Droitture's next two stories share a similar emphasis on borderline physical experiences. The Theban widow Argia does not hesitate to kiss the putrefying face of her beloved husband when, an alternative Antigone, she has found his corpse in a chaotic heap of battle dead. The Roman widow Agrippina, wife of Germanicus, starves herself to death in prison rather than be kept alive by her husband's tormentor, Tiberius. A Theban and a Roman story, together they outline extremes of a self-sacrificing response to the death of a husband. Both sacrifices are significantly situated at the mouth—kissing, eating—providing a congruence with Artemisia's oral incorporation of the husband. Agrippina is too faithful to the dead Germanicus to be force-fed any alien sustenance. Argia can embrace the soul of her dead spouse even through the body's decay.

Boccaccio and Christine equally insist upon the details of the putrefying dead face of Argia's husband, Polyneices:

> O mirum! Semesa iam facies armorum rubigine et squalore oppleta pulvereo et marcido iam cruore respersa, nulli iam edepol cognoscenda, amantissime coniugi occultari non potuit; nec infecti vultus sordes uxoris amovere potuerunt oscula. (p. 124)

> It was a miracle that the half-eaten face, already covered by dust and the rust of arms, dirt and putrid blood, which certainly no one could have recognized, did not remain unrecognized by the loving wife. The filth on his face could not prevent her kisses. (p. 59)

Christine gives the drama a higher torque by allowing Argia a brief speech:

> Car come la face de son mary, par l'enroullieure des armes moittié mengié, et toute emplie de pulenteur, toute ensanglantee, pouldreuse, chargiee et tachiee d'ordure, toute palle et noircie, qui ja estoit comme descongnoissable, ne pot estre mucié a celle femme, tant ardentment l'amoit. Ne la punaise du corps ne l'ordure du viairie n'ont peu empescher qu'elle ne le baisast et embraçast estroittement. Ne le edit et

commandement du roy Creonce ne la pot retraire qu'elle ne criast a
haulte voix: "Lasse! Lasse! j'ay trouvé celluy que j'amoye," et qu'elle ne
plourast par grant habondance. (p. 830)

Even though her husband's face was half eaten away by the corrosion of
his armor and was completely filled with pus, all bloodied, covered
with dirt, smeared and stained with filth, sallow, and blackened—
already practically unrecognizable—it could never be disguised from
that woman, so ardently did she love him. Neither the infection of his
body nor the filth covering his face could stop her from kissing him and
embracing him tightly. Neither the edict nor the order could prevent her
from crying out in a loud voice, "Alas! I have found the man I loved," nor
from weeping profusely. (p. 126)

From the ingestion of a husband's ashes to ardor in confronting the
putrefaction of his dead body, the loyal wife loves her husband at, and
beyond, the point of death, is willing to reach across that boundary,
not recoiling from it as most people would, in revulsion at tabooed
uncleanness. Agrippina, wife of Germanicus, is willing to *cross* that
boundary, starving herself to death, refusing to be kept alive by the
man who murdered her husband. Here loyalty to a husband turns
into violence against a husband's enemy which takes the form of *self-*
sacrifice. Agrippina's desire for revenge echoes the most shocking
addition Christine makes to the story of Argia, where she not only
goes completely counter to the details of Boccaccio's text as she
found them in the *De claris*, but goes also against an entire tradition
of literature from Statius, to Dante, to Boccaccio. In the story of
Argia, Christine radically rewrites the "siege of Thebes." She does so
far more radically than she recasts Semiramis's legend, where she
leaves the details essentially unchanged but simply reinterprets
them.

Boccaccio finishes his version by praising Argia's courage in giving
Polyneices a public, royal burial, against the decree of her powerful
enemy, Creon; in this, Boccaccio is following Hyginus's account
rather than the more common story in which it is the sister Antigone
who buries her brother Polyneices and in which she is, of course,
punished for her transgression by being buried alive in her brother's
tomb. (Antigone's story is an interesting reversal of the story of the
mausoleum-building Artemisia.) In contrast to Boccaccio, Christine

does not end Argia's story with the burial, when she fulfills her pious duty to bury her husband properly by gathering his ashes (as Artemisia did) into a golden vessel. Rather, Droitture goes on:

> Et quant elle ot tout ce fait, comme celle qui vouloit exposer son corps a mort pour vengier son mari, fist tant et y mist tel paine a l'aide des autres femmes, dont grant quantité y avoit, que les murs de la cité furent perciés et guaignierent la ville et tout mirent a mort. (pp. 830–31)

> After having done all this, like some woman wishing to expose her body to death in order to avenge her husband, she struggled and fought so fiercely, aided by a great number of other women, that they pierced the citadel walls, captured the city and put all inside to death. (p. 126)

Christine is not entirely without authorization in describing this revenge—the *Ovide moralisé* explains that women breached the walls during the siege of Thebes.[29] Christine is unique, however, in suppressing mention of Theseus entirely, making the vengeance an accomplishment of the women alone, unaided by men. In excising Theseus from the story of one of his greatest exploits, Christine most pertinently denies a triumph to the Greek hero who conquered the Amazon queen Hippolyta.[30] Nor in denying Theseus his conventional place is she simply rewriting literary history, inserting a new episode for the Theban women (as, for instance, may be the motivation behind Boccaccio's selection of Argia rather than the traditional Antigone as the female intimate who risks all in burying Polyneices). One of Boccaccio's most famous poems—indeed, his attempt at an epic—was the *Teseida*, an heroic poem describing Theseus's exploits. By suppressing Theseus, Christine is writing out of the canon Boccaccio's epic hero.

The entire first book of the *Teseida* is given over to Theseus's attack on Hippolyta's Amazon kingdom; replete with heroic speeches, sea and land battles, and siege machinery, the first book is warfare in fully panoply. When Theseus breaks the siege by digging underneath their city walls, the Amazons sue for terms. Hippolyta had relied on

---

[29]"The *Livre de la Cité de Dames*," ed. Maureen Curnow, 2 vols. (Ph.D. diss., Vanderbilt University, 1975), p. 1088.

[30]Christine had already told the entire story of Thebes in the *Mutacion*, IV.12069–13356, from the birth of Oedipus to Theseus's triumph over Creon.

the walls for her ultimate defense, and when they fail, she makes peace by agreeing to marry Theseus. In a sense, then, she is transformed in the first book of the *Teseida* from an Amazon queen into an exemplary wife.

The second book of the Boccaccio's epic is given over to Theseus's attack on Creon's Thebes. Petitioned by a group of Theban women, who have not been allowed to give their men folk, fallen in battle, a proper burial, Theseus besieges the city and conquers it. After thanking him, the Theban women gather up their dead from the battlefield and ceremoniously burn the corpses, doing them all honor:

> Le donne quasi liete il ringraziaro
> e quindi a fare il loro oficio andaro.
> Esse giron nel campo doloroso,
> dove gli argivi re morti giaceano;
> a ben che fose a l'olfato noioso
> per lo fiato che' corpi già rendeano,
> no fu però a lor punto gravoso
> cercar pe' morti che elle voleano,
> in qua in là or questo or quel volgendo,
> il suo ciascuna intra molti caendo.

> The women thus thanked him
> And then went about their official duties.
> They went out to the sorrowful battlefield
> where the Argives Kings lay dead
> and indeed it was a noisome smell
> which was given off by the corpses
> but they were not deterred in their grave duty
> to search among the dead as they desired
> turning over this one and that one, here and there,
> each seeking her own among the many dead.[31]

Christine's rewriting of events that took place on the battlefield outside the walls of Thebes is more than a preference for one authority (the *Ovide moralisé*) over another, more than the privileging of a French source over an Italian one. Rather, I think we can see

---

[31]Giovanni Boccaccio, *Teseida*, ed. Salvatore Battaglia (Florence: Sansoni, 1938), II, st.77–78; my translation.

Christine here recapturing another city's epic past for the history of women. It was not, she claims, Theseus who revenged the Argive women or who destroyed the tyrant Creon, but a group of women who, we are asked to imagine, included the likes of Argia and Antigone.

Christine may have derived her interest in the part Theseus played in the history of Thebes from the pivotal importance he had in Dante's series of ideal and earthly cities; it is a Dantean pattern we have already seen Christine rewrite in the opening story of Semiramis.[32] In essence, in the stories of the first citizens installed in the city of ladies, we have a recasting of another foundational myth for another canonical city: Thebes is made into a place safe from those who would attack Amazons, such as Theseus, who is here written out of history. Why Christine does not indicate this rewrite, or signal its stance against the alternative tradition, as she does, for instance, in her notation that "some" (meaning an unnamed Virgil) have erroneously supposed that the sibyl led Aeneas to hell, is a bit puzzling. If she doesn't even mention Virgil by name, it is hardly surprising that she would not refer to Boccaccio's alternative tradition of Theseus's heroic generosity toward the women of Thebes. Both Theseus and the poet who made an epic of his exploits, remain unmentioned. Listed at the outset by Reason as one of the cities which, like Troy, did not last, Thebes now becomes newly enrolled, like Babylon, Carthage, and the Amazon kingdom, in a tradition of cities of ladies.

Christine vs. the Auctores: Part II, Sections 17–46

In the central section of part II of the *Cité*—one of the longest stretches of text unarticulated by any other framing device—Christine has recourse to a débat between herself and Droitture by means of which she will group various portraits of women thematically. As Joel Blanchard has usefully pointed out, because she is working as a

---

[32]For a discussion of the function of Thebes in the *Commedia*, see Ronald L. Martinez, "Dante, Statius, and the Earthly City" (Ph.D. diss., University of California, Santa Cruz, 1977).

compilator, the very misogynist materials that Christine refutes form the stuff of her narrative.[33] Seemingly the least "original" of writers, one who simply gathers materials from elsewhere and assimilates them, the compilator is in fact a real original. According to Blanchard, "La compilation est une practique de soi" (p. 154)—compilation is a practice of the self. In Christine's practice, the result is the staging of a relationship with other texts in terms that set up an almost violent opposition. Blanchard provocatively observes that Christine constructed a far more coherent tradition of anti-feminist literature than in fact existed and did so in order to plunder it. The major opposition becomes one between the consensus of an entire tradition that she has set up in order to oppose it and an "élaboration du livre unique" (p. 155)—the elaboration of a single book (her own). While such a suggestion is in danger of denying the actual historical practice of social violence against women, as well as the existence of a literary tradition of misogyny outlined earlier (and "created" also by Chaucer, for use by his Wife of Bath), it does allow us to see the uses to which Christine puts the anti-feminist tradition she may have helped to reify as a "genre," especially in her concerted attack on the *Rose*. Each new story in the *Cité* is a re-beginning of the compilation; more importantly, the series of questions and answers exchanged between Christine and her figures of authority allow her to frame her disparately gathered materials into thematic groupings (of the sort we have been describing) and thereby to analyze them. It is useful to recall that in contrast, Boccaccio supplied no frames for his collection of legends, which were simply arranged in broadly chronological order.

After her distinct intervention into the literature of one pivotal city, Thebes, Christine again returns to direct citation of her anti-feminist authorities, mentioning Jean de Meun, Mathéolus and Theophrastus by name and repeating, specifically, two major complaints gleaned from their tradition: 1) that women cannot love older men and 2) that women and the study of books are mutually incompatible. The complaints are connected: traditionally what these older

---

[33]Joel Blanchard, "Compilation et légitimation au XVe siècle," *Poétique* 18 (1988), 139–57. "Le compilateur ce livre à un bricolage des textes compilés. . . . Il fait une sorte de revue critique de ce qu'il a à piller, et recompose une oeuvre par degrés differents: morceaux choisis illustrant un thème commandé. Il ne faut pas voir dans cette démarche une soumission de la pensée, mais plutôt une recherche triomphante" (p. 153).

men have to offer is wisdom, learning, and political acumen. Droitture gives us numerous examples of such men (Socrates, Cato, Seneca, among them) well loved by their wives. As a means of refuting the misogynists' complaints, the compilation of further exemplary-wife narratives recommences with portraits of two young Roman women whose loyalty to their husbands takes extreme forms.

First, Pompey's young wife Julia is literally frightened to death when she sees what she takes to be the bloody evidence (a torn, blood-soaked robe) of her husband's violent death. Next, young Tertia Aemilia remains loyal to Scipio Africanus even though he has had children by a slave. Christine's aggressive rearrangement of Boccaccio's version of the story of Africanus's wife makes the woman's generous emancipation of her husband's slave/mistress not an attempt to keep his august memory from stain (her motive in Boccaccio), but an act of kindness to the bondwoman who bore her husband children. Lest the point be missed, Christine herself interjects that she has known many modern women to offer similar care for their husbands' illegitimate families. As Blanchard points out in another context, the addition of a further example from Christine's personal experience, in order to round off the list, also incorporates the compilator's authority into the text (p. 148).

The episode of Xantippe immediately leavens these quiescent wives' stories with a dose of healthy anger directed against Socrates, in Christine's rendition, for so pacifically going to his own death. This twist on the legend of the paradigmatic shrew does not exactly prove that women and books mix well, but it does have the effect, as Curnow points out, of demonstrating that Socrates—a wise man—accepts the legitimacy of his wife's anger, based as it is in her deep love for him. Although she finally understands why he goes to his death willingly, she insistently mourns him for the rest of her life, proving her loyalty. Likewise, Paulina, faithful wife to the philosopher Seneca, herself dies from grief, but not before she, like Xantippe (and Argia), has hurled insults at Nero who ordered her husband's death.

Alternating citation of misogynist critiques of female nature with stories that disprove such false claims, the text cites by name Jean de Meun and his authoritative poem, the *Roman de la rose*, specifically recalling its criticism that women cannot keep secrets (misogynist lore illustrated by the tale of Midas). As disproof, Droitture offers the legend of the Roman Portia, Brutus's wife and a famous suicide. To make Portia proof of a female ability *not* to divulge confidences is to pinpoint the most compelling detail of her story—the fact that she dies not by the razor or the sword (though she had practiced these means of taking her own life), but by swallowing live coals. Her "silence" is thus enacted not merely by her having kept her husband Brutus's conspiratorial secrets, but by the violent self-sacrifice of eating her own death: "elle ala au feu, et prist charbons ardans et les avala: ainsi se ardi et estaigny" (p. 845). "She went to the fire, took burning coals, swallowed them, and burned herself to death" (p. 135).

In a sense, Portia's peculiar suicide also connects thematically with the abject borderline experiences of the first loyal wives in this city's citizenship, particularly the incident of Artemisia's eating her husband's ashes. Ingestion is both a gesture of physical intimacy, a way of entering the interior of the body, and a process that usually sustains life. To associate the mouth with death, as in the stories of Portia, Argia, Artemisia, and Agrippina, locates a female act of self-definition at an important physical borderline. The perimeters of the body are unstable margins that can symbolize, as Mary Douglas points out, systemic instability in a society. Instability is usually located at the opened mouth of the loquacious female, often a sign of sexual looseness or nagging shrewishness as well.[34] Portia's death is "la plus estrange dont onques autre mourrast" (p. 845)—"the strangest way anyone ever died" (p. 135). It enacts the most extreme form of self-policing through the mouth. Her swallowing of the coals sets a limit at one of the most culturally important sites on the female body, the site of both nurturance and denial, speech and silence, while it parodies the very preparation of food traditionally associated with female work. Portia's wifely silence may be praiseworthy, but it is achieved at the most extreme cost of self.

The central importance of Portia becomes clearer when we see how she serves as a bridge between the stories demonstrating how women can keep silence and stories proving how disastrous it is for a man not to listen to his wife talk; again, a trace of a gesture at the misogynist tradition (whose authors are no longer "authorities"

---

[34]For a discussion of the relationship between corporeality and verbal excess in the Renaissance, see Patricia Parker, *Literary Fat Ladies: Rhetoric, Gender, Property* (London: Methuen, 1987), chap. 1.

but merely the unnamed "plusieurs dient" (p. 849), "some say."[35] If Brutus had only listened to Portia, if Caesar had only listened to his wife, if Pompey had only listened to his, they would all have lived longer and there would have been no civil war in Rome.

What is at issue in all these stories of exemplary wives and their husbands is female authority within marriage: will women's accurately prophetic speech be listened to, be acknowledged as authoritative? Portia dreamed of Brutus's death, Calpurnia foresaw Caesar's, Cornelia, after a vision of Pompey's death, tried to warn him, just as Andromache had a premonition of Hector's ill fate the day (refusing to heed her) he was slain. Men who listen to their wives' admonitions are the better for it. Such advice needn't even be prophetic: thus the Roman soldier Belisere triumphs over his enemies when he follows his wife Antonia's counsel, and Alexander the Great recognizes his wife's wisdom when she tells him patiently to put his kingdom in order before he dies.

A great roll call of Old Testament heroines is given a typological, prophetic introduction as part of a brief rehearsal of the good granted mankind by the Virgin Mary. By giving birth to God, Mary fulfilled the law that prophesied that women would take Israel out of bondage. So, before her, the Egyptian princess Thermutis had saved the infant Moses from certain death by hiding him.

In similar ways, the heroines Judith and Esther helped to save the Jews—each by a judicious use of sexual power. Judith decapitated her people's oppressor, the evil invader Holofernes, and Esther exposed to her husband the king the treachery of Haman, an oppressor of the Jews, and had him hanged. After these typological legends, the next story may seem something of a surprise: the raped Sabine women are, however, depicted in a way that shows their similarity to Judith and Esther. Like them, the Sabine women managed to turn their own sexual victimization into a city-founding act of peace making. Christine's approach to the Sabine story places an interesting twist on the strategy of empowering women in a situation that would seem to deny them any room for autonomous maneuverings. Having been violently abducted by Roman men, the women are forcibly married and impregnated. Recognizing, however, that their two races are now

[35]Richards, p. 137, translates "plusieurs disent" as "several authors claim," missing, I think, Christine's denigration of the authority involved.

intermixed, it is they who decide that the Sabine and Roman men must make peace. By actively installing peaceful relations between two warring groups of men, they willingly promulgate the end purpose of the violent "traffic in women." Although their activity does, of course, mystify this traffic by making the violence against women end peacefully, Christine shows the Sabines not as passive pieces in the trade, but as themselves actively resolving—as a group—a situation of bloody warfare in favor of a racially intermixed, coherent, and peaceful society.

In seeing how little Christine can actually do to change the story of the Sabine women (except to turn the violence of rape into the female-authored founding of Rome), we see how thoroughly a master discourse constrains the parameters of what can be said.[36] Christine can give the women an active agency in their own determination, but cannot change the details of the story itself (or at least here chooses not to—no doubt because the traditional version institutes another city-foundation under the authority of women).

Although in the Sabine legend, she differs little from Boccaccio, in the story of another Roman woman, Christine makes a significant change, taking away from Veturia, Coriolanus's mother, a striking speech of defiance made to her rebel son. While Boccaccio's mother is a study in vitriolic rhetoric, in Christine's account she receives the homage of her son instantaneously: all she has to do is appear in the field to make her son recant his rebellion. Her power is at once greater and less threatening.

When Droitture turns from her accounts of ancient women to her first mention of the foundation of the kingdom of France, a fascinating anticipatory note intrudes itself into the text. She says that Queen Clotilda is to be praised for making her husband the king convert to Christianity, thus making France a Christian kingdom. This story in itself is insufficient as an account of the founding of France as a Christian kingdom, however, so Christine adds here further commentary on the saints who fed and housed Saint Denis (who brought the faith to France) and his two female companion saints, the woman who saved the saints' martyred bones and the

---

[36]In *Knight, Lady, Priest,* pp. 39–54, Duby outlines the prevalence of "ritual rapine," at first a practical means of mating, which then, under the pressures of the church and older aristocracy pressing for more social order, became "symbolic."

woman who built a chapel to venerate the saints. Such concern for the real woman-authored foundation of the faith in the realm of France mimics the foundational aspects of the historical translation of saints' relics across Europe in the earlier Middle Ages.[37] The reference to the martyrs—whose stories appear in part III—sets up a useful bridge between the women of contemporary France and the women of imperial Rome. Like the dispersal of the saints' remains across Europe, the authority of Rome's founding is gradually interwoven into the fabric of French history through the stories of Roman women. Christine is absolutely explicit about the pivotal part women played in the foundational installation of the spiritual basis for the French monarchy:

> Et les François, qui ont en si grant devocion le cors de monseigneur saint Denis—et a bonne cause—qui apporta premier la foy en France, ne on ylz ce benoit corps et ceulx de ses benois compaignons saint Rustina et saint Electaire a cause d'une femme? . . . Et longtemps aprés, pareillement par une femme fu ou dit lieu premierement faitte chappelle en l'onneur de eulx—ce fu par ma dame sainte Genevieve. (p. 872)

> Do not the French, who have shown such great devotion—and with good reason—to the body of my lord Saint Denis who first brought the Faith to France, have this blessed body and those of his blessed companions Saint Rusticus and Saint Eleutherius, thanks to a woman? . . . Long afterward, likewise, the first chapel in their honor was erected on this spot by a woman—this my lady Saint Genevieve. (p. 152)

This praise of women for their spiritual devotion to the veneration of saints, a veneration institutionally basic to the foundation of feudal political authority, insists upon the foundational nature of St. Genevieve's construction of a chapel for the relics. The ruler Dagobert can only follow her female-based authority by later building a church upon the same site. Genevieve, of course, is the patron saint of the city of Paris. It is important that Christine moves from her to a discussion of women educated in the sciences, again returning from

---

[37]For a discussion of the dispersal of Roman civilization and order along with the saints' relics "stolen" and taken to sites throughout Europe, see Patrick Geary, *Furta Sacra: Thefts of Relics in the Central Middle Ages* (Princeton: Princeton University Press, 1978).

sacred matters to answer typical misogynist arguments that women should not be educated. This time, however, she casts the question not as it appears in the misogynist texts but as it formulates itself in social practice.

> Par quoy je me merveille trop fort de l'oppinion d'aucuns hommes qui dient que ilz ne vouldroyent point que leurs filles ou femmes ou parentes apprensissent sciences et que leurs meurs en empirent. (p. 873)

> Therefore I am amazed by the opinion of some men who claim that they do not want their daughters, wives, or kinswomen to be educated because their mores would be ruined as a result. (p. 153)

More than a juxtaposition of the traditional kind of religious authority often granted women with a discussion of a far less ordinary kind of authority drawn from bookish tradition, the close communion of these two problematically related sorts of authority has much to do with the foundational problems of Christine's text itself as a book. Thus in her two examples of learned women, Hortensia and Novella both owe their educations to the willingness of their fathers to teach them. Hortensia is a peculiarly appropriate case because she defended the "cause des femmes" in the Roman senate with an oration so beautiful all thought it was worthy of her eloquent father.

The final example of the benevolent father is—like other narrations that complete groupings—drawn from Christine de Pizan's own life, although, in fact, this story comprises a twist on the critique of the misogynist tradition she has been promulgating. When Droitture reminds Christine that her own father wanted to educate his daughter, she must also, as we have seen, remind her that her mother refused to allow her to be educated in a way contrary to the ordinary custom for women. Of course, the author is now highly educated. Another proverb—this time one that cuts against her mother's intervention—is fulfilled by Christine's constant interest in study: "Ce que Nature donne, nul ne puet tollir" (p. 875); "no one can take away what nature has given" (p. 155). And so in this context, her mother is depicted as pulling against nature. Christine's mother is not able to prevent her from sustaining a feeling for the sciences which she has "par inclinacion naturelle" (p. 876). Bitterly, Christine replies to Droitture, "ce que vous dittes est voir come *Pater Nostre*"

(p. 873), "what you say is as true as the Lord's Prayer" (p. 155), thus acknowledging that the bookish tradition that she waited so long to enter was distinctly a patrimonial territory.

What is striking about this confession is, again, not only that Christine's real mother is a part of this text and that the bitter conflict between the learned daughter and the traditional mother is staged as part of the business of the text, but also that the admission appears immediately after a mention of the association of female spirituality with the martyrs. Such an anticipation of the martyrs' stories to come in the third section, connected as it is to the mother, begins to gender martyrdom (which is Christine's point) and to associate it as well with conflictual relations with the mother. Sequence in allegory is analytic; it is part of the means by which the text offers a commentary on itself. Not only does the formal arrangement of the text offer clues and the architectural metaphor indicate possibilities of groupings, so too, sheer juxtaposition suggests the possibility of some connection, fully intended or otherwise. The mention of the martyrs closely followed by an indication of the problematic relations between Christine and her mother suggests a subterranean set of relations that will best be discussed in terms of the discourse of martyrdom in the last section. At present it is useful to notice only the close conjunction and to realize that the two are thereby linked.

Bracketing the question of Christian martyrs and the foundational female acts involved in their veneration are more stories of Old Testament heroines, this time introduced as evidence that women can remain chaste. The pattern here basically repeats itself: on each side of Christine's consideration of her relations to her mother, there are a number of Old Testament narratives followed by stories that articulate a further development of the history of Rome. Thus, as the stories of Judith and Esther were followed by narrations about the Sabine women and Coriolanus's mother, now the stories of Suzanna, Sarah, Rebecca, and Ruth are followed by brief accounts of Penelope, Mariam (Herod's Jewish queen), and two chaste Roman women. These latter are Antonia, whose achievement is simply to retain her chastity at the corrupt Roman court, and Lucretia, whose rape and suicide comprise a major event in Roman history, equal in political importance to the rape of the Sabine women.

Unlike Christine's narration of the abduction of the Sabines, the story of Lucretia emphasizes a political change in the state, as opposed to the forming of a communal basis for it. The violence against the female is correspondingly more violent, if also more personal. Introducing this example to demonstrate that, contrary to masculine opinion, women do *not* like to be raped, Christine changes the story from her source in Boccaccio's *De mulieribus claris* in an essential way by shortening the narrative so that the rape and suicide are central. Thus, the husbands engage in no contest about their wives' virtues, Collatine does not boast of his wife's beauty, the men do not come to his country villa, and so on: the drama of the rape is not, consequently, based upon a rivalry among Tarquin, Collatine, and the other Roman men.[38] At this juncture, the source of Tarquin's desire is pure lust; later, Christine will narrate the segment of Lucretia's story which includes Collatine's boast—pivotal to the story's "homosocial" relations—but in her hands the emphasis falls upon the greatness of Lucretia's wifely virtue rather than her beauty. There is no prior acquaintance between Tarquin and Lucretia in Christine's version (as there is in Boccaccio's). Instead, he tricks her by saying he is her husband's friend, gains access to the house, and sneaks into her chamber. When in the midst of his attack he realizes that she would rather die than lose her honor, he resorts to blackmail, saying he will claim that he found her dead body in the arms of a servant. Such coercion prevails and Lucretia submits. Her suicide is her means of making the truth known, for her own honor and for the future honor of all women. Boccaccio's Lucretia exclaims at the moment she plunges the knife into her chest: "Ego me, si peccato absolvo, supplicio non libero; nec ulla deinceps impudica, Lucretie vivet exemplo" (p. 196). "Although I absolve myself of the sin, I do not free myself from the punishment, and in the future no woman will live dishonorably because of Lucretia's example" (p. 102). Boccaccio's Lucretia seems to assume she deserves some punishment for getting raped and suggests that her suicide will be the act by which women in the future should judge their own response to rape. The miniature illustrating this moment in the French translation of Boccaccio's text emphasizes the voyeurism inherent in the scene of Lucretia's self-sacrifice (Figure 24). Lucretia's exemplary act is appreciated by another group of male viewers. Their presence at such a scene of female

---

[38]For a fascinating discussion of Shakespeare's emphasis on the rivalry for rhetorical mastery and political power inherent in this story, see Nancy Vickers, " 'The blazon of sweet beauty's best': Shakespeare's *Lucrece*," in *Shakespeare and the Question of Theory*, ed., Patricia Parker and Geoffrey Hartman (London: Methuen, 1985), pp. 95–115.

24. Lucretia killing herself, *Des cleres femmes*, Ms. Royal 20 C V, f. 76v.
London, British Library, by permission

self-destruction is crucially different from the usual construction of images for the texts of Boccaccio's stories. As Brigitte Buettner has argued, such spectators are usually the kind of characters to be excised from the story when it is condensed in order to be translated into an image: "Spectators are the class of characters the most affected by such excision; after all, they do not have much importance for the action."[39] It is all the more striking then that these spectators are not dropped from the scenes depicting female dismemberments. Their presence is pivotal to the point of the display of the female body.

The male onlookers are particularly important in this miniature because in Boccaccio's version of Lucretia's suicide this moment not only reveals the virtue of a single woman, it is a foundational moment for the city of Rome. Lucretia's rape by Tarquin is thus significant not because she restored her reputation by her self-sacrifice but because by the rape and its consequences "Rome was made free" when Tarquinian tyranny was overthrown and the republic thereby established. The story then—especially with the emphasis Boccaccio gives to the opening scene, in which Lucretia's husband boasts about his wife's beauty thereby tempting the rape—dramatizes the contending struggles between men for mastery not only of the woman but of Rome.

In Christine's version Lucretia's story is repoliticized from its Roman context into a drama of female history. The story is told, for instance, not as the foundation of the Roman republic but as proof that, contrary to masculine opinion, women do not like to be raped. Christine suppresses the boasting session and in general elides the male groups that make sense of the homosocial exchanges in Boccaccio's story. Boccaccio interprets Lucretia's suicide to be the act by which women's response to rape in the future should be judged. By contrast, for Christine, Lucretia slays herself to demonstrate how awful it is to be raped, as well as to save women from feeling shame for her—not to shame them into doing the same. For Christine the crime does not simply end kingship in Rome (a result that she,

[39]Briggite Buettner, "Image et texte dans les 'Clères femmes,' " *Studi Sul Boccaccio* (1990), 281–99: "Les 'spectateurs' sont la classe de personnages la plus frappé part cette éviction, ce qui, après tout, n'a pas beaucoup d'importance au regard de l'intelligence de l'action" (my translation). See also Laura Mulvey, "Visual Pleasure and Narrative Cinema," *Screen* (1975), 8–18.

with her pro-monarchist tendencies, would not necessarily have applauded anyhow); it also catalyzes the institution of a new law making rape a capital crime—"laquelle loy est couvenable, juste et sainte" (p. 887); "a law which is fitting, just, and holy" (p. 162). Boccaccio mentions no such law.

As this brief rehearsal of them makes clear, the differences between Christine's and Boccaccio's versions of these stories are due not so much to historical period as more specifically to gender. Christine rewrites Boccaccio to insert an active female subjectivity into each story. If Boccaccio's text, as exemplified by its reception in the miniatures, reveals an emphasis on the controlling position of the male viewer, then Christine usually elides this "perspective" in her text, taking a resolutely female-gendered position from which to see the story. I want to stress that what the miniaturists reading Boccaccio's text reveal in these pictures is the central position of the male viewer—what the psychoanalytic film critic Laura Mulvey, in discussing the visual politics of classic cinema, has called the controlling male "gaze." The male looks at a woman who is "displayed for the gaze and enjoyment of men." She is for them an icon of their control: over their own act of looking and over the object looked at. But this controlling gaze, according to Mulvey, "always threatens to evoke the anxiety it originally signified." Mulvey, following Freud, names this anxiety the problem of castration which is at the core of male experience of sexual difference (that is, to men women seem to be castrated beings). Again following Freud, Mulvey argues that "the male unconscious has two avenues of escape from this castration anxiety": a voyeuristic pleasure in assigning guilt and in asserting control through punishment or forgiveness (as happens, I suggest, in the stories of Dido and Lucretia), and a "fetishistic scopophilia," the display of the beauty of the female body in objectified fragments, transforming it into an object satisfying in itself. The woman then is no longer a "bearer of guilt, but a perfect product, whose body, stylized and fragmented" is the "direct recipient of the viewer's gaze" (p. 22).

I bring up Mulvey's argument here because I think it suggests a clue to the significance of the spectators in the miniatures of Lucretia's and Dido's suicides, especially as indications of how Boccaccio's text would have been voyeuristically received at the time Christine read it. Her revision of the stories of Lucretia and Dido is, then, a re-seeing not merely of the story but of the way the story, literally, was visualized. Boccaccio intends his text, in its display of violence toward the female body, to be titillating; Christine deploys the female body to far different effect.

The next story Christine narrates stages Rome's imperial violence against its conquered peoples as violence against the colonized female. Boccaccio's version of the story of the raped Galatian queen is an example of the kind of valor even a barbarian woman can reveal; Boccaccio asks, "Who then will not agree that this woman was, I should say, not only Roman but of the same breed as Lucretia, rather than a barbarian" (p. 161). The interesting gimmick in Boccaccio's narrative is that the Roman soldier-rapist does not understand the words in which the Galatian queen commands her servants to murder him, because she speaks in her own barbaric language. So, when he bends over to count the ransom the day after he has ravished her, thinking all safe, he is unprepared for the massed attack by her people. In contrast, Christine's version depicts the queen not primarily as a barbarian but as a woman. Moreover, the mere juxtaposition of her story with Lucretia's (the two are far apart in Boccaccio's text) implies the comparison that Christine need not draw explicitly, in the way Boccaccio does. In her rendition, the raped queen kills the soldier herself with her own knife. In both versions she takes the head of her ravisher back to her husband and shows him how she has taken her vengeance, but in Boccaccio this demonstration bears a very different interpretation: like the exemplary suicide of Lucretia, the Galatian queen's murder of her assailant is the only response— outside of suicide—appropriate for a woman who has been raped.

Et ideo prospectent, quibus inclite pudicitie cura insidet animo, quoniam non satis sit, ad cordis sinceritatem testandam, lacrimis et querelis se violentiam passame dicere nisi, dum possit, quis in vindictam egregio processerit opere. (p. 298)

There, let those women who have within their breast solicitude for glorious chastity see that to prove purity of heart it is not sufficient to say with tears and lamentations that one has been violated, without proceeding to wreak vengeance with noble deeds whenever possible. (p. 162)

The male standard for rape victims is indeed severe.

The Example of the Roman Emperors: Part II, Sections 47–54

Rape is the male/female sexual relationship of dominance at its worst, male violence against the female body enacted at its most sexually specific. Christine does not directly take up the issue of this general cultural violence against women, but does turn to a unique consideration of the example of the male virtù, *in malo*, as a way of defending women. Men, sneers Droitture, have attacked women for failing in virtues that they themselves notoriously lack—as any history of men makes outrageously apparent. Returning to particular misogynist arguments—that women are fickle and inconstant—Droitture narrates an abbreviated list of the "acts of the emperors" in order to demonstrate the vicious evils in which *men* have indulged. The Roman emperors Claudius, Galba, Otho, and especially Nero are described as examples of men who transgressed all human measure in their descent into beastliness. In addition to being utterly fickle and inconstant, they were monsters of lust, gluttony, greed, cowardice, envy, and inhuman cruelty. Nero, for example, ordered saints Paul and Peter "executed as his dinner entertainment" (p. 168): "Il fist decoller a son disner saint Pierre et saint Pol et moult d'autres martirs" (p. 896).

Not only did Nero consent to the murder of his father, he had his mother Agrippina killed as well. In Boccaccio's story of the death of Agrippina, illustrated by Figure 25, the problems of mother/son incest recur through another violent narrative. Boccaccio reports that "some say" Agrippina seduced her son in order to regain the power she had lost. In any event, because "she annoyed her son in many ways," he had her killed, and Boccaccio narrates the almost comically extended measures to which Nero resorted as his mother continually managed to evade his clutches at the last minute, when the roof caved in or the ship did not sink fast enough. Finally, however, she is surrounded by centurions, and when she sees they are going to kill her with a sword, she offers her belly and shouts to them to strike her in the womb.

The miniature from the French translation represents a collapse of two different Boccaccian versions of the moment. In the *De mulieribus claris*, Boccaccio explains only that some authorities report how Nero later saw his mother's corpse and pronounced it beautiful. In

25. Nero having his mother, Agrippina, slit open, *Des cleres femmes*, Ms. Royal C V 20, f. 139r. London, British Library, by permission

the *De casibus virorum*, Boccaccio relates that Nero also had his mother dissected so that he could see the place where he had lain, both as fetus and as lover. The artist (who may well have known the other story from the *De casibus*, for it was illuminated in some of the same ateliers) gives this version of it, only here the conflation of the stabbing of Agrippina and her postmortem dissection results in the image of a far more painful and fully torturous vivisection.

This is imagined violence of an extreme and particular sort launched not merely against the dissected and displayed female

163

body, but against the maternal body. Christine's version of Agrippina's story follows all these details very closely: she reports that Nero, after he had had his mother killed, also had her dead body dissected so that he could see where he had been conceived, and then pronounced that she had been a beautiful woman (p. 167). Christine, however, places the story in an entirely different context. It is not the story of Agrippina herself, but of Nero, in which the detail of the mother is a mere episode in a long list of horrors the man perpetrates against virtually every woman he meets. Nero's vicious history is included in the *Cité des dames* as a touchstone for anti-misogynist argument. Why should women be blamed for inconstancy when one need only think of the Roman emperors to realize the kinds of violence of which men are capable?

> Et se tu veulz que je t'en donne preuves, et de pieça et du temps d'ores, pour ce que, ainsi que se es couraiges des hommes ne eust aucune inconstance ne varieté, ilz accusent tant les femmes de celluy vice, regarde es estaz des plus poyssans princes et des greigneurs hommes, qui est chose impertinant plus que es autres, que te puis je dire des imperiaulx? (p. 893)

> And if you want me to give you proof, from the past and present, of why they accuse women so often of this vice, as well as whether inconstancy or fickleness are found in men's hearts, you need only consider whether the behavior of the most powerful princes and greatest men is more shameless than that of emperors which I can tell you about. (p. 166)

Christine does not mention the rumors of incest between Nero and his mother which Boccaccio reports, and so there is no blame placed on Agrippina, who merely suffers her tyrant son's worst evil along with his other victims. The violence of the text as it was received by Christine's society is both profoundly voyeuristic and analytic: one sees the female body opened up to reveal its secrets to an audience of male spectators. Finally, however, there is no real need for such secrets to be known, as the miniature makes clear: the incision only makes more obvious on a larger scale what is already visible, to the male gaze, about the female body. That is, the wound repeats the cleft mark, sign of the already castrated female genitals.

It is not only the Roman emperors who practice violence against women. Christianity, laments Droitture, proved no guard against masculine evil. Popes and clergymen are not exempt from vicious-ness; like the empire, the church itself, after the Donation of Con-stantine, has become corrupt, and churchmen have grown less holy. In this passage Christine displays a great cynicism—one might even say despair—about the world, implying that the masculine history of the church after it took on its imperial, temporal power has been no better than the history of the evil emperors: "depuis que Constantin ot douee l'eglise de grans revenues et de richesces, la saintité quy y est . . . ne fault que lire en leurs gestes et croniques" (p. 898); "ever since Constantine endowed the church with large revenues and riches the remaining holiness . . . well, you only have to read through their histories and chronicles" (p. 169). Compared with such corrupt men, compared with Judas, even the worst women in history (Jezebel and Brunhilde) seem much less vile.

After this disquisition on the evils of the male sex, Droitture reminds Christine of her opening lament to God—that he had made her be born into the world in a female body—and asks if she doesn't think now that women should praise God for putting the treasure of their souls into female vessels instead of male. In essence, Christine has effected a complete reversal of values. To prove her point, three examples of paradigmatic female virtue follow, each far longer than her usual vignette, examples that taken together offer stunning testi-mony both to the virtue of women and to the capricious willfulness and evil foolishness of men.

By 1405 the story of the suffering Griselda had become famous through a number of important retellings. Its initial appearance as the final story in Boccaccio's *Decameron* inspired Petrarch, who deemed it the one piece of Boccaccio's text worthy of circulation beyond the Italian-speaking public, to retell it in Latin. His version was twice translated into French; Christine knew it in the transla-tion of her friend Phillip de Mézières. She would also have known the Italian version in the *Decameron*. Her choice to follow Petrarch instead may not be mere ease of access, but rather a choice, once again, to move against Boccaccio's authority. Radically condens-ing the Petrarchan prose, Christine proves more sympathetic to Griselda's suffering and by the same token more attentive to her strength. One signal difference between the two versions is the ironic impact of the speech her Griselda gives at the culminating moment of the plot, when she is brought back before the husband who has ostensibly murdered her children and disowned her; she displays a wryness that echoes Droitture's joke that women will only be too happy to follow men's perfection whenever, that is, men manage to achieve it. Griselda has been asked to comment on her husband's new bride, a woman who is—unknown to her—her own daughter. In Mézière's translation of Petrarch's Latin, Griselda directly compares her own strength to the young bride's:

> d'une chose en bonne foy je te veulz de prier et amonestrer, que tu ne veuillez pas molester ceste nouvelle espouse des aguillons, dont l'autre tu as si fort aguillonnée, car ceste est plus josne et plus delicieusement nourie et ne porroit pas souffrir tant comme j'ay souffert, si comme je pense.

> one thing in good faith I pray you take as advice: that you do not molest this new bride with sharp pain as you have needled the other, for this one is younger and more delicately raised and may not be able, I think, to suffer as much as I suffered.[40]

In her revision, Christine drops the direct self-reference and has Griselda cast her chastisement of her husband into the third person; the suffering of wives becomes a more general phenomenon, with the first wife actively achieving something of value, while Mézières' Griselda simply suffered:

> "Mais d'une chose par bonne foy je te vueil prier et admonnester, c'est que tu ne la vueilles pas molestier ne aguillonner des aguillons dont tu as l'autre si fort esprouvee. Car ceste est plus jeune et plus souef nourrie; si ne pourroit pas souffrir par aventure come l'autre fait." (p. 908)

> "I would however make a single request of you and give you only one bit of advice: that you neither trouble nor needle her with the torments with which you so severely tested the other. This woman is younger and has been raised more delicately so that she by chance may not be able to bear as much as your other wife did." (p. 175; revised)

"Par aventure," by chance, this new wife may not be able to suffer in the way that the first did, withstanding the trial of strength with the

---

[40]Elie Golenistcheff-Koutouzoff, *L'histoire de Griseldis en France au XIVe et au XVe siècle* (Librarie Droz: Paris, 1933), p. 178; my translation.

same "virtù." In contrast to Mézières's marquis, who is charmed by his former wife's "bonne chiere" as well as by her constancy, the *Cité*'s husband recognizes the claim of *strength* Griselda's warning makes and, struck by her "grant fermeté, force, et constance" has great admiration for her "vertu" (p. 908). The moral of Christine's story is that Griselda is an exemplary woman by virtue of her strength. Her self-conscious insistence on her extraordinary endurance does not directly detract from the possibility that her daughter might achieve the same strength.

The moral conclusion appended to Petrarch's tale insists that no woman is expected to behave with the inhuman patience Griselda exhibits toward her husband, but rather that all men should suffer the adversities of life with faithful belief in God. Christine's headnote re-genders the interpretation of the tale. Griselda's story is that of a *woman* strong in virtue: "forte femme en vertu" (p. 900). Her patience is something a *wife* must have. To Christine, Griselda is not an exception, as she is for the male authors, but an exemplum that demonstrates an extreme version of the constancy and fortitude necessary for any woman successfully to negotiate the demands attendant upon being a wife.

In conjunction with the story of Griselda, Droitture tells the histories of the Roman wife Florence and of the wife of Bernabo, another character from the *Decameron*. This time Christine takes her stories directly from the Italian text. What these exemplary wives have in common are not only their miraculous healing abilities and intelligence, but also their incredible strength—they are capable of averting their own murders and climbing to the absolute pinnacle of power. The husbands in these stories have in common a strikingly vicious and stupid character. While Christine makes no direct comment on Walter's willful testing of his wife's virtue in the Griselda story, she is contextually commenting on it by placing it in the company of other stories whose male protagonists are willful, brutish, or simply stupid. Florence of Rome's husband and Bernabo, for instance, both consent to their wives' murder; both wives in turn avert their deaths by clever pleading and ultimately gain positions of great power in the world from which they unmask the meanness or folly of their husbands. Florence uses a healing herb given her by the Virgin and unmasks all the men who have tried to harm her; Bernabo's wife, through sheer intelligence and grace, becomes first counselor to the Sultan and is thereby in a position to uncover the trick played upon her gullible husband.

In order to emphasize the underlying masculine violence of these stories, Christine explains that for brevity's sake she has omitted many similar tales told her by Droitture. This is a most unusual rhetorical move; more typically the figure of authority would herself explain that she is going to do some self-editing. The confession makes Christine's own authority as a compiler stand out as distinctly separate from the authority of Droitture, for whom she here does not function merely as scribe. As a result, Droitture is allowed to mention only one further tale of female patience, one about a woman named Leana.

Boccaccio's story of Leana, the Greek courtesan, reveals that for all his praise of female eloquence—and there is a great deal of it in the *De mulieribus,* with countless miniatures representing women sitting at desks (after which Christine's own author-portraits are modeled)—we have a more profoundly earned praise for the silence of women, because it is underwritten by the sufferings of the body. Privy to certain political secrets, the prostitute is tortured to make her reveal the names of her friends, the conspirators. Fearing that she would finally confess their names when weakened by further torture, she bites down on her own tongue, severs it, and spits it out. Boccaccio praises this act as an achievement that wipes out the viciousness of her prostituted way of life. "Certainly," he concludes her story, "first with her silence, and then by biting off her tongue, she gained no less glory than Demosthenes gained among his people with his florid eloquence" (p. 109); "Quo equidem non minus, et muta prius et inde precisa eius lingua, splendoris consecuta est, quam florida persepe oratione apud suos valens meruerit forsitan Demosthenes" (p. 204). Female taciturnity of such a violently self-silencing stripe is the equal of male eloquence in virtue.

Christine tells Leana's story in a single sentence in passing, with no notice of her immoral business life. But the crucial part of the translation, how this particular story of dismemberment is changed as it is taken over into Christine's text, is the placement she gives it. The self-silencing Leana's story is told in a section of dialogue between Christine and Droitture which answers the question that forms the rubric in the manuscript: "Christine luy demande purquoy ce est que tant de vaillans femmes qui ont esté n'ont contredit aux livres et aux hommes qui mesdisoyent d'elles" (p. 923); "Christine asks why the valiant women who have lived have not objected to the books and men who speak badly about them" (p. 184). Leana's self-imposed silence comments by parataxis, simply by its juxtaposition to the question, on the self-imposed silence of women who have not deigned to answer misogynist attack until now. Their constancy, like Leana's, is being rewarded, because Christine is now writing in response to misogynist heresy—because she is now, in fact speaking and not remaining silent.

The detail of mutilation not only refers back to episodes like Portia's burning away her tongue by swallowing coals, but anticipates the torture scenes that will become central to the martyrs' stories in the third section narrated by Justice. In particular, the detail of the dismembered tongue proleptically stages the problematic aspects of the story of St. Christine, in which Christine de Pizan, not surprisingly, displays the most spectacular construction of her own authorship in the text. The mention of a dismembered tongue calls up a basic problem of female authority.

A conversation between Christine and Droitture answers this question about the lack of a female tradition of letters for Christine's own text and essentially turns this lack into a strength. Such is a typical strategy in the *Cité:* for example, if women's bodies are weak, their understanding is therefore sharper. Thus, if there is no tradition to which Christine can point, that same missing set of texts makes her uniqueness all the more important.

> Tu puez veoir par ce que devant t'est dit comment les dames dont je t'ay raconté cy dessus les grans vertus, occupoyent en diverses oeuvres differanciees l'une de l'autre leur entendement et non mie toutes en une meisme chose; ceste oeuvre a bastir estoir a toy reservé et nom mie a elles. (p. 924)

> You can see from what has been said to you before how all the ladies whose outstanding virtues I told you about above have occupied their minds in various specialized works and not at all in any one activity. The composition of this work is reserved for you and not for them. (p. 185)

To explain the immense delay that has occurred before anyone has attempted to set the misogynists right, Droitture has recourse to an analogy with religious heresies—God lets such errors go on a long time before correcting them. In this way, Christine implies that anti-feminism is a heresy and that her book of correction is a divinely authorized act of piety. By such tactics, Christine turns a potential criticism of the weakness of women—their lack of a tradition—into a subtle argument in favor of the importance of this singular book, a proof of Christine's own authority for having been selected to write it, an authority demonstrated by the process of its being written, an achievement unfolding before the reader's eyes. It is doubtless with some sly self-reference, as well as ironical wittiness, that Droitture here makes her nicest punning joke.

> Et les hommes oseroyent dire que toutest femmes deussent estre bonnes, ou celles qui ne le sont que on les doye tant lapider! Mais je leur prie que ilz regardent en eulz meismes; et celluy seul qui sera san pechié, si gette la premiere pierre. Mais eulz meisme que devroyent ilz estre? Certes, je dis que, quant ilz seront parfaiz, que les femmes les ensuivront. (p. 926)

> And men dare to say that all women must be good and that one should stone those who are not! I would simply ask them to look at themselves and then let him who is without sin cast the first stone! And what are they supposed to be? Indeed, I maintain that when men are perfect, women will follow their example. (p. 186)

Consolidating her argument that men are deeply flawed themselves, Christine cites Christ's authoritative protection against the stoning of a woman taken in adultery (John 8:7) and in the process punningly recalls her own city built of "stones," in which the "first stone cast" was the infamous Semiramis. The city and the book are being simultaneously built and written—together they are an "oeuvre" to be built. Lest we miss Christine's insistence upon her authority here and specifically her right to write a book that answers misogynist argument, Droitture goes on to list a few of the works in which Christine has already undertaken to answer no less an authority than Ovid, who argued that women are deceitful. Droitture confesses that one can argue no better than Christine herself has already done in the *Epistre du dieu d'amours* and in the *Epistres sur le Rommant de la rose* (p. 928). So if a tradition of literature which answers misogynist argument is lacking before Christine, Christine can create one out of her own corpus of texts. In the same way, the "pierres" of the *Cité des dames* are there to protect women against the men who, though far from innocent themselves, would continue to throw stones at them. By such behavior, these men betray a basic virtue of citizenship itself.

autre chose n'est bien commun ou publique en une cité ou païs ou communeté de pueple fors un prouffit et bien general, ouquel chascun, tant femmes comme hommes, participient ou ont part. Mais la chose qu seroit faitte en cuidant prouffiter aux uns et non aux autres seroit appellé being privé ou propre, et non mie publique. (p. 928)

The common good of a city or land or any community of people is nothing other than the profit of general good in which all members, women as well as men, participate and take part. But whatever is done with the intention of benefiting some and not others is a matter of private and not public welfare. (p. 187)

Women are people and therefore citizens, and therefore an attack on them is not impartial, harmful to the common good of the city, not a public boon but a private vice. Christine's defense of women against such attack in the titles mentioned is part of the public good; by arguing for the full citizenship of women in the "cité," she implicitly argues that they are a public good in themselves, thus moving women as a group out of the private sphere to which they had been (since Aristotle) confined. Christine here claims a political import to her pro-woman writings; they are not to be viewed as distinct from her direct counsels to king and to queen. She thus bases her authority not merely on the corpus of her written texts, but on the real political effectiveness of her writing—aimed here at the greater public good, because that good must include in its definition all the citizens of a commonwealth, both men and women.

Rewriting the City: Part II, Sections 54–69

In her next major grouping of portraits, Christine is dealing with revisions of a number of legendary stories, told mainly by Ovid. Hence she offers again what she claims to have achieved in earlier texts, an answer to the lies of Ovid. But first she begins the section by returning to Dido, a portion of whose story has already been told by

Reason in part I, when the saga of Dido's founding of Carthage was narrated along with stories of all the other city builders. Immediately after Christine's disquisition on the proper definition of public versus private good, of appropriate citizenship in a community, it is fitting that she should take up the story of a famous city-builder. But Dido, of course, is also a lover, and it is this part of her legend which Christine now considers.

In her use of the story of Dido's love affair with Aeneas, Christine presents an entirely different version from that found in Boccaccio, who ignores Virgil. In Boccaccio's version, Dido, the exemplary wife, has killed herself long before Aeneas could have arrived on the scene. The miniature illuminating this moment in the French translation of Boccaccio, makes the voyeurism surrounding this self-sacrifice recall the illumination of Lucretia's suicide (Figure 26).

26. Dido killing herself, *Des cleres femmes*, Ms. Royal C V 20, f. 65r. London, British Library, by permission

Christine again calls attention to her basic metaphor for her text and remarshalls the tradition of cities into which she is explicitly inserting *her* city of ladies. The installation of Dido's Carthage in the tradition of cities founded by women is here directly counterposed to the founding of Rome. As we have seen, Christine's withering dismissal of Aeneas's faithless ingratitude in the face of Dido's hospitality faults him for his failure to fulfill an ideal of both Homeric and Virgilian epic. *Philoxenia*—hospitality—requires certain behaviors from guests as well as hosts.

> il s'en parti après ce que elle l'ot tout reffait et enrichi d'avoir et d'aise, ses nefs refraischies, reffaictes et ordonnees, plain de tresor et de biens, comme celle qui n'avoit espargné l'avoir la ou le cuer estoit mis. S'en ala sans congié prendre de nuit en recelle traytreusement, sans le sceu d'elle; et ainsi paya son hoste. (pp. 930–31)

> he left after she had restored and enriched him with property and ease, his ships refreshed, repaired, and placed in order, filled with treasure and wealth, like a woman who had spared no expenses where her heart was involved. He departed at night, secretly and treacherously, without farewells and without her knowledge. This was how he repaid his hostess. (p. 189)

In place of Dido's famous curse, Christine substitutes this curt dismissal.

Chaucer also narrates the history of Dido in *The Legend of Good Women*, and his similar rehearsal of the story of a putatively virtuous Dido poses a useful contrast to Christine's. Christine's point is that Dido is more constant in love than Aeneas and while this is also Chaucer's ostensible point, when he has Dido fall to Aeneas's feet and beg to be taken along and "profereth hym to be / His thral, his servant in the leste degre," she loses her dignity and regal bearing.[41]

It is interesting—and puzzling—that Christine does not attempt to rehabilitate Cleopatra, the most famous of all pagan queen/lovers, for her purposes. The ruler of Egypt was an obvious candidate—a highly learned, conquering African queen, notoriously opposed to,

---

[41]Geoffrey Chaucer, *The Works of Geoffrey Chaucer*, ed. F. N. Robinson (Boston: Houghton Mifflin, 1957), *The Legend of Good Women*, ll. 1312–14.

and slandered by, Rome; Boccaccio narrates this pagan woman's legend at length. Chaucer also chooses Cleopatra, "martir," to be the opening story in *The Legend of Good Women*, ironically praising her as the first of Cupid's "saints." As part of Chaucer's narrator's penance for slandering women, the story hardly helps, however, for it works to undercut Cleopatra's virtues at the same time it tries to suppress her vices. It has been suggested that in Chaucer the hyperbolic death Cleopatra achieves by jumping into a whole pitful of snakes (rather than using a couple of asps in a basket) owes something of the genre of actual saint's lives he is obviously parodying in the work. But it is also true that such a death was part and parcel of Cleopatra's love of excess and thus is in keeping with the character Chaucer draws.[42] In any event, Chaucer's Cleopatra is no more ideal than Dido.

Doubtless the sheer weight of tradition was simply too great in Cleopatra's case, for Christine does not even mention her in passing as, for example, an analogy to Dido. Instead, Christine selects Ovidian tales that replay Babylonian themes.

Medea, Thisbe, and Hero are three Ovidian heroines whom Christine enlists in the forces of feminine constancy. In Medea's case— the shortest vignette of the three—Christine simply suppresses the grisly ending of Medea's revenge on Jason's faithlessness and lets her remain an exemplar of the same kind of generosity Dido extends to Aeneas, another woman receiving in return a mendacious ingratitude.

In terms of the alternative tradition of female-identified cities that Christine promulgates in her construction of her cité des dames, the case of Thisbe recalls the rescripting of Babylon that began with the first stone thrown down with the story of Semiramis. Pyramus and Thisbe are citizens of Babylon. The first line of text in the *Ovide moralisé*—Christine's probable source—unequivocally announces this location for the story:

> En Bablione la cité
> Furent dui home renomé

---

[42]See Beverly Taylor, "The Medieval Cleopatra: The Classical and Medieval Tradition of Chaucer's *Legend of Good Women*," *Journal of Medieval and Renaissance Studies* 7 (1977), 249–69.

Dui citeain de grant hautece
De parenté et de richece.

In the city of Babylon
Lived two renowned men
Two citizens of the highest houses
Well connected and rich.[43]

Christine directly cites the *Metamorphoses* of Ovid as her source: "Ovide raconte en son livre de *Methamorphoseos*, si que tu les scez, qu'em la cité de Babilloine ot deux riches citoyens" (p. 933). "Just as you know, Ovid tells in his *Metamorphoses* that in the city of Babylon, there were two rich citizens" (p. 190; revised). Although, as these verbal parallels suggest, Christine had the medieval Ovid open in front of her, the actual Latin verse uses a *periphrasis* that specifically sets the story in *Semiramis*'s city (and Christine might well have known the Latin).

Pyramus et Thisbe, iuvenum pulcherrimus alter,
altera, quas Oriens habuit, praelata puellis,
contiguas tenuere domos, ubi dicitur altam
coctilibus muris cinxisse Semiramis urbem.

Pyramus and Thisbe—he, the most beautiful youth, and she, loveliest maid of all the East—dwelt in houses side by side, in the city which Semiramis is said to have surrounded with walls of brick.[44]

In a famous scene the young lovers speak through the wall that separates their fathers' houses; the mention of Semiramis's construction of a wall of bricks around the city of Babylon therefore not only recalls the Babylonian frame of Christine's own text, but also indicates the important function of the wall within the legend of the tragic lovers themselves. (So important a player is the wall itself that when Shakespeare's rude mechanicals attempt to dramatize the

---

[43]Cornelius De Boer, *"Ovide moralisé": Poème du commencement du quatorzième siècle*, Verhandelingen der Koninklijke Akademie van Wetenschappen, Afdeeling Letterkund, Nieuwe Reeks, 21 (Johannes Muller: Amsterdam, 1920), IV.229–32; p. 18; my translation.

[44]Ovid, *Metamorphoses*, trans. Frank Justus Miller (Cambridge: Harvard University Press), IV.55–58; pp. 182–83.

story in *A Midsummer Night's Dream,* they decide to have one of their actors represent "Wall" in person.) The lovers, of course, meet at the tomb of Ninus on the fatal evening when, like Romeo and Juliet, they commit their loyal but unnecessary suicides. This tomb is, presumably, the sepulcher of Semiramis's husband, the elder Ninus, and consequently it recalls the famous king and his infamously incestuous queen. It also prepares for the single tomb that the two young lovers are to be granted: "En un seul tomblel les poserent" (l. 1165); "they were put in a single tomb" (my translation). And at the site of their meetings, the mulberry tree's berries, formerly white, are now red as a sign of sorrow. The "allegorie" that interprets this story in the *Ovide moralisé* finds Christological enactments in the transformation of the tree and demonic evil in the intruding lion.[45] Pyramus and Thisbe themselves are not judged. In the version Christine tells in the *Epistre Othéa,* the moral is drawn to stress the need to obey one's parents, a moral similar to the one hinted at by Chaucer's irony in the version he uses for *The Legend of Good Women.* While the explicit moral of Chaucer's tale is exactly Christine's— "God forbede but a woman can / Ben as trewe in lovynge as a man!"— in fact, the irony of Thisbe's lament undercuts the claim. According to Elaine Hansen, in Chaucer's version of the story, "Thisbe is less noble than foolhardy, timid, regretful, and desperate to save her reputation in the only way left to her."[46] The narrator is still in the grip of a misogyny for which he is ostensibly doing penance. In the version told by Christine in the *Cité,* there is no undercutting moral: Thisbe's death directly proves her heroic constancy (Figure 27).

In sharp contrast to such leniency, the *Ovide moralisé* harshly condemns Leander's lover, Hero, the heroine of the next story Christine tells, seeing in her suicide not the constancy parallel to Thisbe's which Christine finds but a quintessential dangerous female lust.

> Quar toute la force d'amer,
> Toute la cause et la nature
> Toute femeline luxure
> Naist en sexte, membre de feme.

---

[45]The lion leaves behind a mangled garment, echoing the same incident that scares to death the loving Julia, Pompey's wife, in the earlier story.

[46]Elaine Hansen, "Irony and the Antifeminist Narrator in Chaucer's *Legend of Good Women,*" *JEGP* 82 (1983), 20.

27. Thisbe killing herself, *Epistre Othéa*, Ms. Harley 4431, f. 112v. London, British Library, by permission

Hero tient le brandon qui flame
Dont ele alume son amant.
(IV.3596–3602)

For all the force of love,
All the cause and nature,
All feminine lust
Is born in the sexual member of woman.
Hero holds the flaming brand
Which inflames her lover.

(my translation)

But for Christine, Hero perishes from an excess of love: "Par trop amer fu perie" (p. 937); Christine portrays her as another one of those strong and constant women, who, when they succumb to "folle amour," end tragically, their strength turned against themselves.

The next two stories, which Christine tells in detail, and a third, which she merely mentions, are all taken from Boccaccio's *Decameron*—as she explicitly tells us. Her switch at this point to fuller narration and to Boccaccio's vernacular collection of stories is an interesting recalibration of her narrative tactics. The tales of Pyramus and Thisbe and of Hero and Leander—as their very conventional titles suggest—are in their original forms full narrations, far more than just exemplary portraits of individual women (as are the vignettes in the *De mulieribus*). Christine may be doing no more here than experimenting with Ovidian narrative and Boccaccian tale-spinning in these more extended narrative forms, but the greater concern with plot in this narrative material is itself striking. What is perhaps even more striking, however, is that the two tales she selects from the one hundred at her disposal in the *Decameron* both have to do with tragic love plots in which a part of the body of the beloved male—who has been murdered by the heroine's male relatives—becomes an object of virtually obsessive devotion. In the first tale, Tancred, the duke of Salerno, has the heart of his daughter's lover brought to her in a golden cup, whereupon she waters it with her tears, kisses it obsessively, and then makes herself a poisonous mixture, which she drinks from the cup—heart, tears, and all—and so dies. In the second tale, young Lisabetta discovers her beloved's dead body buried by her brothers in the garden. She takes his head and hides it in a pot of basil, which she waters with her tears until her suspicious brothers remove the pot. She also quickly dies.

The passing mention of another tale from the *Decameron* about a husband who makes his wife eat her lover's heart—so that she never eats again and therefore dies—underscores the peculiar principle of selection for all the stories, with their very pronounced focus on some severed body part. As we saw in her framing of the opening legends, Christine has not previously been much invested in narrative that deal with the dismemberment of the male body: hence it is surprising to see such a singular focus on these details appear toward the close of part II. The disembodied male heart and the decapitated male head function as objects of devotion for their beloveds, as in the case of the woman who kept her dead husband's hand—the male body is not denigrated or rejected as abject by the faithful, loving woman. (We think of Artemisia's ingestion of Mausolus or Argia's loving recognition of Polyneices's partially rotted corpse.) It is possible that these stories of dismembered male body parts are preparation, as it were, for the female martyrs' stories that Justice will narrate in part III; essentially, the same torturing masculine power that subjects the martyrs to violence also caused the dismemberments depicted earlier, exercised at first on the male body.

So too, in the Tancred story, the dismemberment of the male beloved is directly organized by the father in order to provide emotional torture for his daughter. In the oedipal undercurrents of each tale, it is not the woman, but the legitimate, authorized male who causes harm to the less socially protected male. Both Boccaccio's and Christine's texts also make it clear that the father and the brothers have been remiss in fulfilling their patriarchal responsibilities: since they have not married off the woman appropriately, she is exonerated from total blame for having fallen in love on her own.

Beyond these provocative parallels, Christine changes the two stories in ways that emphasize female autonomy; she does not merely condense them for a quicker narrative pace, but in effect accentuates the female's agency in the plot. In Boccaccio's version of the story of Tancred and his daughter Ghismonda, for instance, he lavishes much narrative time on the description of the secret grotto where the young lovers meet and includes careful notation of the leather clothes the beloved servingman must wear in order to protect himself from the briars that scratch at him as he swings on a rope through an air shaft into the grotto. With such flourishes, Boccaccio gives a Douglas Fairbanks slant to the story, one that Christine avoids altogether. In contrast, she provides absolutely no details about the physical meeting place of the lovers (the male hops out of a convenient wardrobe when necessary). Instead, Christine concentrates all her narrative skill on a conversation entirely of her own making which she interpolates into the tale. Unlike Boccaccio's merely sneaky mistress, who communicates her love to her servingman by putting a letter into a hollowed-out cane to be used as kindling (though the item does bespeak the passion she wishes to inflame), Christine's Ghismonda conducts a subtle interview with the man, fully testing his loyalty to her before she confesses her love. She explains that she needs to tell him of a secret love and asks if he can be trusted. Yes, he can, he answers and furthermore swears that he will happily serve whomever it is who has been chosen as her beloved. Only after Ghismonda— "qui l'avoit voulu esprouver" (who wanted to test him)—is certain of his loyalty does she tell him that he himself is the lucky man (p. 940). Thus, while Boccaccio emphasizes the male lover's prowess at feats of physical agility, Christine underlines the heroine's psychological acumen in testing the character of her lover.

Both Boccaccio's and Christine's heroines are proud and blame their fathers for their own waywardness; Christine's Ghismonda is perhaps slightly more condemnatory of her father's culpability for not bestowing her on another husband—and she more particularly pleads that her loyal servingman be spared, arguing that he did nothing wrong in responding to her desires and, indeed, would have been base had he refused a lady of such high standing. Singly responsible for her own misdeeds, she argues that only she should be punished. While both Boccaccio and Christine blame Tancred for his daughter's ultimate death, only in Christine does the father then die of grief. His neglect of his fatherly responsibility is punished to a far greater degree in Christine's book than in Boccaccio's.

In the subsequent story of Lisabetta, the most striking difference between the two renditions is that Christine's heroine intuits her beloved's murder by means of her own wise heart, whereas in Boccaccio the ghost of her beloved comes to her in a dream and reveals that her brothers have killed him and buried him in the garden of their country estate. Boccaccio's heroine finds a whole body when she digs up the new grave in the garden and decides herself to sever the head from the lifeless corpse so that she may have a physical memento of her lover to plant in the pot of basil.[47] Christine's Lisabetta does not molest her lover's corpse. In her version, the ailing heroine is sitting in the garden of the country estate when her heart tells her the whole adventure, "qui le cuer disoit toute l' aventure" (p. 949), and she finds the grave and the head that has already been cut off by her brothers. In Boccaccio's version, the brothers realize when they find and remove her pot that their murder has been discovered, so they flee. Christine is less concerned with the brothers' fate than with that of the constant sister, who, when her memorial pot is taken away, laments the loss and, weeping, dies—another strong woman whose constancy makes her a victim of "folle amour."

The failure of the males (Ghismonda's father, Lisabetta's brothers) to arrange acceptable marriages for these women in each case makes the woman's constancy to the man she herself has chosen exemplary in Christine and even partly praiseworthy in Boccaccio. But their failure also stresses what remains—across classes—the same male responsibility; the major difference between the two stories as Christine's selects and juxtaposes them is the difference in class: one is the story of a duke and his daughter, the other a story of a set of bourgeois Italian siblings. Christine's move to use the *Decameron* rather than the *De mulieribus claris* allows her this switch in class locale for the stories; although there are narratives about women from different classes in Boccaccio's Latin text, the collection of vernacular tales generically tends toward the lower end of the social spectrum, and Christine mines it for two stories that reveal the similar failures of patriarchal responsibility in two separate classes. One of her main considerations toward the end of part II is the explicit inclusion of women from as many different social strata as possible. If they are all to become ladies upon installation in the city—because their womanly virtue is equal—they must arrive there from as many different estates as possible, for virtue is achievable in any walk of life.

Her next grouping of portraits provides a vivid contrast in terms of the level of detail with which Christine narrates each story. John

[47]In "Isabella; or, the Pot of Basil," Keats directly follows Boccaccio (whom he invokes and praises) in all these details of the plot, although (like Christine) he does in his "romance" give greater emphasis to the love, and the grief, felt by the heroine. See *The Poems of John Keats*, ed. Jack Stillinger (Cambridge: Harvard University Press, 1978), pp. 245–63.

Burrow has used the Middle English word "pointing," to mean the selection of different levels of textual detail; it is, he argues, a major resource for the narrative art of the poets working in England at the time Christine was writing and can be seen as a major technical instrument of the time.[48] Whether or not such a technique was shared by Continental artists, Christine certainly juxtaposes some of her most elaborately worked out tales (high relief pointing) with deft rehearsal of summary portraits (low relief pointing): thus the stories of Juno, Europa, Jocasta, Medusa, Helen of Troy, and Polyxena are all polished off very quickly, as examples of women who have become famous in history through accident, either by virtue of their relations to important males or because of their beauty—itself always an accident. Incest between brother and sister, as in the story of Juno's marriage to her brother, or between mother and son, as in the legend of Jocasta's tragic fate, is one of those accidents that may catapult a woman to fame without her having earned a place by her own virtue. Neither is beauty like Helen's either a virtue or a divine power. So, Christine's approach to Medusa's legendary beauty completely refuses any supernatural notion of her charms and interprets her power of petrifaction to be simply a result of her very great physical appeal:

> elle attrayoit toute mortelle creature que elle regardoit si a soy que elle rendoit les gens commes inmouvables. Et pour ce faigny la fable que de pierre devenoyent. (p. 954)

> She attracted to herself every mortal creature upon whom she looked, so that she seemed to make people immovable. For this reason the fable claimed that they had turned to stone. (p. 204; revised)

Like her almost cavalier reorganization of the legend of Semiramis, Christine's astonishing rewrite of the Medusa legend refuses to take as seriously pertinent to her project any male fears that may be engaged by such petrifying details.[49] Her interpretative focus is rather

---

[48]J. A. Burrow, *Ricardian Poetry: Chaucer, Gower, Langland, and the 'Gawain' Poet* (London: Routledge, 1971), pp. 69–78.

[49]Freud's discussion is famous. See "Medusa's Head" in *Sexuality and the Psychology of Love: Collected Papers of Sigmund Freud*, vol. 8 (New York: Macmillan, 1963), pp. 212–13. For an important feminist revision, see Hélène Cixous, "The Laugh of the

on protecting women against the misogynist argument that would cast an immoral light on their beauty—itself accidental and therefore morally neutral, except possibly when they work to enhance their physical charms. Christine threads her way very carefully through the moral minefield of artificial aids to appearance—clothes, cosmetics, ornaments—and argues that should a desire to dress elegantly and behave coquettishly occur to anyone *naturally*—such as it occurred, for example, to the apostle Bartholomew, who liked to dress elegantly—then it would not be a sin. Christine goes on to cite (without agreeing or disagreeing) the opinion of some that in punishment for his sartorial indulgences, St. Bartholomew was martyred by being flayed alive but concludes that only God may judge a soul. Dress (one way or another) is no sign of a good conscience. The story of Claudia Quinta, a Roman woman, is a proof case; in Boccaccio's version, Claudia Quinta dresses sluttishly and wears so much makeup that to serious matrons (gravioribus matronis) she seems not only dishonorable but actually unchaste (non tantum minus honesta, verum et minus pudica). Christine's Claudia, on the other hand, merely delights in beautiful, bizarre clothes and in lovely ornaments:

> Et pource que en ce elle estoit aucunement plus delicative que les autres dames de Romme, aucuns presumerent mal contre elle et contre chasteté au prejudice de sa renommee. (p. 957)

> Because she was more refined than the other ladies of Rome, some people spoke badly of her and of her chastity, to the detriment of her reputation. (p. 205)

Christine here makes certain that it is not Boccaccio's censorious matrons but an ungendered group that judges the young girl. So too, each author draws a very different moral from Claudia's miraculous ability (after she has prayed for a sign that will prove her chastity) to draw a foundered ship safely to shore with her sash, thus demonstrat-

---

Medusa," trans. Keith Cohen and Paula Cohen, *Signs* 1 (1976), 875–93, reprinted in *The "Signs" Reader: Women, Gender, and Scholarship*, ed. Elizabeth Abel and Emily K. Abel (Chicago: University of Chicago Press, 1983), pp. 279–97.

ing to all her purity. Boccaccio moralizes that no one should on this basis presume to request miracles of God—for indeed Claudia's action tempted God, itself a great imposition, not worthy of so small a thing as clearing herself of an assumed crime.

> Velle enim, ut se quis ostendat insontem, id agere quod preter naturam sit, Deum potius temptare est quam obiecti criminis purgare labem. (p. 000)

> For to do something supernatural in order to show that one is blameless is to tempt God more than to purge the blot of an assumed crime. (p. 308)

Drawing an entirely different lesson from the story, Christine explains that we should not simply assume from the results of Claudia's prayer that the goddess to whom she prayed was real. Instead, we are to understand that it was the girl's own magical chastity that saved her and endowed her with the power to draw the ship.

> Et par ce le demonstra que elle ot fiance que la verité de sa chasteté luy fust secourable, laqueelle chose luy ayda et non autre deesse. (p. 958)

> She showed thereby that she believed the truthfulness of her chastity would help her, and indeed it was her chastity which helped her, not some goddess. (p. 206)

The power of virtue is great, as one of the miniaturists who illuminated the Flemish translation of Claudia's story makes clear.

Right after the story of Claudia Quinta, Christine strangely elects to narrate the part of Lucretia's story she had left out when emphasizing the rape. According to Christine, Tarquin is attracted not by Lucretia's beauty but rather by her great virtue: now we hear the episode of the men's betting on their wives, in which the winner is to be the husband whose wife is most honestly occupied at the moment the men burst in on her. Of all the wives, they discover Lucretia to be the one most honestly occupied: she is working in wool and speaking to her women about virtuous things. Whereupon Tarquin falls in love, more smitten by womanly virtue than by beauty. If Tarquin is then an unfortunate example of the allure of virtue, Christine at-

28. Claudia Quinta pulling a ship ashore with her belt, demonstrating the power of her chastity, *De lof der vrouwen*, Ms. Add. 20698, f. 247r. London, British Library, by permission

tempts to correct for the resultant implications by giving a contemporary example from modern French history in which the count of Champagne deeply loves, because of her virtue, the no longer young queen Blanche. He does not, however, press his desires on her in any way, except by writing beautiful poetry. So too, Christine adds from her own experience, many women have complained of being courted far more when they were older than when young; now she realizes that men are attracted more by wise virtue than by mere prettiness. She gives to the experience a generalized voice, almost as if offering to her female readers an object lesson in how to handle this particular problem:

"Dieux! et que veult ce dire? Voyent ces hommes en moy aucune contenance folle par quoy ilz ayent coulleur et cause de pensser que je fusse d'accord de faire si grant follie?" (p. 961)

"Gods! What can this possibly mean? Do these men see in me some foolish behavior which would give them the slightest glimmer of hope that I would agree to commit such foolishness?" (p. 208)

The last vice complained of by misogynist writers is women's supposed avarice, a charge Droitture now explodes. Christine lucidly and wryly argues that because women are kept in such straitened financial circumstances by men, their apparent greediness is merely prudence. Yet even despite their relative poverty, women are great almsgivers now and have often in the past bestowed their jewels to save their cities—as Roman women have famously done. As an example of great female generosity, Droitture briefly sketches a final story from the *De mulieribus claris*, concerning one Busa, who had nursed at her own expense ten thousand defeated Roman soldiers after a major battle with Hannibal, so that they could return to the field and conquer the Punic forces.

Droitture then abruptly cuts from the Roman past to the French present and, in the same breath with which she praises Busa, extols Marguerite, dame de la Rivière, a woman who was alive at the time Christine wrote. Marguerite was famous for having relieved an old soldier imprisoned for debt by sending him the golden chapelet she was wearing at a festive dinner, replacing it with a plain crown of flowers.

Droitture ends part II of the *Cité* by providing a list of living French women—as well as foreigners—who will be included as citizens in "our" city. The Milanese Valentina Visconti now takes her place beside Isabeau of Bavaria and the wives of the dukes of Berry, Burgundy, and Bar, the count of Clermont, and Ludwig of Bavaria, the brother of the queen. In this way, Christine incorporates into her text the circle of women whose families had provided her patronage, praising them and making a bid for their further support. Yet for all her courting of their favor, she insistently includes with them women of lower ranks:

D'autres contesses, baronnesses, dames, damoyselles, bourgoises et de

tous estaz y a tant de bonnes et de belles, malgré les mesdisans, que
Dieux e soit louez qui les y maintiengne. (p. 970)

In spite of slanderers, there are so many good and beautiful women
among the ranks of countesses, baronesses, ladies, maidens, bourgeois
women, and all classes that God should be praised who upholds them
all. (p. 214)

Droitture closes by insisting on the inclusiveness of the city; it has
within it all classes of women, and all of them are ladies.

I'ay bastie de biaulx palais et de maintes belles herberges et menssions,
la t'ay puepplee de nobles dames, tant et a si grans routes de tous estas
que ja est toute reamplie. (p. 970)

I have built it up with beautiful palaces and many fair inns and mansions. I have populated it for your sake with noble ladies and with such
great number of women from all classes that it is already completely
filled. (p. 214)

Such insistence is not merely there to reemphasize the class mixture
of the city, but to underscore as well the experiential tradition upon
which Christine bases her claim for the authority to write such a
text. Just as she is granted the authority to write, so her living
contemporaries are granted the right to enter the city, their city;
there are no lines drawn between dead pagan and living Christian
women, not because of their ideological persuasions or—as it were—
their ontological status. The present is continuous with the past, the
textual fuses with a nontextual tradition, the dead and the living
cohabit easily. This city eschews the barriers normally erected by
men (and most explicitly erected by Boccaccio).

The architecture of the cité des dames is neat and civilized—it
obeys appropriate spatial rules, but by the same token it reorganizes
the grid that usually separates women into classes, into ideological
strata, and into the larger grouping of those living and those dead.
Like the citizens of Dante's Paradiso, all of Christine's women are
joined in a communal harmony.

The last paragraph of this long central section is spoken by the
narrator herself: it is a speech addressed to the readers of her text,

asking them to pray for its author. In its direct address, this call is another transgression of the boundary between the living and the dead: for her prayer includes all princesses of France present and all women who have lived in the past, are living now, and will live in the future. This speech is Christine's appeal to all her female readers and comprises a subtle claim for the lasting fame of her work. This city, she says, will last as long as the world endures—far longer than the work of Ovid, who only hoped that his would be read as long as the Latin language was spoken. Fame helps to break down the final boundary, between the living and the dead. Faith crosses that boundary by transcending mortal limits. It is, finally, that ultimate barrier which is transgressed in the third part of the *Cité des dames*.

Chapter 4

Rewriting the Body:
The Politics of Martyrdom

Unlike man, who holds so dearly to his title and his titles, his pouches
of value, his cap crown, and everything connected with his head,
woman couldn't care less about the fear of decapitation.

—Hélène Cixous

When Perpetua and Justin, along with their Christian contemporaries, acted out their vision of liberty by refusing to sacrifice to the
gods and the emperors, they marked themselves as targets for arrest,
torture, and execution. So long as Christians remained members of a
suspect society, subject to death, the boldest among them maintained
that, since demons controlled the government and inspired its agents,
the believer could gain freedom at their hands only in death.

—Elaine Pagels

Part III

Although the full rubric for the third section of the *Cité des
dames* explains that this final part will tell of further construction, in
fact, the narration of the stories by Justice and the completion of the
city are *not* simultaneous. The rubric reads: "comment and par qui
les haulx combles des tours furent parfaiz et quelles nobles dames
furent esleutes pour demourer en grans palais aet haulx donjons"
(p. 974); "how the high roofs of the towers were completed and by
whom and which noble ladies were chosen to reside in the great
palaces and lofty mansions" (p. 217). Nevertheless, the miniature
illuminating the *opening* of the third section, showing Justice wel-
coming Mary and representative saints, reveals that the city, roofs
and all, is already completed.

The actual construction of the city, as we have seen, is finished

29. Justice receiving the Virgin Mary and other saints into the constructed city, *Cité des dames*, Ms. Harley 4431, f. 361. London, British Library, by permission

midway through part II of the text and forms a major interpretive articulation within that section. By concluding the physical construction with a story about a daughter who breast feeds her mother, Christine has chosen a narrative that designedly recalls and reorganizes the generational relations of the first "stone" to be installed in the foundations, that is, the story of Semiramis with its treatment of non-scandalous mother/son incest. Such maternal physicality (mother/son, mother/daughter) is, however, transmuted by being monumentalized into the metaphor of the city's construction. In contrast, the stories now to be told in part III are not so constrained.

The stories Justice narrates in part III are all legends of saints, most of them martyrs, most, but by no means all of them, virgins. The martyrs occupy an ontological position in the city rather different from that held by the women of the earlier tales, who were not saints. Although the subjects of the last tales narrated in part II are also citizens and not architectural components of the city as are the majority of the tales told so far, the saints of part III are separated even from the preceding citizens, cordoned off into their own section under the aegis of Justice. Theirs is thus a special brand of "citizenship," having a more purely political character than the citizenship of the other women. Unlike the stories in the first two sections about women whose experience is architectural, the saints in this group of narratives are curiously resistant to mutation, not only within the metaphor of the city, but, of course, also within the various *vitae* that Christine recasts.[1] Just as they have already triumphed in life over a politically motivated dismemberment and death, so too, in the text their "bodies" are not transmuted metaphorically into allegorical elements.

The position thus given the female saints' legends within the overall metaphor of the city's now completed construction underscores the text's logic by doubly emphasizing the untransmuted corporeality crucially central to these stories of dismemberment:

[1] It is difficult to render the process visually, although one miniaturist did try to show how the earlier stories, imagined as individual females, could be pictured as being inserted by blocks into a monumental surface (British Library, Ms. Add. 20698, 12ᵛ). For a discussion of Christine's use of Ovidian metamorphoses in earlier works, see Kevin Brownlee, "Discourses of the Self: Christine de Pizan and the *Romance of the Rose*," *Romanic Review* 79 (1988): 199–221.

twice unchanged, both by resisting dismemberment and also by Christine's treatment, the bodies remain sainted forms. As we have seen, in the *Cité* Christine specifically refuses to rewrite the earlier option exercised in the *Mutacion*—that of her own change, under the pressure of fortune, into a man. In the *Cité*, she constructs her authority as one that is embodied most insistently in a *female* corporeal experience. This corporeal existence takes on a final and quite literally spectacular importance in the last section. In the various scenes of the torturing of saints, the display of the body becomes, indeed, a public—and explicitly political—spectacle. The political theater that occurs when the saint's dead body, finally enshrined in a sanctuary, continues to work miracles has already happened even more publicly during earlier scenes of torture when the saint, usually naked, is dismembered before audiences of thousands.

Recent readers of the *Cité des dames* have found it rather shocking and distasteful that the first pro-woman polemic should include narratives about martyrdom, with repetitive burnings, hangings, mutilations, and beheadings, narratives in which the naked bodies of young virgins are beaten and their breasts are ripped off by order of tyrants, most of whom add lust to their cruelty. As Charity Canon Willard explains: "it has been suggested that Christine should have ended her book [after part II], for the stories of saints which make up the third part are sometimes distasteful to the modern mind."[2] That a text as sensitively and sophisticatedly engaged as the *Cité des dames* is in developing a repertoire of strategies for anti-misogynist rhetoric should end on visions of gruesome torture, using the vocabulary of pain, poses critical problems that must be dealt with, most particularly in terms of those very anti-misogynist strategies. Why did Christine decide to write such a conclusion to her self-consciously pro-woman text? The answers to such a question are crucial to our ability to read the *Cité des dames* not only, as Willard points out, in its historical situation as a text written in 1405, but also as a text that may continue to speak to us in the late twentieth century.

First it is necessary to see that by supplying her martyrology, Christine was rewriting her precursor Boccaccio and copying the

---

[2]Christine de Pizan, *The Medieval Woman's Mirror of Honor: The Treasury of the City of Ladies*, trans. Charity Canon Willard (New York: Persea Books, 1989), p. 33.

practice of *his* precursors Dante and Augustine, both of whom contemplate the saints as the quintessentially proper citizens for the civitas dei. In this sense, Christine sensibly continues the readjustment of authority she has given to her auctores in the first two sections. But any answer from literary tradition also needs to take into account problems of history local to Christine's moment, as well as to address far larger questions about her relationship to the institutional authorization of sainthood and martyrdom—which have their own complicated generic and social histories. In attempting to understand why the *Cité* concludes with a martyrology, we need to ask, then, a great many questions of a second sort, such as: what politics could have been involved in Christine's choice in 1405 to use hagiography at all? That is, what impact did the cult of the saints have within the late medieval–early Renaissance polis? Second, what are the internal politics of martyrology itself? That is, what structures of power does it engage in its peculiarly painful narrative display of the body? As Christine persistently genders this body female, it will be important to ask whether her rescripting of martyrology to insist on sexual difference in any way connects the scene of torture to familial practices for engendering appropriate social roles in late medieval women.

The Literary Tradition

The inclusion of a martyrology in the *Cité* forms Christine's major departure from her principal auctor—Giovanni Boccaccio.[3] It is therefore as part of her complicated and highly articulate intervention into the literary canon that she specifically positions herself vis-à-vis authors such as Jean de Meun, Boccaccio, and Dante. In the *De mulieribus claris*, as we have seen, Boccaccio announced that he would not say anything about Christian women because it was inappropriate for pagan and Christian women to be praised in the same terms, since they do not strive for the same goal: "nec equo incedere

---

[3]For another discussion of Christine's use of Boccaccio see Patricia A. Phillipy, "Establishing Authority: Boccaccio's *De Claris Mulieribus* and Christine de Pizan's *Livre de la Cité des Dames*," *Romanic Review* 77 (1986): 167–94.

videntur gradu" (p. 26). He consequently elected not to meddle with any stories of their monotonously virtuous constancy in the face of extreme torture, stories that, as he points out in his prologue, have been told by great and learned men of far more authority than he. Instead, Boccaccio will rest his own claim for his special originality (and thus, in fact, his essential difference from Petrarch) on his being the first to write specifically and exclusively about pagan women.[4] Chaucer's purpose in the *Legend of Good Women* was to judge pagan women by the standards of Christian martyrdom—hence the title "legend"—but he thereby paradoxically condemns them, robbing the valiant of their energy in an effort to make them more "virtuous" and making the patient seem merely silly.[5]

Redressing Boccaccio's emphasis on the distinctions between the two groups and differing from Chaucer's ironic collapse of the categories, Christine's structure resists seeing Christian and pagan females as essentially different. Although the saints in her text are a special case for Justice, all women in the city form a single group in no way striated by divisions of ideology or class—or even the ontological status of living and dead. Hence the city is equally hospitable to both pagan and Christian women, to historical, legendary, and mythical figures, and to women from both the past and the present.

As the subtle erasure of the boundary between living and dead suggests, the choice to narrate saints' vitae in part III, while a major move against Boccaccio's authority, is at the same time a highly allusive reference to the third and last part of Dante's *Commedia*, a paradise populated by saints. Part III implicitly reflects then, what Christine earlier stated directly in her arguments about Jean de Meun: in all ways Dante is a far superior literary model.[6] Although a hierarchy

---

[4]See above, pp. 96–99. It may be useful to remember that Christine's father would probably have known Petrarch personally in Bologna, and she would in all likelihood have been aware of him (Willard, *Treasury*, pp. 18–20).

[5]See Elaine Hansen, "Irony and the Antifeminist Narrator in Chaucer's *Legend of Good Women*," *JEGP* 82 (1983), 11–31.

[6]If in fact the narration of saints' lives in the third section is a further allusion to Dante's practice, Christine would seem to have engaged in the basic move against the precursor, as outlined by Harold Bloom in *The Anxiety of Influence* (New York: Oxford University Press, 1973), although the genders of the poets involved do not fit his psychoanalytic vocabulary. The allusion works to gain access to the authority of a model (Dante) that is prior in time and therefore in authority to Christine's immediate precursor (Boccaccio), a model that was known to have caused Boccaccio anxiety.

is established by the articulation of the architectural metaphor, her city is classless, the uniform class being upper; as the text's very title shows, it is a city of *ladies*. Christine is quite explicit that women of all classes are included and that all are subordinated only to the Virgin Mary, their queen and protector (who announces to Justice that she will happily "live and abide in this city" among all her "sisters and friends"). Any woman who is virtuous can enter the city: "toutes preudesfemes de grant auttorité" (p. 816). None will be "diffamees" (p. 816), as if to be unvirtuous is almost punningly to be not woman. Such virtue is synonymous with an authority over self which makes it possible for women to resist the sins of which they have been accused, including a susceptibility to the lures of foolish love. Among the virtuous, the city explicitly includes "si grans routes de tous estas" (p. 970), "great numbers of women from all classes" (p. 214). In refusing to distinguish among groups of women once they are installed in the city, Christine constitutes them as a group defined by their shared identity. The only boundary marker she institutes is virtue and authority; lack of virtue is by definition succumbing to men's seductive lies about sexual looseness, so that men are proved right about women's weakness.

Dante had demonstrated the classlessness of his empyrean by similar means: for example, pairing his kinswoman Piccarda with the empress Constance in the heaven of Venus in Canto I of the *Paradiso*; both women were allegedly abducted from convents and forced into marriage. Because these are the only two female spirits whom Dante and Beatrice actually meet in paradise, the poet is oddly enough creating a heaven in which the only two females encountered are not in fact virgins, though they are, of course, entirely virtuous. Virtue, not virginity per se, is the central concept for Christine as well; in this she and Dante are both rather at variance from the rest of their culture, which held virginity to be the preeminent state, both the spiritual condition and the physical actuality that was its sign.[7]

---

[7]For a discussion of the importance put on actual physical virginity, an importance that caused the women of the period to disfigure themselves by cutting off noses, lips, etc., in an effort to deflect the threat of being raped before they were murdered (fulfilling their desire for martyrdom), see Jane Tibbets Schulenberg, "The Heroics of Virginity: Brides of Christ and Sacrificial Mutilation," in *Women in the Middle Ages and Renaissance: Literary and Historical Perspectives*, ed. Mary Beth Rose (Syracuse: Syracuse University Press, 1986), esp. p. 50. But for a contrasting emphasis, see Cla-

Yet, if in following Dante she has departed from Boccaccio, she differs radically from Dante as well. Part III of the *Cité* mentions a few males, but all the citizens of this city are of course women, and *all* the stories Justice tells are of *female* saints.

Christine's inclusion of the legends of dismembered saints does not merely allow her to stage her own Dante-authorized difference from Boccaccio by conflating the categories of pagan and Christian he sets up in the *De mulieribus claris*. Her martyrology also permits her to rewrite the display of violence against the female body persistently staged by Boccaccio's text. That such violence was immediately visible to readers contemporary with Christine we have seen in the evidence offered by the miniatures illuminating the French manuscript translations of the *De claris*. Lucretia and Dido's suicides stage the voyeuristic dismemberment of the female body most immediately displayed, as we saw, by the miniature of Nero's disembowelment of his mother Agrippina so that he could see the womb from which he was born (Figure 25). Even Penelope's generically pacific delaying strategies appear to be menaced: the surrounding group of violent-looking suitors seem to threaten to dismember her rather than one another (Figure 30).

By her martyrology, Christine is able to move explicitly against the man who has been her major auctor through most of the narratives in the *Cité* and thus to transform the voyeuristic display of violence against the female body in Boccaccio's text into the sacred empowerment of Christian witness. Not only does she translate the oedipal narratives of dismemberments which are scattered throughout Boccaccio's text locally, she translates the general function of dismemberment. Its violence is turned away from display and in an entirely different genre takes on an entirely different narrative drive. But the genre itself does not merely recontain and recast violence; it makes the violence political, essentially by making female victimization an event undergone by an active narrative agent, whose arena is the polis—the city itself.

Perhaps even more fundamentally, the genre of the martyr's legend

rissa W. Atkinson, *Mystic and Pilgrim: The "Book" and the World of Margery Kempe* (Ithaca: Cornell University Press, 1983), pp. 159–80; she lists a number of married women who became saints, among them Birgitta of Sweden and Dorothy of Montau, whose dates overlap with Margery's (and also Christine's).

30. Penelope staving off her violent suitors, *Des cleres femmes*, Ms. Royal 20
C V, f. 61v. London, British Library, by permission

allows any author who uses it access to a set of narratives where stories with female protagonists have traditionally had some kind of recognized parity with stories about males, a fact the text of the *Cité* takes pains to make clear:

> nous faut loger avec elle les benoites vierges et saintes dames en demon-strant coment Dieu a approuve le sexe feminin parce que, *semblable-ment qu'aux hommes*, a donné a femes tendres a de jeune aage coin-stance et force de soustenir pour sa sainte loy horribles martires. (p. 978; emphasis added)

> We must lodge with her [Mary] blessed virgins and sainted ladies in order to demonstrate how God has approved the feminine sex, because, *as similarly as to men*, he has given to tender young women the con-stancy and force to sustain horrible martyrdoms for his holy law. (p. 219)

The peculiar egalitarianism of the genre (women have equal rights to faith and to the courage to sustain martyrdom for that faith; men are equally enjoined to chastity) may help to explain its attraction for another early woman writer, Hroswitha of Gandersheim, a German nun whose tenth-century Terentian plays took as their subject mat-ter the lives of the saints. Unlike Christine, Hroswitha concerned herself with male as well as female saints, and for both sets, virginity was of fundamental importance, a fact that Boccaccio's ironic dis-missal of the martyrologies' monotonous insistence on chastity had also emphasized. Like Christine, Hroswitha retells the bizarre and uniquely comic story of three sister saints—Agape, Chionia, and Irena—in which a tyrant's henchman is fooled by angelic enchant-ment so that he thinks he is embracing the three nubile sisters when he is, in fact, hugging and making love to kitchen pots, in the process so blackening himself that he becomes indistinguishable from the demon who prompted his lust and, as a result, is punished and mocked by his family and friends.[8] The domesticity of the details of this story, along with the way in which the humor of the joke rests upon hierarchic reversals, obviously appealed to both women au-thors: so much so that Hroswitha named her play for the villain, Dulcitius, and Christine condensed this farce far less than she did the

---

[8]See "Dulcitius," in *The Plays of Roswitha*, trans. Christopher St. John (rpt; New York: Cooper Square Publishers, 1966). In Hroswitha's play, even Dulcitius's wife does not recognize him; Christine does not mention the wife or her unwifely mockery.

much more serious story of St. Anastasia which brackets it in her text.

At the same time, however, that the genre ensures parity by its insistence on chastity (if not virginity) for both men and women, it also tends to subsume sexual difference into a masculine model, without, however, relieving the problem of voyeurism present in stories of female torture.[9] Any martyrdom imitates Christ's; such an imitation does not depend on the specifics of gender. Martyrdom's very lack of dependence on sexual difference is, finally, what makes Christine's rewriting of her specific source for the martyrology so suggestive. It is most important that she not only rewrites Boccaccio simply by including a martyrology, but also revises many significant details in the martyrology of her authoritative precursor for her saints' lives, Vincent of Beauvais. Vincent's versions of the Christian vitae are no less subject to correction than Boccaccio's tales of pagan women.

The incipit illumination to one manuscript of the *Miroir historial*, the French translation of the *Speculum historiale* used by Christine, makes immediately clear that in Vincent, male and female saints have their own distinct—separate and *almost* equal—parts to play (Figure 31).

Clothed in their earthly histories, the bodies of the two sexes are very different in appearance, though organized in parallel panels in the opening illumination. The male is privileged over the female saint, occupying the primary position on the left—as such, the point of entry for any eye reading the illumination from left to right; the males are also placed on a dais slightly higher than the females' platform. The physical representation of the two sets of saints thereby divides them according to gender and stages the male precedence, along with the female parallelism. However, when the saints are depicted naked at the moment of torture, as some representative miniatures from the same manuscript make clear, sexual difference disappears almost completely: musculature becomes similar and the figures are without genital definition (although it is important to see that a voyeurism, here read as bestial desire, remains; Figures 32,33). All such implicit erasure of physical difference (the soul has no sex

---

[9]For a discussion of the chastity central to any saint's experience, see Donald Weinstein and Rudolph M. Bell, *Saints and Society: The Two Worlds of Western Christendom, 1000–1700* (Chicago: University of Chicago Press, 1982), chap. 3.

31. The incipit to the *Miroir historial*, Ms. Ffr. 313, f. 1. Paris, Bibliothèque Nationale

32. The martyrdom of St. Julian, *Miroir historial*, Ms. Ffr. 313, f. 166. Paris, Bibliothèque Nationale

before God), Christine persistently rescripts in her rewrites, reintroducing the specificity of female gender into the vitae.

It is also important to point out that as a set of narratives which uses religion as its major framework, the martyrology closing the *Cité des dames* is fairly unusual in Christine's corpus. She does not ordinarily employ such a specifically religious discourse—her vocabulary is more usually tied to political and humanistic traditions such as Ovidian myth, courtly lyric, and the allegorical quest. While she occasionally wrote a religious poem, such as the *Sept psalm allegorisé* or the *Les heures de contemplation sur la passion de notre*

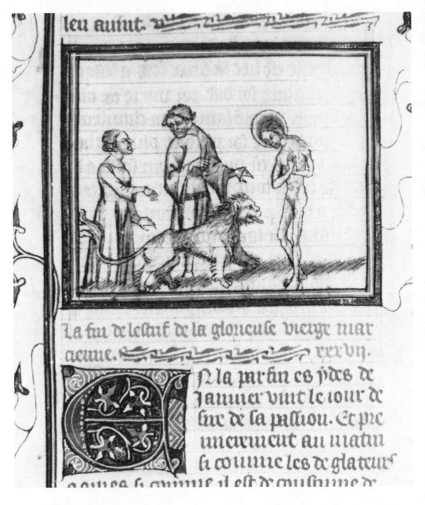

33. The martyrdom of St. Marcienne, *Miroir historial*, Ms. Ffr. 313, f. 276r. Paris, Bibliothèque Nationale

Seigneur, her typical (and quite modern sounding) secularity makes her somewhat unusual among many well-known medieval and Renaissance female writers who claim a divine inspiration for, or at least can point to an institutionally legitimate context for, their authority. One thinks of mystics such as Margaret Prorete or Margery Kempe with their direct inspiration, or Hroswitha and Hildegard of

Bingen, whose religious inspiration was contextualized by their actual institutional affiliation.[10]

Except for her retreat to a convent when forced to flee Paris—from which refuge she wrote the famous *Ditié de Jehanne D'Arc*, a poem as political as it is religious—Christine was, throughout her writing career, a fully secular woman. Unable to appeal to a religious imprimatur, she locates her authority as a writer in various allegorical and prophetic female figures: the sibyls or the personifications of Justice, Reason, and Droitture who narrate the *Cité des dames*. The sequence of narratives that make up the martyrology in the last section of the *Cité des dames* is thus one of the few places where her otherwise secular corpus deploys the discourses of religion. The oddity of the martyrs' legends in Christine's work is worth stressing—female writing in this period was typically couched in religious terms, but Christine's writing was usually of a secular nature. In the last section of the *Cité*, her material is closer to that used by other women writing at the time (as is seen in her choice to narrate a story also dramatized by Hroswitha). In a sense then, Christine's normal practice anticipates the secularity of later renaissance women authors—whose use of religious subject matter was to provide an authorizing discourse for writing careers in fact carried on in secular circumstances.[11]

In an historical sense, the appeal to the saints is the *least* radical element in Christine's program to ground her female authority in the powerful discourses of her society. The more radical part of Christine's claim for authority is actually that based on the new humanist disciplines—her use of Boccaccio, her construction of her own literary tradition with Italian Dante as a founder of the line, her prefer-

---

[10]See Catherina Wilson, *Women Writers of the Middle Ages* (Athens: University of Georgia Press, 1985).

[11]Fredric Jameson, "Religion and Ideology: *Paradise Lost*," in *Literature, Politics, and Theory: Papers from the Essex Conference*, ed. Francis Barker et al. (London: Methuen, 1986), pp. 38–39, has argued about the function of religious discourse in that later Renaissance moment, showing how, in a precapitalist society, religion provided the vocabulary for social contestation: "religious and theological debate is the form, in pre-capitalist societies, in which groups become aware of their political differences and fight them out." A century earlier the public language of sainthood may have provided Christine and her readers with a means for opening a space in which to discuss, with a distinct textual specificity, bodily practices that had immediate political dimensions.

ence for Petrarch's authority over Boccaccio's—all such moves of nascent Italian humanism position her in a very untraditional place. Jacqueline Cerquiglini has emphasized Christine's own triple exile— first as an Italian living in France, then as an author writing in a second language, and finally as a woman who constitutes herself as a writing subject, withdrawn from the world into a new place of the self.[12] Her very authority is based on a "new pride of the writer," "orgueil nouveau de l'écrivain," that later Renaissance literary figures would proclaim (p. 247).

Yet as Pierre Bourdieu points out, "competence" in linguistic performance does not merely mean grammatical correctness or the clarity of communication; rather it includes more fundamentally "the right to speech." By this Bourdieu means the right to speak the "authorized language which is also the language of authority. Competence implies the power to impose reception."[13] In a sense, Christine's pronounced preference for the Dante of the *Commedia* signals her preference for the vernacular—for any vernacular over Latin. Her preference is doubly motivated in the *Cité des dames*—because she is a woman and because her primary audience is made up of women. These two facts are of central importance to the *Cité;* they can be said to constitute an important parameter of the text's production. Her use of the discourses of misogyny—her interpolation of misogynist topoi into her text so that they become the pivot points of her argument—is part of her mastering of the "master discourse," her turning it to speak her own ends.

So too, in telling French stories of the early Christian saints— against the authority of Boccaccio's Latin text (its Latin language indicates its masculine audience) and of Vincent of Beauvais's Latin *Speculum historiale*—Christine makes in part III a move parallel to her use of the texts of misogyny in part I.[14] Martyrology is a well-

---

[12]Cerquiglini emphasizes the gender switch in the *Mutacion de fortune* as another instance of her being "l'étranger à soi meme." See "L'étrangère," *Revue des Langues Romanes: Christine de Pizan* 92 (1988), 239–51.

[13]Pierre Bourdieu, "The Economics of Linguistic Exchanges," in *Social Science Information* 16 (1977), 648.

[14]Maureen Curnow points out that whatever possible, Christine used a translation. In the context of the various audiences possible for a vernacular text in translation, it is interesting that Earl Jeffrey Richards reinstitutes the Latin title for Vincent of Beauvais's collection. Whereas Christine refers to it in its French translation—the *Miroir historiale*—the modern English text published in 1982 prints the Latin *Speculum*

defined, august, fully authorized genre that legitimates narratives of specific female experience. The lives of the saints are written in a vernacular language that, at the same time, has as a language a parallel authority in Latin because the veneration of the saints was institutionalized by the power of the Latin church. Although canonized, the saints were not, however, merely a function of the authority of the Church. With enough popular pressure, the church could be moved—and often was moved very quickly—to canonize individuals the people had chosen.[15] Yet no less a church father than Augustine had already enthroned the saints as the quintessential citizens of the civitas dei.[16] Christine peoples her city with saints on good authority.

It is also useful for Christine's purpose that the saints always appear in Vincent's collection identified by their city—indeed far more often by this means than by their familial relations. Martyrdom was a phenomenon of the late Roman world, when the Roman empire was still intact, exerting its fundamental emphasis upon the city as the basic unit of civilization. Martyrdom in this sense is literally a political process and needs a polis—a city—in which to take place. Each woman whose story Justice relates in part III comes from a different city and is simultaneously taken both into the city of God and into the text of the city of ladies. It is thus of some significance that the first vita Justice narrates concerns Catherine of Alexandria, the famous Egyptian capital. In the late-antique Mediterranean world, the learned virgin-martyr Catherine was the heroine of Alexandria. The selection of Catherine is not in itself at all unusual, but the choice does have the effect of finally bringing that particular

---

historiale. In questions of authority and canonization, the appeal to Latin is a hedge against criticism. Whether or not Christine knew Latin is a real question; in any case, her preference for the vernacular is everywhere. See Curnow, ed., "The *Livre de la Cité des Dames* of Christine de Pisan: A Critical Edition," 2 vols. (Ph.D. diss., Vanderbilt University, 1975).

[15]Catherine of Siena died in 1380 and was canonized in 1411–13.

[16]Hagiography itself as a subject of study does not, however, have the same legitimacy as theology. In his foreword to Peter Brown's *Cult of the Saints*, Joseph Kitagawa speaks of the two-tiered model of religious history which draws a huge distinction between the theology of the elite and the popular superstition of the masses, a codification that studies such as Brown's are helping to change. See Peter Brown, *The Cult of the Saints: Its Rise and Function in Latin Christianity* (Chicago: University of Chicago Press, 1981).

city into the line of cities that have prepared the way for the city of ladies. By this means, Christine fills a noticeable lacuna caused when she refused to name Cleopatra as one of her city's citizens. Rather than treating Cleopatra as a martyr herself—as Chaucer parodically does—Christine reserves a place for the actual Alexandrian martyr. While Catherine and all the female martyrs whose stories follow hers are not a part of the metaphor of city construction, their presence nonetheless translates the notion of the city into a different realm of politics, one that transcends history yet is a part of it.

Local History

In the cité des dames, there are, naturally, no male saints—save for a short list, given, interestingly enough, at the very end of the section, a list in which male saints are mentioned in relation to their being served by exemplary female saints. These women—including St. Plautilla, who comforted St. Paul at his martyrdom, and St. Ephegenia, who built a church to honor St. Matthew—serve (in a closing reprise of the city metaphor) as the "portes et de clostures en nostre cité" (p. 1031), "as doors and windows of our city" (p. 254). The architectural metaphor doubtless reasserts itself in order to bring the work to formal closure; but the device also serves to relegate these handmaiden, secondary saints to a metaphorical position that is distinguished from that of the martyrs. This is not to say that such women's achievements are without merit; indeed, the serving of male saints, the retrieval of relics, and the construction of churches were ways in which women were originally active in the cult of the saints.[17] As part II, however, had segregated women who were "accidentally" renowned by virtue of their relations with men, so the disposition of Christine's city itself privileges those saints who were autonomously active females.

In this sense, as well as in its virtually complete exclusion of male saints, the 1405 Cité participates in a contemporary historical development—the increasingly greater social presence of female saints in

[17]Patrick Geary, Furta Sacra: Thefts of Relics in the Central Middle Ages (Princeton: Princeton University Press, 1978).

late medieval society. Recent work on the sociology of sainthood has discovered through statistical analysis of the vitae that the comparative number of canonized females had been on the rise since the twelfth century, when 11.8 percent of all saints were women, to the mid-fifteenth, when 27.7 percent were women.[18] In *Holy Feast and Holy Fast: The Religious Significance of Food to Medieval Women*, Caroline Walker Bynum suggests that such statistics also reveal a real relocation of female authority towards an increasingly secular place in society—with all its attendant risks. Almost three-quarters of all noninstitutionalized, lay people canonized in the fourteenth century were women, but these secular, outstandingly pious females were at high risk (economically, socially, and politically) simply because of their deinstitutionalized isolation: According to Bynum, after the early fourteenth century "the forms and themes of women's religiosity aroused increased hostility. . . . Although holy women were by the fourteenth and fifteen centuries more likely to be lay and married, to reside in the world, and to have opportunities for significant geographical mobility . . . they were also more subject to male scrutiny and in greater danger of being accused of heresy or witchcraft" (p. 23). As Bynum argues, such increased hostility—and vulnerability—may have been a response to the new possibilities available for women to shape "their own religious experiences in lay communities" by taking on "a clear alternative—the prophetic alternative—to the male role based on the power of office" (p. 22). Such speculation on this "prophetic alternative" lends a contemporaneous sociological weight to Christine's emphasis on various traditions of prophecy, particularly in a text titled for its community of women, the "*City* of Ladies."

The martyred saints in the *Cité des dames* are all early Christians, killed for their refusal to worship the gods of evil pagan emperors and tyrants. If we look first, however, at the life of a saint nearly contemporaneous with Christine, we may be able to sense the cultural possibilities open to spiritual women at the time she was writing. Catherine of Siena died in 1380. She expressed her piety in a way we now label a mental and physical disease. She suffered from what

---

[18]"This increase is even more impressive when we consider that the total number of saints in our sample declined from 153 in the twelfth century to 83 in the fifteenth. In short, the proportion of women in the ranks of new saints continued to increase even during a time of overall downturn." Weinstein and Bell, *Saints and Society*, pp. 220–21.

historian Rudolph Bell calls "holy anorexia," a set of food disorders which ultimately led to her death by starvation.[19] In *Holy Feast*, Bynum also analyzes Catherine of Siena's life as a way of understanding the specially gendered significance that food practices of all sorts—including extreme asceticism to the point of death by starvation—had for women throughout the Middle Ages. Both Bell and Bynum are careful to point out the manifest differences between medieval and modern assumptions about the extremity of such food practices—there is a great cultural gap between holy anorexia and anorexia nervosa. The difference lies in each culture's valuation of extreme fasting, the medieval often deeming it proof of sainthood and the modern deeming it a massive cultural failure of family socialization.

The pertinent point of Catherine's vita for our purposes is the immense political authority she gained over the church hierarchy at the high point of her power: she used this authority to help persuade a pope to return from Avignon to Rome. There was, obviously, more to Catherine than her fasting—but as a central part of her vita, the fasting supports not merely a teenager's rebellion against a constricting family, but her entry into a larger world of public, political activity.

Catherine of Siena is a useful historical example both because such bizarrely extreme food practices indicate some of the religious possibilities in Christine de Pizan's own culture at the time and also because Catherine's self-starvation shares with martyrology a structural feature that most other avenues of saintliness do not.[20] As

[19]Rudolf Bell, *Holy Anorexia* (Chicago: University of Chicago Press, 1985), p. 46: "from the outset her vocation was public and reforming rather than private and penitential."

[20]The connection between martyrdom and anorexia—often staged in an adolescent's struggle with her mother—may help us to connect the martyrology with Christine's distinct emphasis on the position of the mother in the tradition of female authority. As we have seen, the presence of Christine's own mother on the very first page of the *Cité* is the text's first and most distinct gendering; so too, Christine will rewrite all mothers out of the position of the tyrannical parent in part III—it is her most consistent difference from Vincent of Beauvais. The mother/daughter struggle over food fuels the power of Catherine's familial rebellion. See especially Caroline Walker Bynum, *Holy Feast and Holy Fast: The Religious Significance of Food to Medieval Women* (Berkeley: University of California Press, 1987), pp. 223–24: "Thus by a series of ascetic behaviors, Catherine slowly forged for herself, without ever leaving home, a life whose values were utterly different from those of her wealthy

Weinstein and Bell point out, martyrdom "stands dramatically apart from" other categories of sainthood. "In marked contrast to popular notions of the saint as a miracle-working vessel of supernatural power, the martyr is a hero honored as a supreme example of how men and women *by the exercise of their own will* can further God's work" (p. 160; emphasis added). Like the extreme asceticism that became popular during the plague-tormented and penance-ridden fourteenth century, the political defiance of the early martyrs expressed the power of a single human will in combat with repressive institutional forces that would enforce a dominant ideology. Paradoxically, both types of self-"sacrifice" (willed starvation, martyrdom) are enactments of an individual will that take its expression to the absolute boundary of death. The anorexic's insistence that the visions inspired by abstinence come directly from God is in direct opposition to the institutionalized passivity required of women by the church. As Bell goes on to argue, "The holy anorexic never gives in, and ultimately she may die of her austerities. She rejects the passive, dependent Catholic religion of mediation through priests and intercession by saints, and so herself becomes a saint" (p. 19).

Martyrdom even more crucially insists upon the "motif of human agency" (Weinstein and Bell, p. 160). Miracle-working healers are passive conduits for the powerful presence of God. Unlike martyrs, they are not themselves the agents of their power. Of course, all a martyr need do is be killed. However, such a seemingly passive death is almost always the result of an active and individually willed resistance to external pressure from a political power, pressure usually in the form of explicit and detailed torture. In martyrdom, the body becomes a site of dramatic contestation between institutions of power and the self—in Christine's text, the female self—for control over the body. All forms of saintliness have in common this insistence on the body, either its sacrifice (as a sacred offering) or its ritualized control by fasting or more especially, through restraint of the sexual appetite of both men and women. Paradoxically, martyrdom (the ultimate restraint of the body) does not end in a transcen-

---

merchant father and her doting efficient mother with a brood of twenty children. It took a miracle to bring her father to acceptance of her life; and her mother—who understood only too well what it meant—seems never to have been completely reconciled to it."

dence that denigrates the physical vessel in order to exalt the separable soul, but on the contrary constitutes an individual performance of the dramatic centrality of the body to Christian theology. Each martyr's death, as a pattern of Christ's own passion, replicates the Incarnation.

Genre and History

In an argument about the evolving history of genre, Fredric Jameson points out that features that shaped the specific social formation to whose internal contradictions the genre first spoke are still present in the genre's message through later reappropriations of the form. As he puts it:

> in its emergent, strong form a genre is essentially a socio-symbolic message, or in other terms, that form is imminently and intrinsically an ideology in its own right. When such forms are reappropriated and refashioned in quite different social and cultural contexts, this message persists and must be functionally reckoned into the new form. . . . The ideology of the form itself, thus sedimented, persists into the later, more complex structure as a generic message which coexists . . . with elements from later stages. (p. 141)

It is not absolutely necessary to historicize Christine's use of saints vitae by appealing to a generic sedimentation, for as we have seen, saints such as Catherine of Siena were in fact being canonized during Christine's lifetime. Yet she never avails herself of contemporary examples in part III: all of the martyrs she mentions are early Christians, whose legends came from the first centuries of embattled Christianity, before the religion itself became an official state institution.[21] By the same token, one does not have to posit full inten-

---

[21]For a discussion of asceticism in pre-Augustinian terms—before the institutionalization of the church—see Elaine Pagels, *Adam, Eve, and the Serpent* (New York: Random House, 1988); Pagels argues that ascetic practices before Augustine were based in freedom, not in guilt. Early martyrs were not atoning for sins but imitating Christ's transcendence, not taming the flesh but escaping the world. The theology of various ascetic practices has changed through history.

tionality for Christine's use of early Christian saints in order to excavate the particular relevance of their political history to her own. But the notion of generic embeddedness helps us to see how the past social history of hagiography may have continued to inform spiritual possibilities for women within the cults of the later Middle Ages and therefore to shape the function of the saints' vitae within the text of the *Cité*.

If we make an effort to reclaim the charm of the saints, we find ourselves quite quickly in the realm of a paradoxically transtemporal, yet physically embodied, sense of power. In his fascinating study, *The Cult of the Saints*, Peter Brown has argued that the peculiar veneration of the dead in saint cults allowed the late antique world to reorganize its culture in ways that radically changed the face of western Europe. His subtle argument is complex and suggestive, but what is most significant (for the purposes of understanding what a later recasting of vitae might be invoking from the earlier cult forms) is Brown's insistence on two facts: First, in reorganizing the relationship between the living and the dead, the cult of the saints reshaped actual cities, bringing cemeteries inside the walls and allowing for the founding of cities within graveyards. "The impact of the cult of saints on the topography of the Roman city was unambiguous: it gave greater prominence to areas that had been treated as antithetical to the public life of the living city; by the end of the period, the immemorial boundary between the city of the living and the dead came to be breached by the entry of relics and their housing within the walls of many late-antique towns, and the clustering of ordinary graves around them" (pp. 4–5). Brown's second point is one related to the reorganization of the city's public spaces: from the beginning, the cult of the saints had a special appeal to women. Previously, the individual death of an ordinary human was a private, family experience. In the cult of the saints, however, such a death became public, the tomb a place of congregation, and women, as traditional handlers of the dead body, assumed a more prominent, publicly ceremonial function.

The transgressive crossing of boundaries, between city and noncity, dead and living, public and private, allowed a massive restructuring of society—one that located female power in a new arena at the grave site of the saint. This was, we must strive to understand, a very privileged place in the early Christian world: "Filled with great candelabra, their dense clusters of light mirrored in shimmering mosaic and caught in the gilded roof, worship at the martyr's tomb brought the still light of the Milky Way to within a few feet of the grave" (Brown, p. 4). If the cult of the saints became, in Brown's terms, a "public language," it was a language that not only lasted throughout Europe deep into the Middle Ages (p. 49), but a language that, when spoken by a woman, could guarantee her "a public role in the Christianized city" (p. 47).[22]

The position of women both as saints themselves, subjects of their own vitae, and as attendants to the narrative of saints in cult form allows a newly opened *public* space for female political activity— that is, their fully visible activity within the polis, their engagement in the business of the community in nonprivate, public ways. Most importantly, it is this notion of publicness which creates one of the other large differences between the privacy of the merely visionary saints and the public deaths of state-executed martyrs. Christine's specific emphasis is often on the latter type of saints' vitae—with their stagey display of torture in large arenas before audiences of thousands—a public site that guarantees for the scene of torture very real political effects.

The Politics of Torture

In *The Body in Pain: The Making and Unmaking of the World,* Elaine Scarry offers terms we can usefully borrow to see how martyrdom in particular rewrites the politics of torture. First of all, Scarry points out that torture does indeed have a "structure."[23] It is divisible into three simultaneous elements: first is "inflexion"—that is, the

22"The Christian church not only redefined the bounds of the community by accepting a whole new class of recipients, it also designated a new class of givers. For women had been the other blank on the map of the classical city. It was assumed that gift-giving was an act of politics, not an act of mercy; and politics was for men only. By contrast, the Christian church, from an early time, had encouraged women to take on a public role, in their own right, in relation to the poor: they gave alms in person, they visited the sick, they founded shrines and poorhouses in their own name, and were expected to be fully visible as participants in the ceremonial of the shrines" (Brown, p. 46).

23Elaine Scarry, *The Body in Pain: The Making and Unmaking of the World* (Oxford: Oxford University Press, 1985), chap. 1.

actual infliction of bodily pain to a level of intensity approaching the boundary of death, in which the "contents of consciousness are destroyed" (Scarry, p. 31). Simultaneously, there is the second element, the interrogation, staged not to extract necessary information, but to extract by torture a "confession" that is itself an incoherent dramatization of the victim's loss of voice through pain. The loss can then be put to the service of the third process, the translation of the victim's pain into the state's power—a transformation of the objectified attributes of pain into the insignia of power.

At the center of all scenes of torture are these intricately exchanging dynamics between body and voice. As Scarry explains, "The goal of the torturer is to make the one, the body, emphatically and crushingly *present* by destroying it, and to make the other, the voice, *absent* by destroying it. It is in part this combination that makes torture, like any experience of great physical pain, mimetic of death; for in death the body is emphatically present while that more elusive part represented by the voice is so alarmingly absent that heavens are created to explain its whereabouts" (p. 49).

Scarry notes that in the narratives told by torture victims, there constantly recurs mention of some sign that enables the sufferer to persist—be it a smuggled message however anonymous or a mere cry of encouragement in the night—in other words, specifically a verbal sign. Endurance is made possible by the reintroduction of a voice that speaks for and as the victim: "Voices speaking the voice of the person silenced—these acts return to the prisoner his most elemental political ground as well as his psychic content and density" and are "finally almost physiological in their power of alteration" (p. 50).

I have extracted the reciprocal dynamic of body and voice, at the risk of doing some violence to Scarry's nuanced argument, because I think these twin terms of exchange may help to illuminate the structure of a central set of torture scenes in Christine's *Cité des dames*. No legend is more peculiarly poised to represent the problems of Christine's own female authority than the story of St. Christine, her patron saint. In it appear in enhanced form most of the details that so repetitiously pattern many of the legends in part III, those of saints Margaret, Lucy, Barbara, Martina, and others. Significantly, the details of St. Christine's story also speak directly to the question of voice and the subjectivity that the bodily experience of speaking implicitly enunciates.

It is first important to notice that the timing of the narration of

St. Christine's story indicates the difference between Christine de Pizan's own authority and that of her main auctor for the martyrology, Vincent of Beauvais. The position of the story again restages her intervention into the canon of auctores. Although she has been using Vincent for a number of the legends that immediately precede the story of St. Christine, she only names him as her auctor immediately before Justice begins to narrate this central vita. Justice further explains that she will speak at greater length about St. Christine than about other saints, thereby both indicating the greater importance of this pivotal story and implicitly signaling the persistent revisionary differences between Christine de Pizan's and Vincent of Beauvais's versions of the legends.

> Se de toutes les saintes vierges qui sont ou ciel part constance de martire te vouloye racompter, longue hystoire y couvendroit: si comme sainte Ceille, sainte Agnés, sainte Agathe, et inffinies autres. Et se plus en veulx avoir, ne t'estuet que regarder ou *Mirouer historial* la assez en trouveras. Sy te diray encores de sainte Christine: et pource qu'elle est ta maraine et moult est vierge de grant dignité, plus a plain t'en diray de la vie, qui moult est belle et devotte. (p. 1000)

> If you want me to tell you all about the holy virgins who are in Heaven because of their constancy during martyrdom, it would require a long history, including Saint Cecilia, Saint Agnes, Saint Agatha, and countless others. If you want more examples, you need only look at the *Speculum historiale* of Vincent de Beauvais, and there you will find a great many. However, I will tell you about Saint Christine, both because she is your patron and because she is a virgin of great dignity. Let me tell you at greater length about her beautiful and pious life. (p. 234)

The most significant difference between Christine's and Vincent's versions of St. Christine's story is the *Cité*'s treatment of her parents. Christine de Pizan entirely suppresses mention of the saint's mother. She makes the tyrant Urben not merely Christine's father, but her sole parent. A pagan tyrant who tries to coerce his twelve-year-old daughter into worshiping his gods, Urben shuts her up in a tower with twelve ladies-in-waiting so that she may worship the pagan idols placed there (Figure 34).[24]

[24]The only other saint in Christine's collection to be tortured by her own father is also shut up in a tower: St. Barbara's story bears many parallels to St. Christine's. See pp. 998–99; Richards, pp. 232–33.

34. The legend of St. Christine, *Miroir historial*, Ms. Ffr. 313, f. 236v. Paris, Bibliothèque Nationale

The miniaturist who illustrated this scene represents two kinds of idols before St. Christine: the dark one stands for the external infidel, the actual pagan, while the lighter idol represents the "internal" infidel, the heretic in the truth. The nakedness of both speaks to idolatry, always a potential danger, in the intense attractions of sexuality. The young virgin saint gestures as if to protect herself from sexual assault.[25] When St. Christine's waiting women confess that she has not been sacrificing to his idols, specifically to Jupiter, the father god, but has instead been looking out the window to pray to a single celestial god, Urben, enraged by her obstinacy, has her tortured. First, she is stripped naked (as almost all these beautiful virgin

---

[25]Weinstein and Bell report that 80 percent of all saints did not marry; it is by far and away the dominant shared characteristic among all saints. *Saints and Society*, table 3, pp. 146–47.

martyrs are), beaten by twelve men, tied on a wheel over a fire, and has rivers of boiling oil poured over her body. Miraculously, three angles break the wheel so that St. Christine is delivered "healthy and whole." In the meantime, more than a thousand pagan spectators are miraculously slain because they've watched this torture without pity. Their collective cruelty neatly dramatizes the usual boundary of differentiation which, as Scarry argues, is drawn in the scene of torture between the victim, who suffers pain, and the torturer, who by definition suffers none, not even a sensitivity to the pain he is inflicting. Here, however, under the power of miracle, the thousand pitiless spectators become victims themselves and are slain, thereby breaking down the barrier between torturer and victim, as martyr-dom reassigns positions in the scene of torture. The crowd of cruel pagans turned victims is an undifferentiated mass; we are not told exactly what constitutes their infidel nature. The crowd is, of course, explicitly here constituted as alien "others" whose lack of pity legitimates the pitiless exercise of God's power on behalf of the saint. The saint who suffers is not merely passive, but is able to slay whole populations. Such an event demonstrates the fundamental violence of the political power that is exercised in these scenes of retribution.

Urben next decides to drown his daughter; he has his men tie a great stone around her neck and throw her into the sea. Again angels save her, and she is able to walk on the water with them. Praying, she asks that the water be for her the holy sacrament of baptism. At this point Christine de Pizan alters her source in a most interesting way. Her handling of the scene of baptism—which importantly includes the conferral of the name of "Christine"—makes of Vincent's meta-phorical episode a literal event. In his text, the waters are only a "signacle de beptesme" and God's presence is only rendered by signs: first, by a voice saying that "our father" has heard her prayer; second, by a crown and a purple star descending upon the saint's head while angels sing her praises. In the *Cité*, Jesus Christ himself descends in his own person with a great company of angels, baptizes the saint, and names her Christine *from his own name:* "en propre personne a grant compagnie d'anges et la baptisa et nomma de son nom Chris-tine" (p. 1005). He then crowns her and puts a resplendent star on her head. That night her father Urben is tortured by devils, and he dies, his lack of sympathy thereby revealed to be demonic.

The granting of the baptismal name "Christine" from Christ's own name in the *Cité* is nowhere mentioned in the *Miroir*, nor is the baptism the literal sacrament that it is in the *Cité;* Vincent does not reiterate St. Christine's loyal suffering for Christ's "nom." Already infused with voice in Vincent's text, the saint's torture is thereby translated into martyrdom. But Christine further revises Vincent to make the baptism one of two central events in the vita, both of which concern the saint's name. Far from suppressing the victim's voice, this scene of torture completely reverses the dynamic of domination. The death of the father then punctuates the legend by closing the chapter in which the miraculous rebirth of his daughter has been celebrated by her baptism with Christ's own name. The emphasis in Christine's rewrite of the legend of St. Christine on the baptismal granting of the name offers a most significant variation from the usual pattern of saints' lives. As Alison Goddard Elliott explains, "One of the clearest indications of the collective ethos of passion literature is the frequency with which martyrs abandoned their personal names in favor of generic identification, " 'Christianus sum'. . . . Names . . . do not serve to distinguish one saint from another. What the name 'Christianus' does is to distinguish one religion from another."[26] Christine thus takes the generic identification of the term "Christianus" and by wordplay with the name of her patron saint, transforms the generic label "chrestiene" into a fully particularized granting of special Christological authority to the name "Christine." Her own name becomes an allegory of her individual authority.

As the narrative continues, the voice of Saint Christine continues to maintain its supernatural political power throughout the process of physical torture by a second tyrant. To the saint's ability (mentioned in Vincent's text) to make an idol crumble by prayer, the *Cité* adds her capacity under torture to sing and mock her torturers, so that through her, "plus de trois mil hommes furent converties" (p. 1006); "more than three thousand men were converted through the words and signs of this virgin" (p. 238). The language of the saint under public torture has the power not only to destroy masses but also to convert them. The power is represented as political. In some sense, of course, the conversion is no less an annihilation of the "other" than the earlier parallel destruction of a thousand onlookers, for conversion erases otherness by turning it into the same.

After the second tyrant also dies a failure, the third, Julian, takes a

[26]Alison Goddard Elliott, *Roads to Paradise: Reading the Lives of the Early Saints* (Hanover: University Press of New England, 1987), pp. 20–21.

different tack. He has snakes set upon St. Christine. These asps, adders, and vipers merely nurse at her breasts however, in a discomforting image that conflates the visual elements of key Old and New Testament scenes and the image transforms Edenic tragedy into comedy through the powers of motherhood. The sacrificial complications of such an answer to Old Testament stories about snakes are further enacted when Julian has Christine's breasts cut off, and, although she is virgin, they bleed both blood and milk. This miraculous simultaneity of bodily fluids, exhibited by all the mutilated virgin martyrs in the *Cité*, conflates maternality with virginity. Throughout all this torture, St. Christine "san cesser nommoit le nom de Jhesu Crist" (p. 1008), "unceasingly pronounced the name of Jesus Christ" (p. 239), until finally Julian commands that her tongue be cut out so she cannot continue to prophesy.[27] The tongue is duly "coupee." But the saint goes on speaking of divine things even more clearly than before. Hearing God's voice comforting Christine (the voice speaking is, in Scarry's terms, the voice of the person silenced), Julian charges the executioners to cut off her tongue "so short that she cannot speak to her Christ." His henchmen rip out her tongue and cut it off at the root. But immediately:

> Et celle cracha le couppon de sa langue au visaige du tirant et luy en creva l' ueil. Et luy dist aussi sainement que oncques mais: "Tirant, que te vault avoir couppee my language adfin que elle ne beneysse Dieu, quant mon esperit a tousjours la benystra et le tien demourera perpetual en maleysson? Et pource que tu ne cognois ma parolle, c'est bien raison que ma langue t'ait aveuglé." (p. 1009)

> She spat out this cut-off piece of her tongue into the tyrant's face, putting out one of his eyes. She then said to him, speaking as clearly as ever, "Tyrant, what does it profit you to have my tongue cut out so that it cannot bless God, when my soul will bless Him forever, while yours languishes forever in eternal damnation. And because you did not hear my words, my tongue has blinded you, with good reason." (pp. 239–40)

[27]Edmund Spenser may well have known the *Cité des dames* in a 1521 translation by Bryan Aynsley; it is interesting to note therefore that his image for the torture of a poet in the fifth book of *The Faerie Queene* (the book of Justice) presents this figure with his tongue nailed to a post. Spenser also restages multiple dismemberments and mutilations of bodies in his representation of the capital power of the state, most notably the decapitation of an Amazon.

Transformed into a martyr's legend, the narrative of torturing dismemberment not only determinedly refuses to sacrifice the voice to the body, which takes on a virtuous silence as in Boccaccio's story about Leana, but allows the body in pain to continue to speak. In a sense, St. Christine's story translates dismemberment into martyrdom when the tongue puts out the eye of the voyeuristic male gaze; it says, "Hear me speak: understand that because you have not heard me—have not granted me the authority of my own beliefs—I speak to prove you blinded by your gaze."

By putting out the eye of the torturer, St. Christine's tongue reveals by a fleshly metonymy the author's "voice," which is here not only an emblem of the power of martyrdom and of the peculiar dynamics of Christian physical suffering, but also—and most profoundly of all—of Christine de Pizan's own authority. Unlike the women who did not speak in their own defense, unlike Boccaccio's Leana, whose literally tongue-biting silence he celebrates as the best kind of womanly eloquence, Christine de Pizan takes that moment of dismemberment and, rewriting it in the story of her own patron saint, makes it a narrative that authorizes her own peculiarly female authorship—simultaneously authorizing the very writing of the book of the city of ladies.

In the *Miroir*, the saint hurls at the tyrant a less witty if far more gruesome denunciation:

> Je condamne mengie en tenebras les members de mon corps. Tu les avois destruez & tu a trenchee ma langue qui beneissoit dieu. Et pource as tu droicturierment perdue sa veue.

> I condemn you to eat in hell the parts of my body. You have destroyed and torn out my tongue which blessed God. And for that you have rightly lost your sight.[28]

In both texts a literal, physical tongue puts out a literal, physical eye. But the grisly humor of Vincent's version, with its Dantesque contrapasso punishment—whereby the tyrant is doomed to eat the body parts of the saint he has so hideously dismembered—sacrifices

---

[28]Vincent de Beauvais, *Miroir historial*, Ms. Ffr. 313, f. 485, Paris, Bibliothèque Nationale; my translation.

the saint's body, if only metaphorically, to hell. In Christine's text, this body is carefully kept and textualized. In the *Miroir*, "un home de son lignage" writes the saint's legend, after she is finally killed by decapitation—the only method of execution to which the martyrs appear to be vulnerable. Such a vulnerability, however, is triumphant, because the decapitation merely ends the earthly trial, as the saint is freed to take up her citizenship in heaven. In Vincent's text, the masculine gendering of the writer of St. Christine's legend is thus doubly inscribed, first by saying that the author was a man and then by specifying that he was of St. Christine's "lignage." Lineage referred then to agnatic relations defined by filiation through a single male.[29]

In the *Cité*, a more complicated thing happens: "Et un sien parent que elle avoit converti enseveli le saint corps et escript sa glorieuse legend" (p. 1009). A relative of hers, whom she had converted, buried the saint's body and wrote her glorious legend. Not only does the *Cité* keep the body and script more closely connected, describing in a single sentence the care of the dead body and the writing of the text, so that the two events become parallel activities, but the lexical choice also characterizes the writing of the legend as a less resolutely masculine activity: "parenté" is a term which referred to a female-linked, cognatic kindred.

Even the dead body inspires scriptedness. The voice of God in the text, a sympathetic response to the saint's sufferings, authorizes the voice of the sufferer (and through her the author named for her). The text stresses the saint's own sense of the relations between the power of her sacred, fleshly, physical tongue to speak the truth in its continuing miraculous confession of Christ's name and its power over the physical body of the tyrant. If her tongue has the power to blind him, it also makes masses of other people see the truth of that power—for tens of thousands are converted by the saint's miraculous invulnerability to being maimed, and her equally miraculous power to maim. This kind of suffering is not mere passivity. The dismembered tongue is capable of making a political intervention.

As Scarry has pointed out in a related argument, Christianity's innovation was to collect pain and power at the same "end" of the

---

[29]Philippe Ariès and Georges Duby, *A History of Private Life: Revelations of the Medieval World*, vol. 2, trans. Arthur Goldhammer (Cambridge: Harvard University Press, 1988), p. 112.

torture weapon—and indeed, the cross has no handle, no pain end and no power end (p. 213). Pain is empowered by being given a divinely authorized voice, one that in the midst of apparent masochism shows a centralized concern for a sentient human body that keeps its agency and its voice. The central fact of Christian faith— that the word is made flesh—changes torture into martyrdom and the silence of pain into a discourse that speaks to problems of political power.

Oedipal Relations

An apt image of the voice that refuses to be silenced, and therefore a wonderful image of the power of female authority, the narrative fact of the severed tongue continues to enact the painful price paid for that authority.[30] St. Christine's cut-off tongue represents both the power and the precariousness of female speech, especially speech not shored up by the authority of a (masculine) church that can turn narrative facts into a sacred text.

However much a local history may help us to account for the historical instrumentality of the language of the saints—how martyrdom worked to empower previously marginalized groups and how the cult of the saints retained a language that could be spoken powerfully by the weak—we are still left with the pain. We are also left with the violence against the pagan others who may either be destroyed or be converted in these stories; they are thus destroyed as other in one of two ways—by simple annihilation or by becoming the same. Perhaps even more problematically than the construction of public "others," we are left with the intimacy of relations between the victim and the perpetrators; in essence, we are left not only with masochism, but masochism enacted as relationships between intimate family members. In both versions of St. Christine's story, it is clearly established that her first torturer is the twelve-year-old girl's

---

[30]A signal moment in Alice Walker's *Meridian* is the dismemberment of Sojourner. A slave who has told terrifying stories to the master's children, Sojourner is punished by having her tongue cut out; she watches it be kicked through the dust and finally retrieves it to bury it. Where it was buried a huge tree grows; it is this tree in which the college girls sit for the novel's opening scene.

own father. His tyrannical patriarchal authority, of course, easily elides into that of the other city-governors whose political responsibilities are mirrored by his own obsessive need to enforce ideological obedience.[31] There is elision as well into the sexualized position of the tyrants in the other virgin-martyr legends who attempt to force their lustful desires on the young girls.

As a genre, saints' vitae are one of the few medieval forms that pay attention to the familial quotidian—so much so that they can be used as documents for tracing "the texture of changing human relations in the medieval family" (Weinstein and Bell, p. 17). This peculiar domestic particularity of the vitae, their focus on the familial, necessarily invites an emphasis Christine in fact goes on to accentuate in her version of the life of St. Christine and in many of the other legends she has Justice relate. Explaining male hostility to women has been a singular burden of Christine's argument throughout the text of the *Cité des dames*, and her representation of torture in the saints' vitae implicitly acknowledges that while domination exists throughout all levels of society, sadomasochistic family relations are a more intense, one might say a more personal, textbook version of it. Their pathology replicates the larger structure of society, a structure that the city of ladies is being built to counteract.[32]

As we have seen in Christine's references to her own family and to the different behaviors expected of her as a daughter and her brothers as sons, the family is a site of much that profoundly concerns her in the *Cité*. The characteristics of the genre of saints' vitae, moreover, encourage and authorize this kind of domestic emphasis. The spectacular details of Urben's torture of his daughter St. Christine are so close to some central conclusions in Freud's discussion of masochism as to make the psychoanalytic vocabulary at least initially useful for a closer analysis of Christine's text, especially because she so

---

[31]The familial site is, of course, the space of the intersection of a number of important political moves in the evolving history of Christian politics. The call to a disciplined ascetic Christian life included the rejections both of private family responsibilities and of public care for the pagan political world. The early Christian radical emphasis on celibacy was a concerted attack on pagan practices based on family; the "family" thus has a specific history local to the moment of the early martyrs. See Pagels, *Adam, Eve,* pp. 81–96, for the anti-family politics involved in virginity.

[32]For a discussion of the virtually generic conflict between family and saint, see Weinstein and Bell, *Saints and Society,* p. 67.

explicitly genders the parent male, by entirely excising a mother who is dramatically present in Vincent's version.

Freud's most specific pronouncements about masochism are in the essays "A Child Is Being Beaten" (1919) and "The Economic Problem of Masochism" (1924). Although there is much complicated trading around of the gender identities of those doing the beating and those being beaten in the fantasies Freud surveys, his proposition in the earlier essay is that "in the case of the girl the unconscious masochistic phantasy starts from the normal Oedipus attitude; in that of the boy it starts from the inverted attitude." He concludes, however, that "in both cases [of male and female children] the beating-phantasy has its origin in an incestuous attachment to the father."[33] The 1924 essay, distinguishing among three kinds of masochism, the "erotogenic," the "feminine," and the "moral," focused on the issue of the eroticization of suffering, or the "lust of pain."[34] But in both essays, it is the incestuous desire for the father which is thought to fuel the pleasure of pain. In this sense, Freud is associating normal femininity with masochism: whereas, for a male, masochism is an inversion, in which the boy plays the woman's part. Although Freud does not discuss "feminine masochism" in females (because of the nature of his material), it is inescapably his assumption that masochism attends the normal female's progress through the oedipal process. Early Freudian theory spilt much ink over this characterization of female sexuality; more recently feminist qualifications and critiques have readjusted the discussion, which, to say the least, remains profoundly problematic.[35]

---

[33]Sigmund Freud, *Sexuality and the Psychology of Love: The Collected Papers*, ed. Philip Rieff (New York: Macmillan, 1963), 7.127.

[34]Sigmund Freud, *General Psychological Theory: The Collected Papers*, ed. Philip Rieff (New York: Macmillan, 1963), 5.192.

[35]For a brief summary of the subsidence of the importance of the identification of masochism with feminine nature in contemporary psychoanalytic theory, see Jessica Benjamin, *The Bonds of Love: Psychoanalysis, Feminism, and the Problem of Domination* (New York: Pantheon, 1988), pp. 80–82 (and notes). Benjamin's own position is that the prevalence of female fantasies of masochism has something to teach us about domination at large: "From a psychoanalytic point of view, it is unsatisfactory to merely attribute the pervasiveness of submission fantasies in erotic life to cultural labeling or the derogation of women. The alternative to a biological explanation of masochism must be sought not only in culture, but in the interaction of culture and psychological processes. Cultural myths and labels, while undoubtedly destructive,

Freud's basic first emphasis on incestuous desire as the root of masochism is still very suggestive for our purposes, especially because of the contextualizing sequence in which the St. Christine story is placed. Announced by Justice, as we have noted, with a fanfare that calls attention for the first time to Vincent, Christine's literary *auctor*, St. Christine's legend is followed immediately by a set of brief tales about mother saints who have seen their children martyred, curious stories we will take up in a moment. Immediately after this group, and thus bracketing the mother saints, come two fuller vitae about nonmartyred cross-dressed saints which form a curious pair of father/daughter relationships. Of course, many of the other saints' lives are concerned with parent/child relations, but the stories of St. Christine and the two cross-dressed saints are focused on the father to an extreme—both in terms of Christine de Pizan's reorganization of Vincent's details and in terms of the sequence in which they are placed. By comparing Christine's renditions of these three extended vitae with Vincent's versions, we can see her regrouping the various elements of the oedipal triad into interesting variations on her precursor's set text. The sequence of stories reads like a series of puzzle pieces being rearranged in new configurations until they fit a discourse about child/parent relations that speaks to a specifically female experience.

Christine's revision of Vincent's legend of St. Christine makes the father's position more centrally and personally problematic. In contrast to Vincent's scene in which the saint's father merely misunderstands her promises to worship correctly (he assumes she intends to worship Jupiter, whereas she is talking about the Christian God), the *Cité* shows father and daughter carrying on an involved conversation about their various responsibilities to each other. Urben explains that he is torn between loyalty to his own flesh and to his gods; St. Christine grants her father power over her flesh, while granting her spirit to another, higher father. Distraught, Urben tells her, "Fille, pitié naturelle destraint durement mon couraige de ainsi tourmenter

---

still do not explain how the 'essence of trained femininity' gets into women's heads and is there converted into pleasurable fantasies of erotic submission. To begin to explain it, we must start with the way in which the mother's lack of subjectivity, as perceived by both male and female children, creates an internal propensity toward feminine masochism and male sadism" (p. 81).

toy qui es ma char; mais la reverence que j'ay a mes dieux me contraint a ce fair pource que tu les despites" (p. 1003). "Daughter, natural affection wrings my heart terribly to torment you who are my own flesh, but the reverence I have for my gods forces me to do this because you scorn them" (p. 235). On her side, St. Christine specifies the limits of his biological rights: "Tirant, que je ne doy appeller pere, ains annemy de ma beneurté, tourmentes hardiement la char que tu as engendree, car ce puez tu bien faire; mais a l'esperit, cree de mon Pere qui est ou ciel, n'as tu povoir d'atouchier par nulle temptacion: car Jhesu Crist, mon sauveur, la garde" (p. 1003). "Tyrant who should not be called my father but rather enemy of my happiness, you boldly torture the flesh which you engendered, for you can easily do this, but as for my soul created by my Father in Heaven, you have no power to touch it with the slightest temptation, for it is protected by my Savior, Jesus Christ" (p. 236).

In part what is effected here is simply a trade of one father for another, a substitute authority figure. The threatening personal patriarch is supplanted by a more distant (more authoritative) father who is mediated by a self-sacrificing son.[36] The personal quality of this conversation, however, with its adjudication of rights in terms of flesh, locates the familial tie in the physical, fleshly bond; and as we have seen, Christine de Pizan tends to present the physical flesh in a less derogated status than Vincent. A more radical difference (one that helps to explain the closer personal ties Christine sets up between father and daughter) is the substitution of this conversation for one that has been utterly excised between the saint and her mother. This suppression is a pivotal one.

In the *Cité des dames*, St. Christine has only one parent, her father; in the *Miroir*, the twelve year old also has a mother. The first result of the *Cité*'s excision is that the mother need not be in any way involved in the torture of her daughter; this effect provides one clear mark of the gendered difference of Christine de Pizan's authority. As she had earlier defended Semiramis's right to practice mother/son incest as an honorable, prelegal practice, her move here would seem to be a similar one: to remove the mother from any potential blame

---

[36]But see Caroline Bynum, *Jesus as Mother: Studies in the Spirituality of the High Middle Ages* (Berkeley: University of California Press, 1982) for discussion of the son's maternality in both male and female mysticism.

for the torture of her daughter. The mother, however, is not only absent, but also in a sense suppressed—the father serving as a portmanteau person for both himself and her—and this suppression raises complicated issues about the gender politics of Christine's text.

In Vincent's *Miroir*, the pagan mother has some very interesting things to say for herself. Named there only as mother and wife, St. Christine's mother is overwhelmed by a paroxysm of grief the moment she hears that her daughter is being tortured by her husband. She immediately goes to visit her child in prison and there pleads with her to relent.

Et donc sa mere femme Urben ouyante que sa fille avoit suffert si grant peine derompit ses vestemens et mist cendres sus son chief et alla a la charte et cheut aux piedz dicelle a pleur disante. Ma seule fille ayez pitie de moi qui alaictas mes mammelles qui ta len fait pour quoi tu aoures ung estrange dieu.

And then her mother, Urben's wife, hearing that her daughter had suffered such torture, tore her clothes and put ashes on her head. She went to the prison and threw herself at her child's feet, and crying said: "My only daughter, have pity on me who nursed you with my breasts: why do you worship a strange god?"[37]

St. Christine answers her mother very harshly, completely abjuring the filial relationship: "Why do you call me daughter: for you have no one in your lineage who is called a Christian [chrestienne]. Do you not know that I have my name from Christ my savior? He is the one who tests me in celestial chivalry and has armed me to conquer those who do not understand." Hearing this, the mother gives up, returns home, and denounces her child to her husband: "Et la mere oyant ce retourna a la maison & denonca tout a son mary" (II.clxxv^v).

Christine de Pizan, of course, simply translates the saint's abjuration of her mother into her rejection of her father's fleshly claims, just as later in the story she will restage the pun on the name Christine/Christian as a fully dramatized baptism. But in the process, she places the boundary between parent and child at a very different

---

[37]Vincent de Beauvais, *Miroir historial*, trans. Jean de Vignay, 5 vols. (Paris: Petit, 1531), II:clxxv^v; my translation.

place: in the *Miroir* the saint refuses to recognize her mother as a mother at all; in favor of a spiritual lineage, she denies the human bond entirely. In the *Cité*, on the other hand, the saint admits her father's legitimate claims and then argues that by his torturing of her, he has ceased to be a proper father. In both texts, the parents insist upon the connection through the flesh, the mother through her feeding of her child, the father through his engendering her; only in Christine's version does the saint acknowledge the very real claims of this flesh.

The presence of the mother is not completely lost to the third section of the *Cité* because Mary, the mother of Christ, announces, "I am and will always be the head of the feminine sex." Like Mary, the women in the stories narrated just after the legend of St. Christine have witnessed the deaths of their own children, for these are legends of "plusieurs saintes qui virent martirer leurs enffans devant elles" (p. 1010); "a number of saints who saw their children martyred before their own eyes" (p. 240). Allegory, as I have emphasized, often organizes its analysis of narrative materials by sequence. Here the sequence instantly restages the scene that in Vincent's text St. Christine's mother had tried to stop: the torture of her child. There is, however, this large difference: Vincent's pagan mother attempts to dissuade the daughter from sacrificing herself, while the *Cité*'s Christian mothers actively offer their own children for sacrifice. For Christine's saints, maternal love must be second to love of God:

O! quel est au monde plus tendre chose que mere a son enfant, ne plus grant douleur que son cuer seuffre quant male luy voit endurer? Mais par ce que je voy encores est foy plus grant chose.... Si avoit cest bonne dame oublié couraige maternel quant au corps pour l'amour de Dieu. (pp. 1010–11)

What in the world is dearer to a mother than her child, and what greater grief than that which her heart suffers seeing her child in pain? Yet ... I maintain that faith is a much greater feeling.... Thereby this good lady forgot her mother's heart as far as physical comfort was concerned for the sake of the love of God. (pp. 240–41)

Christine presents three such sacrificing mothers, and she names them explicitly, while the children (who are given names in Vincent's text) tend to lose their particularization in the *Cité*. The narration of the stories of the mothers, immediately following the legend of St. Christine (from which the mother who objects to torture has been suppressed), returns the mother to narrative status in a very different position—she shifts from speaking against martyrdom and in support of the existing political structure to speaking for martyrdom and against the present established power. Through the persona of Justice—the most political of the three figures of authority—Christine also points out directly that the maternal affection that is here conquered by faith is an affection involving the *physical* well-being, the "corps"—of the children who are sacrificed. What we see therefore are three mothers' relationships to suffering which authorize a powerful position for the mother and stage the central dramatic conflict between love and faith not in terms of a child's obedience (or disobedience), but as a conflict internal to the maternal psyche. At its most personal level, Vincent's version stages the parental conflict in terms of a triumphant statement by a daughter who abjures her mother as mother. In Christine's text, this scene is excised and then immediately transformed into a celebration of mothers capable of going so far in faith as to allow their own children to be sacrificed. In doing so, of course, they only ask of the children what the mothers themselves expect to suffer and indeed suffer—in one case dying simultaneously with the child (p. 1011).

In contrast to these quick vignettes of martyred mothers and children, the next two legends in the *Cité* abruptly switch to father/daughter relations, as expressed in the legends of two cross-dressed saints: the young virgins Maryne and Euffrosine, who dress as men in order to enter monasteries. Their legends dominate the brief section devoted to saints who were not martyrs but performed physical miracles just as astonishing as St. Christine's ability to speak without a tongue. What their stories have in common with St. Christine's is that their entry into these monasteries is directly instigated by their fathers' plans for them, though these paternal desires are very different. Maryne's father has entered the monastery before her, wishing to live a holy life there; he finds, however, that he misses his daughter terribly and with her contrives a secret plan: he asks the abbot if he may send for his son. When the loyal young Maryne enters the monastery cross-dressed as a man, she is accepted by all as her father's son, a role she continues to play after his death.

In contrast to the obedient Maryne, Euffrosine enters the monastery disguised as a man in order to *escape* her father; like so many ill-advised parents, he wishes to marry her to an unwelcome suitor. Like joining the convent (indeed, like sainthood or martyrdom), her entering a monastery is an effective way of frustrating his plan and of interrupting this one particular exchange in the generalized traffic in women. Euffrosine's disguise is also successful and she lives out her life as a monk. The sexual identity of neither woman is discovered until she dies. At that point, her dead body reveals the truth. In the case of Maryne, moreover, only at that point is her true patience in suffering adversity made known, for she had many years before been falsely accused by a peasant girl of having fathered the girl's child. Rather than prove her innocence by revealing her true sex, Maryne does not deny the false accusation; instead, she not only raises the child, she does penance through all those years, taking care of the monastery's latrines and serving its food: "the abbot ordered her to perform all the filthy and servile duties inside, to fetch water for the latrines and to wait on everyone" (p. 243). These domestic chores are, of course, two traditionally female operations, both dealing with the physical requirements of the body, its tabooed issue and its equally gendered nourishment. Ironically, the "brother" is punished by being made to perform female tasks.

Christine gives extra stress to the physicality of the revelations in Maryne's story. In contrast to Vincent's version, in the *Cité* the saint's dead female body turns out to be capable of performing great miracles. At her funeral the monks gather round:

> La vindrent tous le moines, dont un, qui n'avoit qu'un oeil, s'inclina sur le corps, le baisant par grant devoccion, et tantost la veue luy fu restituee. Ce mesmes jour celle qui avoit eu l'enffant devint hors du scens et crioit son pechié: et elle fu menee au saint corps et recouvra santé. (p. 1015)

> All the monks were there, including one brother with sight in only one eye who knelt over the body, kissing it with deep devotion, and immediately his sight was restored. On this same day the woman who bore the child went out of her mind and cried out her sin, whereupon she was led to the holy corpse and recovered her health. (p. 243)

Miracle-working Maryne has lived as a pariah in her monastery, but Euffrosine by contrast is a great star in hers, where she is known as Brother Sinaroth, famous for the great effectiveness of his sympathy. In Vincent's version, when the father of the missing Euffrosine comes to the monastery for solace at the loss of his daughter, the abbot sends him to this same sympathetic brother "Sinaroth." Recognizing her own father, the disguised Euffrosine promises him that he will in fact see his daughter again before he dies. In most of these details Christine follows Vincent quite closely. At the close of the story, however, in her handling of the saint's revelatory dead body, she differs most radically from her source. In Vincent's version, a dying Euffrosine reveals herself to her father and they become reconciled; on her death bed, she asks that no one touch her corpse but her father. In Christine's text, the living saint does not reveal herself to her father; instead the dead body itself communicates the daughter's identity.

> Un escript tenoit en sa main que nul ne luy povit oster. L'abbé et tout le couvent s'i vint essayer; mais reigns n'y faisoyent. Sur ce, la vint le pere a gran pleurs et a grans cris pour son bon amy qu'il trouva mort, ouquel estoit tout son reconfort. Et aussitot que il s'approucha du corps pour le baisier, devant tous, il ouvry la main et luy bailla l'escript. Et cil le prist et lut dedans comment elle estoit sa fille et que nul ne touchast son corps pour l'ensevelir fors luy. (p. 1018)

> The dead monk held something written in his hand which no one could remove. The abbot and all the monks tried, but they could do nothing. Thereupon the father approached in tears, sobbing for his good friend whom he saw dead and in whom had been all his consolation. As soon as he approached the body to kiss it, its hands opened in front of everyone and gave him the writing. He took it and read within how she was his daughter and that no one should touch her body to bury her except for him. (p. 245)

The newly added detail of the script in the dead body's hand is similar in its miraculous instrumentality to the still functional (if more aggressively so) tongue of the martyred St. Christine. Both bodies, one dismembered, the other dead, still have a remarkably tenacious agency. In both cases, as in the case of Maryne, the saints' bodies remain actively engaged in influencing the world of the living beyond the normal limits of the flesh. The detail of the opening hands is further connected to the legend of St. Christine because it is, in fact, a substitute embellishment for the excised miracle of the monk's restored eyesight which Christine has transposed from the story of Euffrosine to that of Maryne; this transposition of miraculous eyesight links both narratives to a central detail of the St. Christine legend: that her tongue had put out the tyrant's eye.

In trying to account for the marked insistence on incidents of blindness and restored eyesight throughout the transpositions of these legends, it will be useful to recall for a moment Freud's indication of the symbolic function of blindness as a representation of the fear of castration associated with incestuous desires—as in Oedipus's own story. In these terms, we might say that Christine takes the elements of Vincent's male vision of generational conflict and rearranges them to suit her differently gendered considerations.[38] What, for instance, is the effect of taking the miraculous restoration of eyesight from Euffrosine and giving it to Maryne? Aside from any reconsideration of the value the substitution may assign to the relative merits of an obedient versus a disobedient daughter, the transposable eyeball, so to speak, emphasizes the problem of sightedness and blindness in all three legends and thus abstracted, brings up the oedipal question directly. On the one hand, the capacity to restore eyesight bestows a miraculous power on Maryne's body—a body that was falsely accused of impregnating a woman, a body that did *not* function as a father. It grants to that body an active, magical agency that further authorizes the female-based penitence of Maryne's life— her penance becomes not merely privation but a miracle-ensuring

---

[38]Much feminist psychoanalytic argument takes off from the problem of specularity in Freud's theory, but a particularly resonant strain is to be found, not surprisingly, in film theory, dependent as film is on vision. The classic article is Laura Mulvey's "Visual Pleasure and Narrative Cinema," *Screen* 16, no. 3 (1975), 8–18, which argues that the female body is represented in film in accordance with a dominantly male scopic economy. Another extremely suggestive account that argues that the female voice is also carefully controlled to produce gender is Kaja Silverman, *The Acoustic Mirror: The Female Voice in Psychoanalysis and Cinema* (Bloomington: Indiana University Press, 1988), especially chap. 1. Silverman points out the constant slippage between the (male) viewing subject's sense of lack and a projection of that lack onto the female spectacle, as in the quick elision between the "glanz" in Freud's discussion of fetishism, meaning both the "look"—that is, the act of viewing—and a "shine"—or that which is seen (p. 20). The classic cinema, according to Silverman, is organized "to divest the female subject of any claim to discursive authority" (p. 21); a reinvestment involves then the authorizing of the female voice and includes the possibility of its speaking its own desire as author (p. 218).

patience. For Maryne, the normal round of debased female labor becomes a foundation for the miraculous power of healing. Allied with her father, herself suffering punishment for a sham fatherhood, her miraculous female body revalorizes female labor, making it the penitential equal of, if not superior to, a fatherhood that was supposed to be sinful. Her restoration of a man's eyesight is explicitly connected to the question of paternity: the episode elicits the lying woman's confession and thereby establishes the truth of a mystified fatherhood.

On the other hand, for Christine to take *from* Euffrosine the power to work miracles through the agency of her corpse is to take potency away from the *dis*obedient daughter. Such a move withdraws power from a female protagonist who, for all the particulars of the story, might just as easily have been a male: St. Francis's going naked in rejection of his father was not much more scandalous than Euffrosine's cross-dressing in rejection of hers. Yet the substitution in Euffrosine's legend of her script-bearing dead body for the restoration of another's eyesight makes the two actions at least potentially parallel. Euffrosine's announcement of her identity through the note offered her father by her dead body in a sense replicates the miracle of restored sight: in each case the miracle is connected to a revelation about paternity. Both these saints have no mothers; they are identified only in relation to fathers to whom they both offer solace— Maryne from the very first and Euffrosine at the end in the guise of the sympathetic monk. And although Euffrosine was initially disobedient, she teaches her father through her patience that (though he had been blind to this truth), her desires *had* been legitimate. In Freud's terms, Oedipus blinded himself because he was afraid of facing his desire; in these stories, as retold by Christine, female saints restore eyesight when they become able to identify themselves to their fathers in order to comfort them.

The crucial difference between the fate of St. Christine, of course, and those of the cross-dressed Maryne and Euffrosine is that the last two saints are not martyred. There is no dismemberment in either tale; the blindness is an occurrence outside of the frame of the narrative of the vita, significant only by its undoing within the boundary of the story when the saint miraculously restores the eyesight. Christine's text might then be said to take up father/daughter desire not under the aegis of dismemberment, but under that of crossdressing—protected by disguise, the daughter is not desired, is not *seen*, by the father. The daughter's self-identification is finally and simply that she is female. After the prolonged successful disguise, such a revelation is akin to miracle (and is authorized by miracle). Here, incestuous desire of daughter for father (and vice versa) does not seem to require a deeply masochistic narrative, such as we saw in the story of St. Christine. Freud's insistence that masochistic fantasy is based on desires connected specifically to the father would seem not to be borne out in Christine's revisions of the legends, but to be undermined by the lack of any physical beating or dismemberment in the stories that most protractedly deal with father/daughter relations.

As we have seen, the personal dynamic between St. Christine and her father Urben is, in the text of the *Cité*, a substitute for another conversation between the saint and her mother in the *Miroir;* Christine de Pizan's father/daughter conversation could be said to have borrowed its positional intensity from the mother/daughter relation acted out with such pathos in Vincent's text. In essence then, it would seem, by its contextual juxtaposition so close to the father/daughter narratives, that the relation with the mother suppressed out of Christine's vita of her own patron saint may be in the *Cité* the more crucial familial connection. As noted earlier, the very next set of martyrdoms Justice presents after the story of St. Christine concern mothers watching their children be tortured before they themselves are led off to martyrdom. This sequence intervenes between the legend of St. Christine and the two father/daughter stories.

Such a sequence in Christine de Pizan's text invites us to consider the place of the mother in the discourse of martyrdom; martyrdom's necessarily masochistic component may, in fact, be found not in the relationship with the father but in the relationship with the (absented) mother. Such a notion finds support in some of the more recent developments of psychoanalysis, especially those branches concerned with making psychoanalysis an accessible vocabulary for feminist gender theory.[39] Jessica Benjamin's recent argument about the problematic cultural domination of women, for instance, locates

---

[39]Freud's conclusion about the parent significant to masochism may be seen as something of a piece with his mistaken notions about the male gender of the pivotal adult in his famous study of hysteria in the case history of Dora. See particularly Toril Moi, "Representation of Patriarchy: Sexuality and Epistemology in Freud's Dora," in *In Dora's Case: Freud-Hysteria-Feminism*, ed. Charles Bernheimer and Claire Kahane (New York: Columbia University Press, 1985), pp. 181–99, but also passim.

the origins of domination in an oedipal complex paradoxically mis-understood by classical psychoanalytic theory. Her solution may be stated simply because it is something like Alexander's solution to the Gordian knot: "The father's ascendancy in the Oedipus complex spells the denial of the mother's subjectivity, and thus the breakdown of mutual recognition. At the heart of psychoanalytic theory lies an unacknowledged paradox: the creation of difference distorts, rather than fosters, the recognition of the other. Difference turns out to be governed by the code of domination" (p. 135). Her solution to the problem of dominance calls for inserting the mother's subjectivity into the oedipal triangle.

More specifically relevant to a reading of the extreme visions of torture and dismemberment in the *Cité des dames* is another at-tempt by a female psychoanalyst to understand the problem of a culturally experienced masochism. In *Powers of Horror: An Essay on Abjection*, Julia Kristeva analyzes the results of an insufficient dif-ferentiation between the subject and the "abject" in relation to the maternal body.[40] Her argument is an important means of opening up questions about the *Cité*, both because she discusses the abject in relation to the maternal body and because she suggests that the experience of abjection—that "crossroads of phobia, obsession, and perversion"—is involved with the project of writing itself.

Masochism and Motherhood

What Kristeva calls the "abject" is a failure of the development of a proper set of relations between the person as subject and the first parental objects, mother and father. Abjection involves a lack of boundary between subject and object, between the self and an engulf-ing maternal body. Food, excrement, blood, and milk all blur the borderline necessary for the creation of identity, system, order; it is a borderline that de-marks the difference between the maternal body and the "clean and proper self."

[40]Julia Kristeva, *Powers of Horror: An Essay on Abjection*, trans. Leon S. Roudiez (New York: Columbia University Press, 1982).

The body's inside . . . shows up in order to compensate for the collapse of the border between inside and outside. It is as if the skin, a fragile container, no longer guaranteed the integrity of one's "own and clean self" but, scraped or transparent, invisible or taut, gave way before the dejection of its contents. Urine, blood, sperm, excrement then show up in order to reassure a subject that is lacking its "own and clean self." The abjection of those flows from within suddenly become the sole "object" of sexual desire—a true "ab-ject" where man . . . crosses over the horrors of maternal bowels. (p. 53)

Both male and female "devotees of the abject . . . do not cease looking, with what flows from the other's 'innermost being,' for the desirable and terrifying, nourishing and murderous, fascinating and abject inside of the maternal body" (p. 54).

According to Kristeva, the indistinguishable confusion of boundaries, inside and outside, subject and object, pain in pleasure and pleasure in pain is bound up in the incestuous desire not for the father but for the mother. Such abjection is a pervasive experience and is due to the simple weakness of the incest prohibition, upon which so much culture rests: following Georges Bataille, Kristeva argues that "the symbolic 'exclusory prohibition' that . . . constitutes collective existence does not seem to have . . . sufficient strength to dam up the abject or demoniacal potential of the feminine" (pp. 64–65). In *Erotism: Death and Sensuality,* Bataille goes even further in arguing about the obverse side of abjection: "The inner experience of eroticism demands from the subject a sensitiveness to the anguish at the heart of the taboo no less great than the desire which leads him to infringe it. This is religious sensibility, and it always links desire closely with terror, intense pleasure and anguish."[41]

Making use of Mary Douglas, Kristeva notes that many religious rituals of defilement are instituted to set up boundaries in order to ward off "the subject's fear of his very own identity sinking irretrievably into the mother" (p. 64). Dietary laws, such as prohibitions against the use of milk, all construct boundaries and operate under a logic of separation. Milk is interdicted not as food itself in injunctions such as the one against stewing a kid in its mother's milk, but

[41]Georges Bataille, *Erotism: Death and Sensuality,* trans. Mary Dalwood (San Francisco: City Light Books, 1986), p. 39.

as it may be intermixed with impurity: "such a dietary prohibition must be understood as a prohibition of incest" (p. 105). The taboo of the mother seems to be the "originating mytheme" of the "tremendous project" of separation expressed in the Old Testament dietary prohibitions in their entirety.

Christianity radically rearranges the pattern of difference and separation set up by the Old Testament. In Kristeva's terms, abjection is no longer outside, to be organized by rules about physical practices. To install the great difference, Christ consorts with sufferers from leprosy, a disease of the skin, the membrane that functions as boundary between bodily exterior and interior. So too, Christ eats food with pagans, taking impurities inside himself. He also has power over impure spirits, expelling them from the bodies of the afflicted. This deliberate confusion of categories means that in Christianity's radical rearrangement of Judaism, the abject is no longer exterior but has become interiorized, or, as Kristeva most suggestively explains, the abject has become "reabsorbed into speech." Kristeva points out that for all the changes, the maternal principle "is not for that matter revalorized." Yet with the Incarnation the question of flesh becomes heterogeneous. With the Crucifixion, pain can underwrite discourse.

> The avowal of faith is thus from the very start tied to persecution and suffering. This pain, moreover, has wholly permeated the word 'martyr,' giving it its basic, ordinary meaning, that of torture rather than testimony. Speech addressed to the other, not sinful speech but the speech of faith, is pain; this is what locates the act of true communication, the act of avowal, within the register of persecution and victimization. Communication brings my most intimate subjectivity into being for the other; and this act of judgment and supreme freedom, if it authenticates me, also delivers me over to death. . . . avowal absolves from sin, and, by the same stroke, founds the power of discourse. (pp. 129–30)

Kristeva's argument serves to reinforce the earlier discussion of the power of the voice and of language in martyrdom and the profound thematic importance of St. Christine's tongue for Christine de Pizan's text. Rather than the regulation of food intake established in Judaism by categorizing food as clean or unclean, in Christianity it is the acts of speech that are categorized and stigmatized and ritualized in auricular confession—that alone has power to render clean the

improper and polluted body. Marking in a different way the same
boundary between speech and purity, St. Christine tells her father
that she does not want him to kiss her, because she wishes to keep
her lips pure to pray to God:

> Et celluy cuida que elle voulsist dire a Jupiter, et fu joyeux et la voulst
> baisier: mais ele s'escria "Ne touches a ma bouche, car je vueil offrir
> offrande nette a Dieu celestre." (p. 1002)

> He thought she meant Jupiter and he was overjoyed and wanted to kiss
> her, but she cried out, "Do not touch my mouth, for I wish to offer a pure
> offering to the celestial God." (p. 235)

If we take Christine de Pizan's ultimate subject in the *Cité* to be
the creation of female subjectivity, that is, the construction of her
own authority as a specifically female-gendered author—a strikingly
modern agenda—then it is important that we have a sense of the
necessary part that, in Kristeva's terms, abjection plays in writing in
and of itself. The vocabulary for a female subjectivity simply did not
exist in 1405 (indeed, neither did the vocabulary for male subjectivity, at least not as we know it). As one of the first authors to
attempt not merely the expression of the female subject but of subjectivity itself, Christine finds in the saint's life a genre that can
begin to speak the creation of the "self" (that of the nameable, historically particular saint) at the site—the family—where the individual
is shaped into a particular social being.

The frequent and idiosyncratic appearance of Christine's own
mother in its text suggests that the author's relationship to her
mother was a foundational one for the writing of the *Cité des dames*.
We recall that contrary to all generic expectations, her mother appears on the very first page of the allegory. This might not be at all
surprising in a text that seeks to establish a female tradition of
authority, except that it is absolutely different from the way in which
all other medieval authors open allegorical debate poems. And so,
from the first page, Christine indicates that motherhood will necessarily be a part of her topic. Moreover, Christine's mother not only
appears on page one, she arrives to offer food, which the daugh-
ter/author leaves her study to eat before she undertakes to write her

text; we are thus invited continually to keep in mind the relationship between the two activities—feeding and writing. In the second section, Christine's mother appears a second time, as we saw, when Lady Droitture reminds Christine that daughters are more faithful than sons (pp. 112–13). Her third appearance occurs when Lady Droitture reminds Christine that her mother was the major obstacle to the author's obtaining the education her father had intended her to have (p. 155).

When Christine's mother does not appear directly in the last section of the text, that is doubtless part of the point. Abjection is the language for discussing relations with the maternal, especially maternal relations as prominently problematic as Christine's own—as she has made explicit elsewhere in the text. For all the mother's absence in part III, there is a boundless maternal power residing in what Kristeva has called "the flows" which course through its pages. This final section retrospectively reshapes the first: Justice's collective prayer to Mary, God's mother, addresses her as if she were a fountain. The assembled citizenry of the city pray that all "de la fontaine de vertus, qui de toy flue, elles puissent boire et estre si rassadiees que pechié et tout vice leur soit abominable" (p. 976), "may drink from the fountain of virtues which flows from you and be so satisfied that every sin and vice be abominable to them" (p. 218). Mary, the flowing mother's body, rewrites the auctores—"grant foyson de autteurs and ce propos que je ramentevoye en moy mesismes l'un aprés l'autre, comme se fust une fontaine resourdant" (p. 619); "like a gushing fountain, a series of authorities, whom I recalled one after another, came to mind, along with their opinions on this topic" (p. 4). Such bad influence has been transformed into the miraculous flows of the female body in martyrdom: Martina's body, slashed all over, "yssoit laict pour sanc et oudeur grande rendoit" (p. 987), "instead of blood, poured milk from all its wounds and she gave off a sweet scent" (p. 221). The maternal milk tags the miraculous suffering as participating in the processes of motherhood. The broken, mutilated bodies of Marcia, Lucy, Barbara, Eufemia, and other female saints are miraculously healed and made completely whole. Such corporeality, however, underwrites speech. The pivotally dual nature of the third section and its martyrdoms may be sensed in two separate visions of Mary offered by two different miniaturists of the *Cité*.

In the miniature illuminating the opening of the third section in the earlier manuscript (a miniature possibly overseen by Christine herself), Mary carries a book (see Figure 29). In a later fifteenth-century illumination, the book has been transformed into a baby (Figure 35).

The substitution plays, of course, with the notion of the infant Jesus as the Logos. But it also makes the queen of the city a mother, and the section in which she is introduced is thus by implication devoted to the idea of motherhood. The very brief martyrology of part III—it is only one-eighth as long as the other sections—is a set of narratives, placed within the confines of the city Christine constructs, to query the problematic powers of motherhood—its abjections, its ideals, its costs, and its relations to fatherhood. Significantly, Christine herself, usually a very active interlocutor, speaks at only two points in this section and never to Justice; unlike parts I and II, where the conversations between Christine and Reason or Christine and Droitture are almost stichomythic, the third section is almost entirely one long monologue by Lady Justice. Perhaps even more pointedly, Justice addresses Christine only as "friend," whereas the other two figures of authority, Lady Reason and Lady Droitture, often addressed her as "daughter." Within a recitation where she does not speak, within a display of authoritative narratives for which she chooses not to play interlocutor, Christine apparently stages here her own *lack* of a distinctly different speaking position.

The only two moments in which she represents herself as speaking in this last section are, first, in her prayer to St. Christine—an interposition of another genre that breaks through the boundary of her literary text—and second, in a final direct address to her female readers, present and future, in which she gives them advice that would be generically appropriate to the most conservative of conduct books, a book, indeed, that she would soon write.

The prayer to St. Christine is a direct address by the author to the saint:

O! benoite Christine, vierge digne et beneuree de dieu, tres elitte martire glorieuse, veuilles par la sainteté dont Dieux t'a faitte digne prier pour moy, pecharresce, nommee par ton nom, et me soyes propice et pieteuse marraine. Si voir que je m'esjoyes de avoir cause de enexer et mettre ta sainte legende en mes escriptures, laquelle pour ta rever-

35. Justice leading Mary into the city, *Cité des dames*, Ms. 1177, f. 95v. Paris, Bibliothèque Nationale

ence ay recordee assez au long. Ce te soit aggreable, pries pour toutes femmes, auxquelles ta sainte vie soit cause de bon exemple de bien finer leur vie. Amen. (pp. 1009–10)

O blessed Christine, worthy virgin favored of God, most elect and glorious martyr, in the holiness with which God has made you worthy, pray for me, a sinner, named with your name, and be my kind and merciful guardian. Behold my joy at being able to make use of your holy legend and to include it in my writings, which I have recorded here at such length out of reverence for you. May this be ever pleasing to you! Pray for all women, for whom your holy life may serve as an example for ending their lives well. Amen. (p. 240)

If Reason, Droitture, and Justice are ultimately only mediated figurations of the authority of Christine's voice, so too this prayer stands outside the fiction of the text; here is a "real" appeal by a living Christian to a functioning saint. As a figure of church history, as a construct of legend, St. Christine is one of the citizens who will dwell in the Cité. But of course she also already dwells eternally in the civitas dei and is thereby transtemporally accessible to the author in this prayer. The prayer thus transgresses the boundary of the fiction of the text and enacts language as agency before the reader's very eyes. The literal prayer, fully functional as active language, collapses distinctions between saint's legend, author's "escriptures," and the instrumental effect Christine hopes her text will have on female readers in her political present—the French court in 1405— and on readers in the future. Punningly calling attention to the divine authority of her own name, Christine de Pizan authorizes her own voice by dramatizing in this prayer Christ's naming of her patron saint.

Her prayer to St. Christine uncannily anticipates the terms in which she will address Joan of Arc in the poem she will write nearly a quarter of a century later. But its special significance is already marked in the Cité by the way it reverses the dynamics of the prayer that closed the second section of the book. At the end of part II, Christine prayed to all the present princesses of the court and to "all women," whether living or dead or yet unborn. That address, as we saw, overtly broke down the usual boundaries between different categories of existence—economic, social, temporal, ontological. In the same way, the prayer directed to St. Christine enacts the utter dissolution of that boundary. The prayer to the saint is also preparation for the prayer that closes the text. By far the longest, this third prayer addresses all ladies as a group of readers. In it Christine instructs various groups of women in the proper behavior appropriate to their several callings, to their relational and class status—wife, widow, virgin, noble, bourgeois, lower-class; above all, she warns them of the deceptive seductions of men and of the need for patience in all things.

Prayer was quite traditional a means of imposing closure on a text in the late Middle Ages, and Christine's prayers are not therefore in themselves unusual.[42] What seems important about them is their ability to emphasize the structural articulations of her text. And simply because prayers are conventional methods for gaining closure, the interpolated prayer to St. Christine, set in the middle of the third section, stands out all the more. Not surprisingly, it occurs precisely midway through the small final section.[43] If one counts the chapter titles in the table of rubrics for part III, the "Item, de sainte Christine, vierge," occurs at the exact midpoint of the text, with eight saints' lives preceding it and eight succeeding. As in the repetitions of the name Christine throughout the text, numerological patterning gives a further boost to the dramatic staging of Christ's baptismal conferral of the saint's (and author's own) name. Furthermore, and more importantly, the baptismal naming of Christine's patron saint recalls quite specifically the numerologically central episode of Canto XV of Dante's *Paradiso*, in which the poet comes upon his great-grandfather, Cacciaguida. In imitation of Book VI (the central book) of the *Aeneid*, in which Aeneas meets his father Anchises, in this canto Dante hears his great-grandfather speak about numerological matters he does not really understand concerning his baptism and the granting of his name in the baptistery in Florence: "Insieme fu cristiano e Cacciaguida" (XV.135); "simultaneously I was Cacciaguida and Christian." In passing, Cacciaguida speaks of the Florence of the century before Dante, when morals were not corrupt and life was simple, a time when, while spinning thread, women

---

[42]Rosemarie P. McGerr, "Medieval Concepts of Literary Closure: Theory and Practice," *Exemplaria* 1 (1989), 149–79.

[43]I am indebted to Kevin Brownlee for the following points about the placement of the legend of St. Christine.

spun tales about the founding of cities—Troy, Fiesole, Rome. Then at the very close of his speech, Cacciaguida confesses that he was also a martyr.[44]

Cacciaguida's taciturn, old crusader's confession of his martyrdom is a far cry from Christine's elaborate rehearsal ("assez long") of the baroque details of St. Christine's torture, but there are so many elements to interest Christine in the canto in which Cacciaguida appears that one cannot help wondering if the difference between the two figures is as carefully arranged as the echoes must be. The greatest difference, of course, is that Dante's canto celebrates a paternal lineage, while Christine's interpolated prayer establishes a bond between a saint's legend and her own writing. It is a prayer asking for aid for the whole female community, set in a text building a city of maternal lineages; the only male in it is Mary's baby, the son of God, in whose name the martyrs died.

Stephen G. Nichols has recently argued that hagiography is a mediated, scripted genre controlled by the institution of the church, designed to marginalize unauthorized prophetic voices, such as those of women. The only body that speaks in a hagiographical text is a dead body; it speaks, moreover, by having been turned into a text.[45] But Christine's rewrite of Vincent's details, as I have tried to suggest, reinvests the body with a living instrumentality, even as it is being dismembered. In Christine's revision of her auctor, the mediated, interpreted events of St. Christine's legend in Vincent's rendition are made literal, present events. Mere signs become actual events: the waves, formerly a mere "segnacle," become actual baptism; a crown and disembodied voice are transformed into the actual person of Christ. The prayer to St. Christine also functions to bring the possibilities of a present power into the text, which, while it remains a mere written record, makes contact with a transtemporal and prophetic present. Christine's revisions of Vincent begin to turn hagiography into prophecy and to connect the saints' legends of the last section of the *Cité* with the persistent emphasis on prophecy in the first two.

At the end of her life, Christine de Pizan took to actual prophecy.

---

[44]I am borrowing an argument from Kevin Brownlee, who first pointed out in conversation the possible connection between the central episode of the *Paradiso* and the legend of St. Christine.

[45]Paper presented at the University of Pennsylvania, Spring 1987.

But before we can see what the historical occurrence of Joan of Arc may have to say about the decades-long defense of women mounted by Christine, we need to take into account the practical manual Christine wrote immediately after the *Livre de la cité des dames*, a manual that she titled the *Trésor de la cité des dames*. The *Trésor* is itself, in fact, an extension of the advice-giving prayer Christine uses to close the *Cité des dames*.[46] In a similar sense, the *Ditié de Jehanne D'Arc* can be said to take up the rhetoric of direct address found in the prayer to St. Christine. Both texts then, the practical manual in prose and the poem of prophecy, derive from and continue the *Cité des dames*. The militancy of the legend of St. Christine may be said to find its fullest expression in Christine's celebration of Joan, and the *Trésor* is equally significant for an understanding of the socially conservative prayer that closes the *Cité des dames*. If the book's opening—the radical revision of the scene of reading, with its installation of the problem of actual and historical motherhood (and daughterhood) at the threshold of the text—is an unorthodox manipulation of the genre to introduce female-authored issues about sexual difference, then the closing prayer by its very conventionality (wives, be patient; widows, be prudent; virgins, stay chaste) seems a distinct rejection of the anti-misogynist thrust of the main discourse and its willingness to court a scandalous originality.

As we shall see, the main note at the opening of the *Trésor* is a bizarrely explicit fatigue and exhaustion on Christine's part that contrasts strongly with the energy of the revisionary scene that opens the *Cité*. It is tempting to dismiss the ending of the *Cité* as the first effect of the failure of will of a weary author who faces the real world in which the textual construct is only that, a fiction. Edmund Spenser had also closed his incomplete allegory with a similar exhaustion and an explicit denunciation of his audience and of the way his text had had to withdraw from its own most effective modes of narration. So too, William Langland had rewritten *Piers Plowman* three times. Allegory by generic bent remains a narrative form incomplete until a reader "interprets" it. The unsatisfactory oddity of Christine's closure, which provides no visionary ending—the

---

[46]Charity Canon Willard, *Christine de Pizan: Her Life and Works* (New York: Persea Books, 1984), p. 145, also argues for the similarity: "The final chapter of the *Book of the City of Ladies* serves as an introduction to the second undertaking, *The Book of the Three Virtues*."

blessed Virgin Mary, for example, hovering with angelic chorus over the completely constructed city—but instead preaches an admonition to the readers, may be due to the generic requirements of her narrative mode. At least what she does is what other allegorists have done. Whatever the reason, the ending points to the possible continuation of the problems in a new key in the *Trésor*. A brief consideration of that manual's advice will help us to decide if Christine's rhetoric is a collapse into conventionality, a recourse to Machiavellian modes of deception, or if it contains some savvy realpolitik hints at how to maximize power when given limited room for maneuver. In other words, the *Trésor* may have been written as a how-to manual designed for a period when a woman, an inhabitant of a real and not a fictional city, could not count on God to intervene directly to raise her and her sex to national prominence as the saviors of her realm. And the *Ditié* was written because Christine believed a woman could save—and was at that moment, saving—France.

Chapter 5

The Practice of History

On July 12, 1405, when Louis of Orléans and his sister-in-law Isabeau of Bavaria, queen of France, were out hunting in the countryside around Paris, their sport was interrupted by a violent thunderstorm. While Louis of Orléans took shelter with the queen in her coach, the horses became so frightened that they bolted and ran headlong into the Seine; the coach would have followed had the coachman not cut the traces just in time. During this same thunderstorm, a stroke of lightning hit the castle where the dauphin was living, charring a room close to his own. We know of these events on this specific date because the thunderstorm was widely considered to be a divine portent, a direct warning to Louis and Isabeau to cease their extravagant and luxurious spending, to end a notorious financial spree that was overburdening the common people and disturbing the stability of the realm.[1]

In part because of the interpretations of this portentous thunderstorm, it was assumed until quite recently that the queen and her brother-in-law were having an adulterous (and, given their fraternal relationship, necessarily an incestuous) affair. So abrupt was the queen's precipitous switch of allegiance in 1405 from the duke of Burgundy (the king's uncle) to the duke of Orléans (the king's brother), sexual attraction seemed to provide a reasonable answer.[2]

[1]For the thunderstorm, see Jean Verdon, *Isabeau de Bavière* (Paris: Librairie Jules Tallandier, 1981), p. 104.
[2]See Mathilde Laigle, ed., *"Le livre des trois vertus" de Christine de Pisan* (Paris:

Now, however, most scholars agree that there probably was no sexual liaison; the rumors about an affair date only from many decades later.[3] Still, it is true that in 1405, Isabeau of Bavaria "ceased," as Mathilde Laigle puts it, "to enjoy the public's estimation" (p. 20). The scandal about Isabeau and the "dishonesty" of which the chroniclers generally complain appear to have been due fundamentally to the queen's extravagant expenditures, as well as her apparent carelessness about her tragically insane husband's state at that time. (Charles VI wandered castle halls ill-kempt, unwashed, and vermin-infested.) She was also criticized for her neglect of her royal children's education.

Whatever the actual reason for Isabeau's change of allegiance, it is important to realize that when she so abruptly lost all public estimation, she was a reigning queen. In 1402 she had been granted absolute power to rule in her mad husband's absences, and it was then that she first made peace between the warring Armagnac and Burgundian factions. Although her authority was somewhat limited by subsequent ordinances, she had, in the words of one historian, "emerged as the only person eligible to watch over the interests of the immediate royal family and act as mediator in the ducal quarrels" (Famiglietti, p. 27). She was granted these powers because she was expected to be impartial and to make peace.

The *Trésor de la cité des dames*

More significant for us than the fact that Isabeau's loss of her former popularity occurred during a single year is the date of that

---

Honoré Champion, 1912), pp. 20–24. Charity Canon Willard accepts the view that there was an adulterous relationship between sister and brother-in-law; see *A Medieval Woman's Mirror of Honor: The Treasury of the City of Ladies*, trans. Charity Canon Willard; ed. Willard and Madeleine Pelner Cosman (New York: Persea Books, 1989), p. 41.

[3] Isabeau's most recent French biographer argues at length that there is no basis in fact for assuming a sexual liaison; see Verdon, *Isabeau de Bavière*, pp. 103–5, 138–39. Even more persuasive is the argument of R. C. Famiglietti in *Royal Intrigue: Crisis at the Court of Charles VI, 1392–1420* (New York: Abraham Magazine Service Press, 1986), pp. 42–45.

year—1405, the year in which Christine de Pizan wrote both the *Livre de la cité des dames* and the *Trésor de la cité des dames*. At the beginning of 1405, when Christine would have been writing the *Cité des dames*, Isabeau was still working to keep peace in the realm. Indeed, Christine compliments Isabeau specifically as a reigning queen: "a present par la grace de Dieu raignant, en laquelle n'a raim de cruauté, extorcion ne quelconques mal vice, mais toute bonne amour et benignité vers ses subgiez" (p. 967); "at present by the grace of God reigning, in whom there is no cruelty, extortion, or any kind of vice, but only good and benign love for her subjects" (p. 212). Figure 36 is the incipit to the entire presentation volume Christine put together for Isabeau.

Laigle argues that by the time Christine wrote the *Trésor de la cité des dames* (also called *Le livre des trois vertus*) during the summer of this same year, Isabeau had lost her popular renown and, therefore, a great deal of her power. Christine dedicates the *Trésor* not to Isabeau, but to her daughter-in-law, the duchess of Guyenne, wife of the dauphin. It is almost as if she had given up on Isabeau and was turning to a younger, less tainted generation to carry on the cause of peace. Not surprisingly, the *Trésor de la cité des dames* is not included in the copy of her works Christine presented to Isabeau.

Shortly after the composition of the two *Cité* texts, Christine wrote a letter directly to Isabeau, dated October 5, 1405. In this letter she passionately argues that Isabeau should do all she can to make peace among her family members, praying in particular that she may be able to make "par cy que prouchaine paix entre ces II haulz princes germains de sanc et naturelment amis, mais a present par estrange Fortune meuz a aucune contencion"; "peace between these two princes of the same blood [Orléans and Burgundy, the king's brother and uncle respectively] and who are loved ones by nature, but who are at present brought to a quarrel by strange fortune."[4] Christine mentions three reasons Isabeau should undertake this task. First, the avoidance of war would be a Christian act of supreme value for the realm; second, peace would protect her own noble children (and their subjects). The third and striking reason is

---

[4]Christine de Pizan, *The Epistle of the Prison of Human Life, with an Epistle to the Queen of France, and Lament on the Evils of the Civil War*, ed. and trans. Josette A. Wisman (New York: Garland, 1984), pp. 72–73.

36. Christine de Pizan presenting her works to Isabeau of Bavaria, Ms. Harley 4431, f. 1. London, British Library, by permission

the restoration of Isabeau's personal glory: "Le tiers bien, qui ne fait a desprisier, c'est qu'en perpetuelle memoire de vous, ramenteue, recommandee et louee en croniques et nobles gestes de France, doublement couronnee de honneur seriez, avec l'amour, graces, presens et humbles grans merciz de voz loyaulz subgiez" (p. 74). "The third good, which is not to be despised, is that in eternal remembrance of you, you would be remembered, commended, and praised in the chronicles and noble tales of France, twice crowned with honors, with love, presents, graces and humble and deep gratitude from your loyal subjects" (p. 75). Christine thus not only appeals to a humanist ideal more usually associated with masculinist enterprises—historical fame and personal glory—she includes an implicit threat by hinting at the opposite reputation in the present and in the future:

the ingratitude, the hate, and disloyal rebelliousness of the common people now and the harsh criticism of historians later. Isabeau is given a choice: either to be remembered as a Queen Blanche who, when the barons rebelled against her infant son, made peace among them, or to be remembered as a false queen Jezebel. In essence, Christine is counseling Isabeau to return to the activities she had been pursuing before her alliance with the king's brother, to become again a peacemaker between the houses of Burgundy and Orléans. Laigle has argued, not surprisingly, that after Christine sent her letter to Isabeau of Bavaria, she precipitously lost the queen's favor.[5]

In order to understand the developing practice of history in which Christine was engaged at this time, it is important to note the specific position of authority from which she speaks in the letter to the queen. She presents herself there as a mouthpiece of the common people, those who are already suffering the most from the present wars and who, Christine predicts—if not with prophetic insight, then with acute political realism—will bear the heaviest burdens should France be attacked by outsiders while vulnerable because of internal strife. Self-described as "povre, ignorant and indigne," Christine says she speaks for the "supplians Françoys . . . qui a humble voix plaine de plours crient a vous, leur souveraine et redoubtee Dame, priant, pour Dieu mercy, que humble pitié vueille monstrer a vostre begnin cuer luer desolacion et misere" (p. 72); "supplicant French people so full of affliction and sadness, and who cry with tearful voices to you, their supreme and revered Lady, praying, by the mercy of God, that a humble pity may show to your tender heart their desolation and misery" (p. 73). In fact, she is asking the queen to do what she, Christine, is doing, that is, to serve as a female mediator between the suffering people and male warriors: inspired by these same laments Isabeau must persuade them to stop fighting.

Christine's manual for successful female maneuvering in the early fifteenth-century world, the *Trésor de la cité des dames*, dedicated as it is to the dauphin, is less direct in its approach to the queen, but it reads very much like a guide of reparative instructions for her, a book about how to regain her former power. Christine describes in the *Trésor* how a woman may gain power by appeasing all parties. Since

[5]Laigle, *"Trois Vertus,"* p. 33: "Isabeau va recevoir l'Epitre de Christine en octobre 1405 et saura lire entre les lignes. Sa largesse ne s'étendra plus sur ce gênant auteur."

Isabeau has lost her reputation through her own financial extravagance and the scandalous behavior of her court (fifteen of her ladies-in-waiting were later arrested for improper conduct), Christine outlines a program of scrupulous and publicly displayed adherence to the strictest rules of moral virtue whereby a woman of authority may establish and maintain an excellent reputation. It is essentially this burden of public display which makes the *Trésor* so different from the *Cité des dames*. In the earlier text the women were metaphorically safe from history, impregnable in their transtemporal city. In the sequel text, they are as vulnerable to social realities as Isabeau of Bavaria. In consequence, the whole first book is given over to advising the woman of authority; the second book is dedicated to the court lady and her responsibilities. Both must practice chastity, sobriety, and prudence in order to insure a good reputation. This is the precondition to being granted power; it also becomes the method for exercising it.

In the *Trésor*, Christine stops short of the reasoning Machiavelli would enjoin a hundred years later; Christine's counsel is for the "sage dame"—the woman of authority—*both* to be virtuous and to have a reputation for virtue. Like Machiavelli, Christine's real emphasis falls on the need to maintain the *appearance* of virtue. While she never goes so far as to take Machiavelli's final step and to argue that the appearance is more important than the actuality, still— given the vulnerable situation of Queen Isabeau at the time Christine was writing—it would seem that, especially because Isabeau herself may have been innocent of any actual wrongdoing, Christine is politically right to emphasize the importance of appearance. The English would later start the rumor that Isabeau's last son, the dispossessed dauphin (and future Charles VII) was illegitimate; his own later involvement in the scandalous murder of Jean Sans Peur, then duke of Burgundy, was thus—according to rumor—actually motivated by filial revenge for the duke's earlier murder of his putative father, the duke of Orléans.

As in Machiavelli, in the *Trésor* the public perception is all: thus tactics for creating and controlling one's reputation are given far greater weight than the actual possession of virtue. Praising what she specifically calls a "juste hypocrisie" (a justifiable hypocrisy) for instance, Christine argues that when giving alms the great lady should take care that her charity is as public as possible: "mieulx seroit la donner publiquement que en secret"; "it would be better to give publicly than in secret."[6] The woman who follows this advice of the figure Worldly Prudence will hobnob with churchmen and clerks, both of whom are powerful formers of opinion. Of the usefulness of churchmen in particular, Christine explains that on the one hand the good and devout will pray to God on her behalf, and on the other hand: "Et l'autre pour ce que elle soit louee d'eulx en leurs sermons et collacioans, si que leurs voix et leurs paroles lui puissent estre se mestier est, escu et deffense contre les murmures et rapors de ses envieux mesdisans et les puissent estaindre" (p. 203). "She may be praised by them in their sermons and homilies so that, if the need arises, their voices and words can be a shield and defence against the rumours and reports of her slanderous enemies and can negate them" (p. 71).

Christine's concern for the structures creating reputation (and fame) speaks directly to the problem Isabeau was facing at the time the *Trésor* was written. But it also speaks to Christine's sense of the powerful role the people's opinion played in the politics of the day. Because Christine's views on the people and their place in the political process has come under recent attack by Sheila Delany, it will be useful to see in this practical handbook how Christine posits the relationship between the ruler and the ruled. A "juste hypocrisie" is "necessaire" she argues, "a princes et princepces qui ont a dominer autrui" (p. 205); "to princes and princesses who must rule over others" (p. 72). So great a care for reputation recognizes the remarkable power subjects have over rulers.

> la sage princepce doit mettre peine et cure de se mettre bien de ses subgies. . . . Et ce pourroit sembler a aucuns mal avisez que chose superflue soit de ce dire, et que il n'apertient point que princepce preigne cure d'attraire ses subgies . . . et qu'ils doivent obir et mettre peine de l'attraire a amour, et non mie elle eulx, ou autrement ne seroient mie subgies et elle maistresse. (p. 208)

> the princess ought to be well regarded by her subjects. . . . Some might think that it was not the princess's business to court her subjects . . . and

---

[6] Lore Loftfield Debower, ed., "*Le Livre Des Trois Vertus* of Christine de Pisan" (Ph.D. diss., University of Massachusetts, 1979), p. 204. Translations are from *The Treasure of the City of Ladies or The Book of the Three Virtues*, trans. Sarah Lawson (Harmondworth, Middlesex: Penguin, 1985), p. 72.

her subjects ought to obey and take pains to court *her* love and not the other way around, or otherwise they will not be subjects and she the mistress. (p. 73)

Such currying of favor with all the people seems so important to Christine that she repeats it over and over: "quoy que le prince soit seigneur et maistre des subgies, toutevoies les subgies font le seigneur, non mie le seigneur les subgies" (p. 208); "though the prince be the sovereign and master, the subjects nevertheless make the lord and not the lord the subjects" (p. 73).

The power of the mediator, then, comes from voicing the needs and opinions of the people; when the lady has won her husband's trust by her prudent, chaste, and sober management of herself and her household, he will delegate power to her (as Isabeau received it). Her job then is to mediate disputes between powerful men of the upperclass, but also to translate the needs of the common people, to ensure that those needs are fulfilled so that her husband (and she) can govern in peace, undisturbed by rebellion. The interstice where the lady locates her power, then, is close to the people's specifically constitutive power. It is as a spokesperson for the people, at that borderline between suffering subject and heedless queen, that Christine placed herself in her letter to Isabeau.

Given the trying circumstances of Christine's rhetorical position vis-à-vis the queen in her letter, it is perhaps not surprising that she complains at the very opening of the *Trésor de la cité des dames* about her exhaustion. The incipit illuminations in the manuscripts make her fatigue quite clear; in these, although she is approached by the three figures of authority, Christine is shown asleep. Figure 37, the earliest of the manuscripts and therefore the one closest to Christine's own practice, shows Christine asleep on the bed, with the three figures hauling her out of bed by the arm.[7] On the right-hand side of the miniature, Dame Prudence reads from a book to women of different social classes (some wear crowns, while others wear plain headdresses like Christine's own). The opening sentence of the sequel makes sheer weariness the connecting link between the *Cité des dames* and the *Trésor de la cité des dames*.

---

[7]Debower, "*Trois Vertus*," p. 108, points out the general agreement among art historians that this miniature was done in the atelier where the so-called "Christine de Pizan Master" worked.

37. The three virtues pulling Christine out of bed to begin work on the *Trésor de la cité des dames,* and Worldly Prudence lecturing to women of different classes, incipit illumination, Med. Fr. Ms. 101, f. 1. Boston, Public Library, by courtesy of the Trustees

Apres ce que j'oz ediffiee a l'ayde et par le commandement des troys dames de vertus, c'est assavoir Rayson, Droitture, et Justice, la cite des dames par la fourme et maniere que ou contenu de la ditte cite est declairie, je comme personne traveillie de si grant labour avoir accompli et mis sus, mes membres et mon corps lasses pour cause du long et continuel exxercite, estant en oyseuse et querant repos, s'apparurent a moy de rechief, gaires ne tarderent, les susdittes troys glorieueses, en disant toutes trois paroles d'une meismes substance en telle maniere (p. 122)

After I built the City of Ladies with the help and commandment of the three Ladies of Virtue, Reason, Rectitude, and Justice, in the form and

254

manner explained in the text of that book, and after I, more than anyone else, had worked so hard to finish the project and felt so exhausted by the long and continual exertion, I wanted only to rest and be idle for a while. But the same three ladies appeared to me again and all three lost no time in saying the same kind of thing to me. (p. 31)

Later fifteenth-century illustrations of this sentence preserve the weariness of the author, who sits slumped over in the characteristic chin-in-hand posture of the earlier *Cité des dames* miniatures, but this time with her eyes closed (Figures 38, 39).

Such weariness may indeed be a counterpart to Christine's shame and despair at the opening of the *Cité*, a way of staging her unworthiness in the face of the eager authority of the august figures who wish to complete a task they judge yet undone. But its emphasis may also signal her frustration at the reality of the limitations faced by a woman who would have power in this world. No Semiramis, the "sage dame" whom Christine's manual first addresses in the *Trésor* must begin by fearing the Lord and learning to be humble, however rich she is: "une simple femmellete qui n'as force poissance ne auttorite se elle ne t'est donne d'autrui" (p. 140); "a simple little woman who has no strength, power, or authority unless it is conferred on [her] by someone else" (p. 41).

Although in the incipit miniature Christine is quite recognizable, a major difference between the two works is that Christine never names herself in the text of the *Trésor*. Instead the first-person speaker varies through several different identifications. Or, as Lore Loftfield Debower summarizes this curious use of Christine's usual signature "je":

It is easy to wish to identify the "je" of the text with Christine, but in truth the Virtues narrate the work. They in turn speak for others. Christine is present in the text as "je" only at the beginning of the text "Apres qu j'oz ediffie . . . la cite des dames" and at the end when she is "tres resjoye" to have completed her text. The other times that "je" appears in the text the careful reader can identify it as one of the Virtues, Prudence Mondaine, a character in one of the anecdotes, or the reader herself who is always present in the text. The Virtues imagine arguments that the reader might raise and speak directly to their students. (p. 93)

38. The virtues pulling Christine out of bed to begin work on the *Trésor de la cité des dames*, Ms. 427, f. 1r. New Haven, Beinecke Rare Book and Manuscript Library, Yale University

Christine also stages conversations between other barely named interlocutors—imagining, for instance, what God says, or what the sage princess might say to herself under the sway of evil. The rhetorical position of all speakers is, then, not clearly marked; the three

39. The virtues waking Christine to begin work on the *Trésor de la cité des dames*, Ms. Ffr. 1177, f. 3v. Paris, Bibliothèque Nationale

figures collapse into one "nous"; in contrast to the particularly differentiated figures of the *Cité*, they are in no way distinct from each other; indeed their "nous" collapses into the "je" of Prudence Mondaine and so on.

The effect of this narrative blend keeps the *Trésor* from attaining the distinctive clarity of the three-part specificity of Reason, Droitture, and Justice in the *Cité*—in the *Trésor* none of the advice given belongs specifically to Reason or to Justice or to Droitture. In terms of its allegorical analysis, the sequel seems far more analytically relaxed or exhausted than the discursive structure arranged for the construction of the *Cité*. The new structure also has the further result of silencing Christine's own voice. Whereas in the earlier text her authority becomes a subject dramatized by the text, in the sequel it is submerged in the indistinct welter of authorities.

The weariness marks a sense of constraint, a compulsion to write differently because of external circumstance. That external circumstance appears very early in the text. Second only to the lady's need to intercede for the poor is her duty to make peace between any barons who happen to be warring. This is the very first lesson:

> Ou se il avient cas que aucun prince voisin ou estrangier vueille mouvoir guerre pour aucune chalenge a son seigneur ou que son seigneur la vueille mouvoir a autrui, la bonne dame pesera moult ceste chose en pensant les grans maulx et infinies cruaultes, pertes, occisions, et destruction de paix et de gent qui a cause de guerre viennent, et la fin qui souventes fois en est merveilleuse. Si avisera de toute sa poissance se elle pourra tant faire en gardant l'honneur de son seigneur que ceste guerre puist estre eschivee. Et en ce se vouldra traveillier et labourer sagement en appellant Dieu a son aide, et par bon conseil. Et tant fera se elle puet que voye de paix y sera trouvee. (pp. 158–59)

> If any neighboring or foreign prince wishes for any reason to make war against her husband, or if her husband wishes to make war on someone else, the good lady will consider this thing carefully, bearing in mind the great evils and infinite cruelties, destruction, massacres and detriment to the country that result from war; the outcome is often terrible. She will ponder long and hard whether she can do something (always preserving the honour of her husband) to prevent this war. In this cause she will wish to work and labour carefully, calling God to her aid, and by good counsel she will do whatever she can do to find a way of peace. (p. 50)

Written at about the same time as the letter, the *Trésor* states more obliquely what Christine's letter says directly. Its point would have been obvious to anyone who had observed Isabeau's successful rise to power. Christine merely counsels Isabeau to return to a successful program that, all scholars of the period agree, enabled her to win political power. As a mediator between the two warring factions of Orléans and Burgundy, she had become indispensable; it was for this that Charles VI made her regent with full power.

Yet the mediation first stressed in the *Trésor* is concerned with conflicts not merely between different elites but also between different classes. The text first insists upon the importance of the lady's intercession for the people. She mediates on behalf of the people by carrying their needs to her lord, and she also mediates for him, excusing him to them.

> Si fera sa response sage et convenable . . . excusera son seigneur, et en dira bien. Se aucunement pour quelque cas s'en tiennent mal contens, dira que elle se charge de son pouoir d'en faire la paix ou d'estre leur bonne amie en la peticion que ils demandent, et en toutes autres choses de son pouoir. . . . Ainsi ceste noble dame respondra tant sagement aux ambassadeurs du peuple ou des subgies que ils s'en partiront si contens que se ils avoient devant aucune rancune, rebellion, ou murmure en courage ils seront tous pacifies. . . . Sans longue dilacion, parlera a son seigneur bien et sagement. . . . tres humblement suppliera pour le peuple, moustrera les raisons de quoy elle sera tres bien informee, comment il est necessaire que prince, se longuement il veult regner en paix et glorieusement, soit amez de ses subgies et de son peuple. (p. 157)

> She will reply wisely and suitably . . . she will excuse her husband, and speak well of him. If for any reason her subjects feel disgruntled with her reply, she will say that she promises to try her best to make peace, or to stand as their good friend in the petition they are making and in every-thing else in her power. . . . In this way the noble lady will reply so wisely to the ambassadors of the people or of her subjects that when they go away from her they will be satisfied to the extent that if they previously had some grievance, rebellion, or quarrel in mind, they will all be pacified. . . . without long delay she will . . . speak to her husband well and wisely. . . . She will show the reasons, which she will understand thoroughly, and she will show how it is necessary for a prince, if he wishes to reign long in peace and glory, to be loved by his subjects and by his people. (p. 49)

Through a curious amalgam of Christian charity and cross-class mediation, the wise woman gains her own "pouoir"; from having had none of her own before, she appropriates both the power of her lord and of his subjects. Borrowing real power from both, the lady makes peace and her own authority. In particular, it is the very real power held by the common people, which Christine emphasizes in this 1405 text, that provides the woman of authority the potential for her own power.

Such arguments about how to turn an apparent weakness into a strength are the hallmark of Christine's strategy throughout the manual, which takes place at the level of tactical advantage, not principle. For instance, in advising her readers how to deal with enemies in the close courtly milieux, Christine counsels absolute dissimulation: pretend you don't know they hate you, but be certain to be a good actress, for if once they suspect you, you are ruined and they will think you dissemble out of fear of them and not out of policy. Thus, in the argument for mediation, the Christian virtue of charity toward the poor leads to power. In the argument for deflecting hostility through subterfuge, the forgiveness of enemies also leads to power; justifiable hypocrisy and discreet dissimulation are allowed because they enhance the authority of the woman who would make peace in a warring kingdom.

Sheila Delany has roundly criticized Christine's ideological conservatism and prudish moralizing, taking her to task for espousing the role of the "angel in the house," that is, one who is "socially an agent of control on behalf of the ruling elite."[8] If, as Delany argues, Christine's politics could be boiled down to the role of the "angel in the house,"—a term borrowed from Sandra Gilbert and Susan Gubar's influential discussion of Victorian women (whom, they argue, twentieth-century women must learn to "kill" in themselves)[9]—such a fact would not so much be grounds for Christine's dismissal from serious scholarly (or feminist) consideration as it would be an issue of some historical importance. One could then locate, if not the origin of a very long-lived myth of womanhood, at least a role that reappears at different times because it offers useful leverage for women within existing power relations. Nina Auerbach has argued, in fact, that the angel is always part demon and that even in the nineteenth century, "when properly understood, the angel in the house, along with her seemingly victimized Victorian sisters, is too strong and interesting a creature for us to kill."[10]

[8]Sheila Delany, " 'Mothers to Think Back Through': Who Are They? The Ambiguous Example of Christine de Pizan," in Medieval Texts and Contemporary Readers, ed. Laurie A. Finke and Martin B. Schichtman (Ithaca: Cornell University Press, 1987), pp. 177–97, quote from p. 190.

[9]Sandra Gilbert and Susan Gubar, The Madwoman in the Attic: The Woman Writer and the Nineteenth-Century Literary Imagination (New Haven: Yale University Press, 1979).

[10]Nina Auerbach, Woman and the Demon: The Life of a Victorian Myth (Cambridge: Harvard University Press, 1982), p. 12.

Even though Delany's point is primarily one about Christine's specific politics, she is right in insisting on Christine's effort to contain energies directed against the social hierarchy. It is quite true that when Christine gives advice to a woman in the lower ranks of society, her counsel for traditional virtue is less a means of granting the woman leverage (as it is when she argues for virtue in the elite) than it is a counsel that upholds the traditional, hierarchical status quo. If the common people in this text have rights to petition their ruler and justly can be considered the formative agent of his rule, they also have responsibilities that it is the duty of the common laborer's wife to urge her husband to fulfill. Thus the wife must advise her laborer husband not to cheat his master: "Ne mucent pas les bones berbis ne les meilleurs moutons chieux les voisins pour paier le maistre. . . . Et quant ils sont commis par leurs maistres de prendre des autres ouvriers se ils les louent .vi. blans le jour ne facent mie acroire que .vii. coustent" (p. 404). "Don't hide the good ewes or the best rams at the neighbors in order to pay the master with inferior animals. . . . When the master commissions [his laborers] to hire helpers, if they are hired at six groats a day, they should not pretend they cost seven" (p. 220; revised).

Perhaps more to the point of Christine's bias toward the ruling elite is her condemnation of otherwise excellent servant women who manage, in entrepreneurial fashion, to cheat their rich employers. In the process of condemning such women, who are able to cheat so well because they give the best of service, Christine paints a detailed portrait of the possibilities for personal enrichment in the domestic sphere; clever servant women are able to hire out their own work, becoming middle managers, so to speak, by giving away the food and wine of the house to friends and family.

Car le beau service que faire sceuent leurs flateries bien apareillir a mengier tenir tout nettement et ordonneement belparler et beau respondre aveuglent tellement les gens que on ne s'en prent garde de leurs tres grans mauvaistes. Car elles meslent de devocion parmy pour mieulx tout couvrir et vont au moustier a tout Pater Nosters, et la est le peril. (p. 392)

Because of the excellent service that they know how to give and their flatteries, and by preparing meals well, keeping the house neat and

40. The virtues lecturing to court women of different ages, *Trésor de la cité des dames*, Ms. 427, f. 72r. New Haven, Beinecke Rare Book and Manuscript Library, Yale University

clean, and speaking well and answering questions politely, they blind people so much that no one is on the look-out for their wicked deeds. The better to cover up everything they pretend to be pious and go to church for all the prayers, and therein lies the danger. (p. 171)

What is most heinous to Christine about such a woman is not her success or her hypocrisy in gaining it, but the danger she poses for a young and inexperienced mistress; someone who does not hesitate to cheat in household accounts will also be willing to serve as a pander for would-be lovers who would seduce her mistress. Such servants are only a cut above prostitutes—who are given counsel in the very next section of the *Trésor*. While prostitutes merely sell their bodies, the pandering servant prostitutes the ideal of service.

Christine's *Trésor* is organized hierarchically downward, so that wives of laborers and poor women come last. If the wicked chambermaid deserves condemnation like that given to the prostitute, she does so because she poses added danger to the vulnerability of her mistress to slander and immortality. The precariousness of a woman's fame, open to harm from both external enemies and intimate domestics, is a major burden of Christine's text. At all levels, the ideal of service requires that women work together to protect each other. Thus, the proper behavior for the court lady is to protect her mistress, even when she knows the lady to have done something wrong; she is not to be envious, to gossip, to carp and quarrel, to carry tales, or to aid a would-be lover in his approach. In Figure 40, the three virtues lecture a group of court women and children. Just as the wife is enjoined to be loyal to a husband who is bad, so a woman is told to serve a mistress well, even if she is evil; such good service includes every effort to turn the wrongdoer away from the evil activities. All court ladies are enjoined to be sober and virtuous for their own good, but also for the good of their mistress.

L'une qu'on juge communement a l'estat et maintien qu'on voit a la maignee de l'estre et condicion du seigneur ou de la dame. Pour quoy se les femmes n'estoient de belle ordonnance aucuns pourroient supposer que non fust la maistresse. Laquelle chose pourroit estre desacroiscement de l'honneur d'elle. (p. 235)

One commonly judges the quality and status of the lord or the lady by the conditions and conduct that one sees in the household, so that if the women did not behave well, some could suppose that the mistress did not either, and the lady's honour could suffer. (p. 86)

The dangerous notoriety of Isabeau of Bavaria's ladies-in-waiting, fifteen of whom were later arrested during the Cabochien revolution that swept through the court in 1413, may stand behind the great number of pages Christine devotes to the need for subordinates to conduct themselves for the honor of their mistresses. The elaborate outline of the conduct proper to an older woman chaperon in her tutelage of a young woman owes much to the powerful stance of counsel the subordinate has in relationship to the superior. Such moralizing counsel is a pattern repeated throughout the different classes of society, an ordered pattern allowing legitimate moral petition and advice from the subordinate to the superior, a duty equally necessary for the bourgeois woman employed to tutor a young married princess and for the wife of the common laborer. Each counsels the social superior not to cheat.

It is just such an emphasis on maintaining social hierarchy which leads Delany to chastize Christine.

> For Christine, social justice and harmony consist in each rank fulfilling its divinely appointed duties according to its divinely determined nature. . . . By the fifteenth century this model was sadly outmoded, completely out of touch with late-medieval social life and political theory. The image that comes to mind is of King Canute trying to beat back the tide with a broom; so Christine tries to beat back the tide of social change, of protest and nascent democracy. . . . In a time when even courtiers and clerics wanted change, Christine continues in her quiet neo-Platonic hierarchies and her feudal nostalgia. (p. 188)

Delany is right in her evaluation of Christine's emphasis on keeping social order; she gravely overstates the case, however, for advances in political theory. Because Delany's critique of Christine's regressive politics rests on the charge that she was reacting against theories for possible social change at the time, it is crucial to Delany's argument that there be some nascent democratic thought in Christine's society, at least a potential questioning of the validity of hierarchy. If Christine is legitimately to be charged with being "plus royaliste que le roi," it is necessary to find a body of opinion that questions the king's absolute authority.

A major proof for Delany of the possibilities of social change is the Cabochien revolution of 1413, centered in Paris and fomented in part by the duke of Burgundy in his continued bid for power. It was a revolution Christine saw with her own eyes and responded to directly in the *Livre de la paix* of 1413. Her response to that summer of upheaval was to withdraw from the position taken in the more hospitable *Trésor* and to show no further sympathy for rule by the common people. In the *Paix* she cautions the dauphin, the duke of Guyenne, to learn from the past and not to raise the common people to positions of government:

> tu n'eslieves point ceulx que nature commande estre bas, car un petit ruissiau desrivé, il est plus aspre que une grant reviere de non eslever

trop gent de commun, et que peril soit, et non leur bailler ou souffrir avoir charges ne estas plus grans en autres que ne leur appartient, c'est qu'ilz n'aient auctorité de quelconques office ne prerogative de gouvernement de cité ou ville, lesquelz choses sont partinens aux bourgois notables et d'ancienne ligneés de degré en degré, selon la faculté des dis office commes des personnes.

do not raise up those whom nature decrees low, for a little rivulet gone beyond its banks is harsher than a great river; do not raise up the common people whatever the danger, and do not give nor suffer others to have charge or estate greater than belongs to them, for they have no authority for any office whatever in the government of the city or town, which rather belongs to the notable bourgeois or to those of ancient lineages in various degrees, according to the said ability of such people for office.[11]

Although Christine recognized in the *Livre de la paix* the ability of the common people to govern themselves in their guilds in order to earn their livings at their trades, this private self-government within the various corporations did not, in her view, qualify them for public office; they did not know the law nor how to speak reasonably in public assembly (p. 131). Finally, whenever they gained power they misused it—and robbed, murdered, and put to death; they menaced even innocent women and the children.

What this rejection of the people's authority over Paris can teach us is the peculiar need to construct female political authority by appropriating the authority of those who are similarly marginalized, just as Christine had spoken for the suffering poor in her letter to Isabeau. Here she specifically rejects the rights of the people to self-government. Are her strictures, however, different from the very demands made by the Cabochien revolutionaries themselves? Alfred Coville, an authority on the Cabochien revolution and its Ordonnance, explicitly states that the Ordonnance published in May 1413 "represents less the new ideas of a revolutionary movement, than the experience of the past; it was the legislation of an entire century, renewed and summed up."[12] Coville does argue that the acceptance

[11]*The "Livre de la Paix" of Christine de Pisan,* ed. Charity Canon Willard (The Hague: Mouton, 1958), p. 130; my translation.

[12]Alfred Coville, *Les Cabochiens et L'Ordonnance de 1413* (Paris: Librairie Hachette, 1888), p. 322.

of the principle of elections—which were in 1413 a matter of ordinary procedure in both the government of city guilds as well as in the university—provided part of an advance in the direction of democracy and helped to make possible the early coalition between members of the university and such guilds as the butchers (pp. 122–24). Both the guilds and the university had immense popular power in the city of Paris; in particular, the university had taken over the role of the church, then undermined by schism, in advising the king. But when it came to civic government, the central focus of all possible political activity remained in theory, and in practice, the king.

As Coville explains, "all the daring of the reformers, armed with full powers in a time of demagoguery and daily riots, resulted in nothing truly subversive of traditional order" (p. 320). He goes on to add that "Liberal tendencies hardly appear in elections and deliberations, for it was merely the agents of royal power which were chosen and decided and in the last resort it was always the king who spoke" (p. 320). The very language in which the Ordonnance is cast makes the fact of royal cynosure clear; each of the 258 ordonnances begins with the formula "Comment le Roy ordonne." Number 102, for instance, has the king ordain that if there are three persons to be chosen in an election, one should come from the clergy, and also ordain that receiverships be elected without gifts (that is, bribery). But even this reformist interest in elections specifies that the elected should be taken from among "good, rich people and men of social position, who are knowledgeable about justice."[13]

The framers of the Ordonnance were, of course, the same men of position who ultimately abhorred the violent excesses of mob rule and who, in September of 1413, sided with the dauphin and helped to end the Cabochien rule.[14] Between mob rule and the Ordonnance, there was no middle ground where truly democratic thought might

[13]*L'Ordonnance Cabochienne (26–27 Mai 1413)*, ed. Alfred Coville (Paris: Librairie des Archives nationales, 1891), p. 45. Caboche himself, the butcher for whom the revolution was named, was a very wealthy man. Writing in 1931, the scholar James Westfall Thompson in his *Economic and Social History of Europe in the Later Middle Ages (1350–1530)* (1931; rpt. New York: Ungar, 1958), pp. 300–301, reckoned that a comparable butcher whose will was contested by his family in 1380 owned three country houses in addition to his townhouse, possessed farms for stock-raising and cattle pens in Paris, and held a fortune of $30,000 in hard cash and $9,000 in jewels (this in depression dollars).

[14]See Willard, "*Livre de la Paix*," pp. 24–25.

emerge. At the height of the powers of the Parisian populace, when a mob entered the dauphin's quarters and demanded the arrest of fifty of his servants, the people of Paris could still only ask for reform in the name of helping the kings. The people's spokesman demanded: "véez-cy les Parisiens, non point tous, en armes, que de par cest ville de Paris, pour le bien de vostre père and de vous, requièrent que on leur libre aucuns traistres qui sont en vostre hostel de présent" (Coville, p. 188). "Here are Parisians in arms, not at all the whole, that require by this city of Paris and for the good of your father and you, that you deliver to them certain traitors who are presently in this house" (my translation). Astonished by their own victory, the butchers, Coville points out, "felt that they possessed little authority of their own, either in material or moral force, with which they might sustain the role which they had taken on through violence" (p. 192).

Caboche himself finally owed his election to Charles VI who, in his madness, had appointed Caboche and his confreres to important posts.[15] It was, in essence, the king's eccentric friendliness to the people's cause which allowed the revolution to flourish for as long as it did; Christine counsels the king's son against such a course in the *Livre de la paix*. She explains to him that the common people are not capable of rule and that, contrary to his father's practice, he should not appoint them to government positions. It could hardly have been necessary to say this to the duke of Guyenne who, all commentators agree, was deeply angered after having seen some of his favorite ministers arrested out of his own house and sent off to execution.

Not even Jean Gerson could question the centrality of the king. He was, of course, Christine's onetime ally in the quarrel about the *Roman de la rose*; as chancellor of the University of Paris he was an exceedingly powerful man, a theologian and also a theorist of government. His widely influential sermon of 1405, "Vivat Rex," outlined the ideal government in terms of an hereditary monarchy in which the king is the minister of God on earth and is therefore required to have every virtue. If, indeed, the king were not capable of living up to

---

[15]Famiglietti, *Royal Intrigue*, pp. 124–32; "letters show that the duke of Guyenne was no longer a free agent and that he was doing what the Cabochiens required of him. He was forced into this passive role because the king had pronounced himself in complete accord with the Cabochiens. No action was to be taken against them, Charles VI had declared, and thus, if the dauphin overtly sought their downfall, he would make himself a target for a charge of treason" (p. 126).

the ideal, he would then become a monstrous tyrant, and, Gerson, argued, it would be legitimate to kill him and to deliver the realm from his tyranny (Coville, p. 132). Driven by humanist theory into a radical-sounding stance that merely changed kings, Gerson staked out a position that was not espoused by a single activist reformer, all of whom claimed to be operating in the name of the king. In essence, as Coville summarizes, "nothing" about the Cabochien revolution, "marks the advent of new rights" (p. 320).

If, as Coville also argues, there was anything tending toward the democratic in the politics of the time, it was the transferal of the elective and collective decision-making processes from the usual internal self-governing procedures of the guilds and the university into the public sphere. But even here the potential for real political innovation vanished when these institutions were incorporated into the very traditional structure of kingly rule: they were only there to counsel the king, to act as advice givers. The ultimate authority remained with the king.

Thus, for Sheila Delany to insist that Christine is very much in the rearguard of social thought of her time and especially to cite the Cabochien revolution as an example of such forward-looking political thinking, is to misrepresent the historical facts. It is true that Christine does not formulate any theory to articulate popular rule or to give coherent speech to Parisian mob-leaders who themselves could not think past a language of central royal authority even as they were exercising real power in the face of it. But then, no one else offers such a formulation, not even the very leaders of the revolution who are bound by exactly the same ideological limit as she. For Delany to argue that Christine had less sympathy for the sufferings of laborers and poor people than other of her compatriots had is also to ignore the way in which she gives voice to their pleas in, for instance, the earlier 1405 letter to Isabeau of Bavaria, a letter in which she prophesies the foreign conquest of France if the queen fails to make peace between the warring barons. It is, she says, the people who will suffer the most:

> Helas! Et qu'il convenist que le povre peuple comparast le pechié dont il est innocent! Et que les povres petits alittans et enfans crisassent aprés leurs lasses meres veufves et adolues, mourans de faim, et elles, desnuees de leurs biens, n'eussent de quoy les appaisier! Les quelles voix,

comment racontent en plusiers lieux les Escriptures, percent les cieulz par pitié devant Dieu juste et attrayent vengence sur ceulx qui en sont cause.

Alas! That the poor people should have to pay for the sins of which they are innocent! That the poor little infants and children should cry for their miserable and suffering widowed mothers, in a state of starvation, and their mothers, deprived of all their goods, should not have anything to appease them! Their pitiful voices, as the Holy Scriptures tell in several passages, pierce the heavens before God who is just and ask for vengeance on those who are the cause of it. (Wisman, *Epistle*, pp. 78–79)

As a court poet and political propagandist, in the *Livre de la paix* Christine espoused the political doctrine most friendly to her own class—the haute bourgeoisie. She inhabited the middle position, both by class and by design. From this position she had argued that the court lady could exercise real power, serving as mediator between factions and classes, appropriating power from both sides in the conflict but especially borrowing the moral authority of the suffering poor people.

Christine's conservatism in the face of potential political innovation may indicate something centrally significant about the political affordances accessible to women at any given moment in history. By "affordances" I mean what might or might not conduce to women's greater liberation at specific local periods of historical possibility. Democratic processes do not in themselves conduce to female authority. The elective processes that Coville sees as basic to the democratic potential inherent, but never realized, in the Cabochien revolution in fact stem from the corporate practices of two distinctly all-male institutions. The university was a masculine institution, greatly increased in power because of the vacuum caused by the schism in the church. The university, in effect, had come to exercise in its far more democratic way the advisory power of both institutions, that is, the church and university together. So too the guild of the Grande Boucherie was instituted as a male domain and was, in fact, much more exclusive in its criteria for membership than the university, which was itself open to all classes of society (indeed, the various guilds were among those agencies then providing scholarships for students). Membership in the butchers' guild, in contrast, was by inheritance only; only the sons of masters had the right to enter and therefore to exercise the trade, which, in some sections of the city included the right of appointing apprenticeships. Thus a boy could inherit the right of mastership at the age of seven years and a day. If a place should fall vacant due to lack of an heir, only someone born in the neighborhood could take the empty place. The single exception to such close-knit neighborhood exclusiveness was that the king had the right to name a butcher to the Grande Boucherie. As Coville points out, it was in part this remarkable closeness of the guild which gave it its power to exert force in the political scene (p. 102).

In contrast to two such fully authorized and self-sustaining institutions (the university and the butchers' guild, which, in joining forces, together became a powerful instigator of social action), Christine's was a lone and singular female voice. Like the corporations and the university, she could merely advise. If they, with all their independent power, could not think past assumptions about the royal cynosure, it is not surprising that Christine did not, since she was enfranchised only by that central royal authority and therefore was far more dependent upon it. It would perhaps be more convenient for the political programs of our own day if Christine had experienced the precariousness of her position in a way that allowed her to question the entire apparatus of social structure and hierarchical authority. Her failure to do so should make us ask why and come up with a better answer than a mere condemnation of her politics.

Lacking any other authorizing agent, Christine, as a woman, was more dependent on her existence as a subject to royal authority than were her male contemporaries. Member of no corporation, student of no university, Christine de Pizan, as we saw at the outset, named her authorizing position only as a woman writer, an inhabitant of an allegorical land at the margin of articulate territory: "femme soubz tenebres." Her letter to Isabeau becomes useful in this regard if read to understand the collective political dimension of the speaking positions Christine felt able to occupy; in it she appropriates the authority of all the loyal subjects of the queen. "Si finaray a tant mon epistre, suppliant vostre digne majesté qu'elle l'ait agreable et soit favourable a la plourable requeste par moy escripte de vos povres sujiez, loyaulz François"; "Thus I will finish my epistle, begging your worthy majesty that she receive it well and that she be favorable to the teary request of mine written on behalf of your poor subjects, the loyal French people" (pp. 79–80).

In an exceedingly interesting correction of Althusser, Peter Stallybrass has recently argued that in early modern history, ideology does not interpellate the individual as a subject (to repeat Althusser's famous formulation) so much as, historically, the subject precedes the individual. That is, the political experience of being the subject of an absolute authority predates in the collective historical experience of Western Europe the collective experience of enfranchised autonomous individuality.[16] Subjection to an absolute sovereign was, historically, the precondition in all Western European nations for the development of the notion of the free individual. In a related argument about seventeenth-century English absolutism and female subjectivity, Catherine Gallagher has demonstrated that the language most available to early proto-feminist writers at that time for giving voice to a self-consciously active subject position, whereby a woman could speak her own political desire, was the language of loyalist faithfulness to absolute monarchical rule. Tracing what she calls the "paradoxical connection between the *roi absolu* and the *moi absolu*," Gallagher argues that "the ideology of the absolute monarchy provides, in particular historical situations, a transition to an ideology of the absolute self."[17] Lacking any other agency by which they might conceptualize a fully authorized subject position for women, seventeenth-century women writers such as Margaret Cavendish and Mary Astell borrowed from arguments for absolute sovereignty in order to authorize an articulation of the autonomous agency of an "individual" woman. Some historians have tried to account for the disturbing Toryism of the first feminists in seventeenth-century England by explaining that "as middle class men acquired new political, economic, and educational advantages, aristocratic ladies and gentlewomen may have felt a relative erosion of their social power" and hence their Toryism stemmed from a perceived loss of status that could be restored only by restoring the shaken hierarchy (Gallagher, pp. 24–25). Such an argument does not, however, explain the wide

[16]Peter Stallybrass, "Shakespeare, the Individual, and the Text," in *Cultural Studies Now and in the Future*, ed. Larry Grossberg, Cary Nelson, and Paul Treichler (London: Routledge, forthcoming).

[17]Catherine Gallagher, "Embracing the Absolute: The Politics of the Female Subject in Seventeenth-Century England," *Genders* 1 (1988), 24–39.

spectrum of partisan political activity on the part of a large number of nonwriting aristocratic women (Gallagher, p. 5n). Gallagher further argues that political absolutism offered something particular to the proto-feminist writing woman: "the foundation for a subjectivity that would make its own absolute claims" (p. 27). Moreover, in quite particular terms, the absence of absolute monarchy in England during the interregnum made such sovereignty all the more metaphorically accessible as a subject position.

> During the years when the Cavendishes, like the rest of the English court, were exiled in France and Holland, Charles II was himself the ruler of a kind of fantasy kingdom. In a sense, the exile literalized the monarch's metaphoric significance. The real king had become the ruler of what amounted to a microcosm, had almost been reduced to a private kingdom, and hence had practically enacted the metaphorical equivalence of sovereign monarch and sovereign private person. (p. 29)

Paradoxically, because she lacked actual legal subjecthood, a woman might the more easily take on the position of sovereign individual. Such an identification would also have been made easier in England *because* "women were excluded from all state offices except that of monarch" (p. 27).

Seventeenth-century England had an entirely different political climate from early fifteenth-century France of course; Cavendish and company were writing at the end of absolutism in England, while Christine wrote at the very opening of absolutism's three-century domination of France, so any similarities between the two writing practices must be treated cautiously. But Gallagher's argument about the seventeenth-century proto-feminist writers can help us to see how, in the midst of a vast amount of articulate cross-class revolutionary theorizing, other self-consciously pro-woman polemicists could find an absolutist vocabulary helpful in their search for a way to articulate an active female subject position.

The exile of Charles II of England bears an interesting similarity to the mediated rulership of Charles VI of France, who was often barred by his madness from direct personal rule. Christine wrote to Isabeau specifically as a reigning queen, that is, as an individual woman exercising the position of power for the king. The major trajectory of Christine's advice to women in the *Trésor* is how to win, exercise, and keep that appropriated social power. Throughout the *Cité des dames,* we have seen Christine construct her own authority as if she were a figure of authority herself, a named self-conscious subject in the position of the active speaker: "Je, Christine." In the *Trésor* she loses that particular named position, but in sharing her voice with other authorities, she articulates what is in fact subjected, that is, thrown under, hierarchically subordinate, in the position of woman. She speaks *as* a loyal subject, constituting her own nameless authority in that text by articulating the behavior necessitated by the hierarchy, holding her power to speak from the traditional role of loyal, advising subordinate who counsels a superior by borrowing the voice of those lower down the hierarchical scale.

Finally, Delany has argued more generally that Christine is to be faulted for not responding to the radicalism of her period: "Those who are not familiar with the period of transition from feudalism to capitalism—Christine's period—are often surprised by its radical aspects, for it was a self-consciously modern age that had begun in theory and in practice to attack traditional ideas and institutions. What was the social context in which Christine lived and wrote? What would 'radicalism' actually mean in early fifteenth-century Europe?" (p. 183)

As I hope I have shown, the radicalism of revolt never became fully articulated. So too, in a recent Marxist investigation of that problematic development from feudalism to capitalism, *The Lineages of the Absolutist State* Perry Anderson has characterized the transitional period specifically in terms of its absolutism that, he argues, was less a "balance" between the nobility and the bourgeoisie, as Friedrich Engels had argued, for instance, and was more a "redeployed and recharged apparatus of feudal domination . . . it was the new political carapace of a threatened nobility."[18] What Delany sees as the possibility for new, "radical" political thought was in fact peasant unrest in rural areas coupled with the activities of urban economics "freed from direct domination by a rural ruling class" (p. 21). This activity, as Anderson argues, was a real product of feudalism, not part of its dissolution; "towns . . . were never exogenous to feudalism in the West . . . the very condition of their existence was the unique 'detotalization' of sovereignty within the politico-economic order of feudalism" (p. 21). Yet the aristocracy, according to Anderson, "had to

---

[18] Perry Anderson, *The Lineages of the Absolutist State* (London: NLB, 1974), p. 18.

adjust to . . . the mercantile bourgeoisie which had developed in the mediaeval towns," a presence that prevented the Western nobility from settling its accounts with the peasantry in the Eastern fashion, "by smashing its resistance and fettering it to the manor" (p. 21). Such a recognition of the feudal nature of city activity is important, both for any claims one might wish to make about Christine's emphasis on the city as a liberal humanist political center (it is not liberal in the political sense) and also to make clear the political repercussions of revolt during the Hundred Years War. In essence, "the political order remained feudal, while society became more and more bourgeois" (p. 23).

Even though the transition from feudalism to capitalism had, as Delany rightly points out, allowed radical possibilities to surface, what triumphed at the end of the fifteenth century was, as Anderson points out, nevertheless political absolutism: "This was precisely the epoch in which a sudden, concurrent revival of political authority and unity occurred in country after country. From the pit of extreme feudal chaos and turmoil of the Wars of the Roses, the Hundred Years War, . . . the first 'new' monarchies straightened up virtually together" (p. 22).

Full-blown absolutism did not come to France until the seventeenth century, but the process had begun with the reign of Charles VII. In one very real sense then, in opting for an absolutist political organization, Christine was very much at the forefront of history, if not of political theory. Christine's feudalism was not so much nostalgia, as Delany suggests, as it was prophetic of the absolutist state that constituted everywhere in Europe the transitional political form between feudalism and capitalism.

The *Ditié de Jehanne d'Arc*

It may be perhaps easier to put Christine's royalist politics into the "radical" possibilities of her time if we consider the monarchical focus at the heart of the very last poem she penned in her lifetime, the last day of July 1429. It is the poem she wrote about Joan of Arc. And, as the woman-to-woman salutation of the "Ditié de Jehanne d'Arc" provided the opening to our exploration of Christine's construction of her female authority, so this last poem may also provide a fitting close to our discussion of the process whereby even transgressive female authority constitutes itself in direct relationship to a royal cynosure.

Christine addresses not only "Jehanne" in the poem and does so in the familiar second person ("Tu") but also Charles VII, the rejected son of the legitimate king—"le degeté enfant / Du roy de France legitime."[19] Disbarred from the succession to the French crown not because of his suspected illegitimacy but by political negotiations, the last son of Isabeau and Charles VI since the Treaty of Troyes in 1420 had been king of only part of France. The treaty granted the realm to the offspring of Catherine of France and of King Henry V of England. By its terms, Charles VI was undisturbed in his power; it was the dauphin who was disinherited. Henry V did not, of course, live to see his son inherit France; he died in 1422, two months before the death of Charles VI. From then until 1429, France was ruled by a Bedford, that is, an English, regency. Many recognized Charles VII as king. As his biographer points out, there was no real need for Jehanne d'Arc to crown him at Rheims because he was already a crowned king, being at the time she did it already in the seventh year of his reign: "The coronation at Rheims was thus . . . otiose."[20]

Just as Jehanne insisted on the coronation, so Christine's poem, written shortly thereafter and in direct celebration of the event, proves how symbolically important that gesture was. Christine describes Jehanne leading the king "par la main" to the coronation:

> A tresgrant triumphe et puissance
> Fu Charles couronné à Rains,
> L'an mil CCCC, sans doutance,
> Et XXIX, tout sauf et sains,
> Ou gens d'armes et barons mains,
> Droit XVIIe jour
> De juillet.
>
> (ll. 385–91)

[19]Christine de Pisan, *Ditié de Jehanne D'Arc*, ed. and trans. Angus J. Kennedy and Kenneth Varty (Oxford: Society for the Study of Mediaeval Languages and Literature, 1977), ll. 33–34.

[20]M. G. A. Vale, *Charles VII* (Berkeley: University of California Press, 1974), p. 57.

It was exactly the 17th day of July 1429 that Charles was, without any doubt, safely crowned at Rheims, amidst great triumph and splendour and surrounded by many men-at-arms and barons. (p. 48)

Christine goes on to hail the miraculous recovery of king and kingdom through God's direct intervention in history, an intervention that proved his love for the female sex: "Hee! Quel honneur du feminin sexe! Que Dieu l'ayme il appert" (ll. 265–66). It was by miracle that a sixteen-year-old peasant girl led her king to victory:

> Consideré ta persone,
> Qui es une jeune pucelle
> A qui Dieu force et povoire donne
> D'estre le champion et celle
> Qui donne à France la mamelle
> De paix et doulce nourriture,
> Et ruer jus la gent rebelle,
> Véz bien chose oultre nature!
> (ll. 185–92)

When we take your person into account, you who are a young maiden, to whom God gives the strength and power to be the champion who casts the rebels down and feeds France with the sweet nourishing milk of peace, here indeed is something quite extraordinary. (p. 44)

Christine directly addresses the city of Paris, warning it of impending attack by the king. Counterpoised to the combined authority of the hereditarily legitimate king and the divinely sanctioned woman warrior is the disloyal city:

> O Paris tresmal conseillié!
> Folz habitans sans confiance!
> Aymes-tu mieulz estre essilié
> Qu'à ton prince faire accordance?
> Certes, ta grant contrariance
> Te destruira, se ne t'avises!
> Tróp miulx te feust par suppliance
> Requerir mercy. Mal y vises!
> (ll. 433–40)

Oh Paris, how could you be so ill-advised? Foolish inhabitants, you are lacking in trust! Do you prefer to be laid waste, Paris, rather than make peace with your prince? If you are not careful, your great opposition will destroy you. It would be far better for you if you were humbly to beg for mercy. You are quite miscalculating! (p. 49)

In chastising the city from which she had gone into exile eleven years earlier, fleeing the excesses of the newly regnant Burgundians, Christine sees the political unit of the city preeminently in terms of its subjection both to the sovereign authority of the king and to the divinely authorized woman; she also counsels all the other "disloyal" towns that have accepted Burgundian/English rule to beg pardon and surrender without a fight to avoid any further bloodshed. Christine's poem, then, contains not only threats but also a plea for the end of the war. No less than Jehanne d'Arc herself, Christine understands the political necessity of the war-torn moment in terms of the need to legitimate a central royal authority. One might argue that Christine ought to have been able to come up with a better political agenda than an ill-educated, lowborn teenage girl. But the prejudice toward a royal cynosure she shares with Jehanne demonstrates how much she was at one with the moment Jehanne d'Arc also inhabited: Once again naming herself as author, "Je, Christine," she sees Jehanne through the lens of the martial maid's legitimating activity of crowning the king; ultimately in the poem all three—king, maid, and author—are poised against the disobedient city.

Christine also shares another interesting habit of mind with Jehanne d'Arc: both women prophesied. One of the backward-looking features of Christine's conceptual framework which makes her so outmoded in Delany's view is her interest in astrology and prophesying, an interest she would have acquired from her astrologer father. In fact, in addition to doing a great deal of prophesying in the "Ditié," Christine also points out that the advent of Jehanne had long been foretold. Part of the Maid's persuasive historical presence is owing to a tradition of prophecy which promised her advent.

> Car Merlin et Sebile et Bede,
> Plus de V^c ans a la virent
> En esperit, et pour remede

> En France en leus escripz la mirent,
> Et leurs prophecies en firent,
> Disans qu'el pourteroit baniere
> Es guerres françoises, et dirent
> De son fait toute la maniere.
>
> (ll. 241–48)

For more than five hundred years ago, Merlin, the Sibyl and Bede foresaw her coming, entered her in their writings as someone who would put an end to France's troubles, made prophecies about her, saying that she would carry the banner in the French wars and describing all that she would achieve. (p. 45)

Christine's career-long investment in sibylline prophecy, from the early text of the *Epistre Othéa* to this last poem, conformed to a widespread belief in fifteenth-century France in prophecy and sorcery. Jehanne's own prophesying and "voices," of course, are part of what made her most vulnerable to the charge of heresy and witchcraft. But astrology and divination were also predilections Jehanne and Christine shared with their king.

Charles VII was widely known to be interested in astrology and the arts of prognostication. M. G. A. Vale speculates that this interest may have indeed led to Jehanne's introduction to him. According to Vale, it may have been the faction of Charles's mother-in-law, Yolande of Aragon, which first introduced Jehanne to the king in Chinon during February 1429. One of the Maid's first public acts was a visit to one of Yolande's ailing relatives, René of Anjou. Although Jehanne was unable to heal him, she did ask him to help lead her into France. As Vale provocatively guesses: "To introduce a prophetess to the impressionable Charles could have been a stroke of something approaching political genius" (p. 50). Vale further guesses that the party that might best profit from such a plan was Yolande's.

Jean Gerson was said to have authored a tract, *De quadam puella*, justifying Jehanne, allegedly written between March and his death on July 12, 1429. Recent scholars dispute this attribution, but the spuriousness of the claim does not detract from its suggestion that Gerson could have been thought capable of supporting Jehanne at the time. Although warning against the easy claims to inspiration made by women, the writer judges Jehanne to be given to "devout beliefs,"

in no way against the faith.[21] Christine's poem, written in the isolation of the convent at Poissy, celebrates Jehanne as prophetic proof of
God's divine favor toward women; in it she adds her voice to pronouncements in favor of the Maid, which many assumed had been
made by Gerson. Again, as before in their "querelle de la *Rose*," the
issue of legitimate female authority was at stake.

It is not necessary to argue for any further connections between
Christine de Pizan and Jehanne beyond the fact that hers is the only
signed poem written during Jehanne d'Arc's lifetime explicitly to
celebrate her miraculous deliverance of France. Christine herself saw
Jehanne as proof of the rightness of her programmatic argument for
the divine favor God had shown to women. The Maid was living,
incontrovertible proof of what Christine had been arguing all along.
When we note, furthermore, that Yolande of Aragon was a strong
woman who greatly influenced her son-in-law, Charles VII, we may
begin to sense the potentiating part Christine's decades-long argument for the authority of women may have played in preparing the
dauphin and his court to accept a low-born female teenager as a savior of France. Yolande of Aragon had married a man whose mother,
Marie of Blois, was mentioned in the *Cité des dames*, where she is
extolled as one who rules her territories during her children's minor-
ities, quelling rebellion and dealing out justice with a firm, fair hand
(p. 671). And of course, even before Charles VII came under the sway
of his mother-in-law Yolande at age ten, he would have been ruled by
his own mother Isabeau, herself the cynosure of Christine's most
urgent advice. Although Charles was born only two years before
Christine wrote the *Cité des dames* and would have been only fifteen
in 1418, the year Christine chose silence and exile in a convent at
Poissy, he would not necessarily have grown up outside of the orbit in
which Christine's authority had had such wide dissemination. Indeed, Charles's older sister was a member of the convent in which
Christine had placed her own daughter and to which she later retired,
seeking refuge from the wars (Verdon, p. 70). So too it was Charles's
older brother who was the patron for whom Christine had written
the *Livre de la paix*. That women could have special prophetic au-

---

[21]Georges and Andrée Duby, *Les procès de Jeanne d'Arc* (Paris: Editions Gallimard,
1973), p. 12.

thority in advising and guiding kings would not have been an unusual idea to a man like Charles VII.

It cannot be entirely an accident then that the unique and singular female writer in late medieval France should so overlap the advent of the unique and singular female warrior; although it is not possible to prove such things, it does make sense to suppose that Christine's arguments, so highly visible to all court members, may have helped prepare them to accept a woman's authority. Her constant retelling of the Amazon myth, arguing for their legitimate domain in a martial realm of their own in text after text, could very well have prepared the culture at court to see a woman warrior as something other than a monster. And this preparation would not have hurt Jehanne's chances for being well received by that court (Figure 41).

Jehanne appealed to the same prophetic tradition by which Christine had claimed part of her own authority. It is not merely that they shared an acute awareness of their time, demonstrated by their success in gaining the attention of the court through claiming prophetic powers. Christine uses prophecy in the *Ditié* to authorize her own celebration of Jehanne's advent: such prophecy is, of course, only one among numerous other general and specific prognostications that heralded Jehanne's miraculous arrival.[22] But hers was a very distinctive one, and she remains the only author of a signed poem written during Jehanne's lifetime.

In the *Ditié*, Christine prophesies that Jehanne will lead Charles VII on a victorious crusade to Jerusalem, a symbolic recognition of the underlying fact that what Jehanne had most usefully accomplished was the conversion of the protracted Anglo-French conflict into a religious war (Vale, p. 55). In this particular prognostication, of course, history has proved Christine a false prophet. And, indeed, many who narrate the end of Christine's life prefer to spare her the knowledge of Jehanne's fate by suggesting that she may well have

---

[22]Marina Warner in *Joan of Arc: The Image of Female Heroism* (New York: Knopf, 1981), pp. 98–200, makes a very interesting point about Joan of Arc's name having less to do with the family name than with the subterranean Amazonian message it carries, the "arc" being the bow the famous warriors carried. Although Christine herself does not call "Jehanne" an Amazonian warrior, her presentation of Joan as authorized by sibylline prophecy connects her to the sibyls prominent in the *Epistre Othéa* and the *Cité des dames.*

41. Hippolyta and the Amazons, *Epistre Othéa*, Ms. Harley 4431, f. 103v. London, British Library, by permission

died before Jehanne was captured by the Burgundians in late May
1430 or at least before Jehanne was executed as a heretic a year later
in May 1431. Christine was definitely dead by the year 1434 when
Champion celebrated her fame.

But I question the need for this particular gesture of narrative
closure. It is of course unlikely that we will learn anything new
about the relative dates of the deaths of Jehanne, woman warrior,
and Christine, woman writer. It is possible, however, to conjecture
whether the capture and death of Jehanne would necessarily have
made Christine revise her assessments of the heroine's earlier triumphs. Jehanne herself said that her voices and her mission ended
with the coronation. There was, in addition, an option for Jehanne's
triumph in the future, one Christine could have hoped for her even at
the stake. In the twentieth century history has finally exercised that
option—Jehanne was canonized a martyr saint in 1920. Christine
thus may be said to have prophesied more compellingly in the Cité's
martyrology what actually happens to the kind of woman she celebrated within it, than she did in the Merlinic mix of Jerusalem-bound
prophecy she actually gives in the Ditié. And it seems likely that the
author of the Cité might have been able to appeal in the face of
Jehanne's execution to the faith underlying the martyrology of the
Cité. If the martyrology of the Cité can be read in terms of the full
historical practice of the Ditié, we can see more immediately the
political power engaged by actual martyrdom, both the politics that
sent Jehanne to her death and the slow, centuries-long political process that canonized her. If we read the prophecy of the Ditié in terms
of the end of the Cité, that is, as Christine's unique sense that the
advent of Jehanne was a true historical marker for one kind of female
heroism, never to be forgotten by the world, then Christine's attempt
to foretell the future doesn't seem so mistaken after all.

Finally, if we read Christine's texts in terms of their potential
preparation of the dauphin's society to welcome Jehanne d'Arc as a
legitimate savior of the realm, then we begin to perceive the very
historical instrumentality Christine everywhere positions her text
to achieve. If the politics are absolutist rather than liberal in the
modern sense, they are no less engaged in the founding of female
authority. An apt poet for singing the praises of the warrior woman,
Christine shares many of her heroine's desires. But like Jehanne, she

also stands as a figure worthy of study (if not emulation), a pivotal early character crucial to any full accounting of women's achievements, as well as one of the first woman writers of their neglected history.

Index

Library of Congress Cataloging-in-Publication Data

Quilligan, Maureen, 1944–
  The allegory of female authority : Christine de Pizan's Cité des dames / Maureen
Quilligan.
    p. cm.
  Includes bibliographical references and index.
  ISBN 0-8014-2552-2.—ISBN 0-8014-9788-4 (pbk.)
   1. Christine, de Pisan, ca. 1364–ca. 1431. Livre de la cité des dames. 2. Feminism and
literature—France—History. 3. Women and literature—France—History. 4. Author-
ship—Sex differences. 5. Authority in literature. 6. Women in literature. 7. Allegory. I.
Title.
PQ1575.L563Q54 1991
841'.2—dc20   91-55069